An Introduction to Middle English

An Introduction to Middle English

Simon Horobin and Jeremy Smith

OXFORD
UNIVERSITY PRESS

In memory of David Burnley

Oxford University Press

Oxford New York

Auckland Bangkok Buenos Aires Cape Town Chennai

Dar es Salaam Delhi Hong Kong Istanbul Karachi Kolkata

Kuala Lumpur Madrid Melbourne Mexico City Mumbai Nairobi

Sao Paulo Shanghai Singapore Taipei Tokyo Toronto

Published by Oxford University Press, Inc.
198 Madison Avenue, New York, New York 10016
by arrangement with Edinburgh University Press Ltd
22 George Square, Edinburgh, United Kingdom

Oxford is a registered trademark of Oxford University Press, Inc.

Library of Congress Cataloging-in-Publication Data available

ISBN 0-19-521949-X (hardback)
ISBN 0-19-521950-3 (paperback)

Typeset in Janson by Norman Tilley Graphics

Printed and bound in Great Britain by
MPG Books Ltd, Bodmin, Cornwall

Contents

113/60

Abbreviations

>	becomes
<	derives from
C	consonant
CHEL	*Cambridge History of the English Language*
CSD	*Concise Scots Dictionary*
EETS	Early English Text Society
EME	Early Middle English
EModE	Early Modern English
ETOTEL	*Edinburgh Textbooks on the English Language*
GenAm	General American
HTE	*Historical Thesaurus of English*
IPA	International Phonetic Alphabet
LALME	*A Linguistic Atlas of Late Mediaeval English*
LME	Late Middle English
LOE	Late Old English
ME	Middle English
MED	*Middle English Dictionary*
MEOSL	Middle English Open Syllable Lengthening
ModE	Modern English
MS(S)	manuscript(s)
NF	Norman French
OE	Old English
OED	*Oxford English Dictionary*
OF	Old French
ON	Old Norse
PDE	Present-Day English
RP	Received Pronunciation
V	vowel; verb
WS	West Saxon

To readers

This book is designed as a linguistic introduction to Middle English for undergraduate students who have already encountered the language, perhaps through reading Chaucer's works or having undertaken a general 'survey' course on the history of the English language. We have attempted to make the book a bridge between elementary surveys of the kind to be found in beginners' readers and more sophisticated (and theoretically oriented) work; thus in the last chapter we point forward to issues which are part of recent scholarly debate. Our view is that it is important for all students, as colleagues in the discipline, to be aware of current controversies; however, we have tried to avoid such controversies in the body of the book so that not too strong a 'party-line' is pushed. Even so, it would be foolish to deny that there is an overarching approach, which may be defined as linking concerns often described as 'linguistic' (theory-centred) with 'philological' (text-centred) ones.

We envisage our book being used, at an early stage, as part of an undergraduate Honours course on Middle English. In order to enhance its usefulness (and indeed to keep overall costs down) we have supplied a reader of illustrative texts, but ideally students will supplement this with other collections. We especially recommend Burnley 1992.

The authors would like to acknowledge with gratitude the patience and tolerance of Sarah Edwards and James Dale. We are also much indebted to the very helpful and detailed comments on the first draft made by Donka Minkova and Heinz Giegerich, which saved us from many infelicities, drew attention to flaws, and were invaluable in clarifying and correcting our arguments. We were also very grateful for early sight of parts of the companion ETOTEL volume on Old English, by Richard Hogg. However, we take full responsibility for any errors of omission or commission which remain.

Although we collaborated closely in the writing of the book, JJS was primarily responsible for Chapters 1 to 7; SCH undertook the editing and annotation of the Appendix of Texts, and supplied textual material at various points elsewhere.

1 Introduction

1.1 The purpose of this book

The purpose of this book is to introduce you to Middle English (ME), the form of the English language which was spoken and written in England between c.1100 and c.1500. If you have read any of the poetry of Geoffrey Chaucer, who died in 1400, then you have read a kind of ME. It is hoped that when you have finished working with this book, you will have a good understanding of the range of linguistic choices available to writers like Chaucer. We also hope that you will understand how ME came into being as a distinct form of English, and how the study of ME helps you to engage with key questions about the processes of linguistic change.

ME may be distinguished from Old English or Anglo-Saxon (OE), the form of the language spoken and written before c.1100, and from Modern English (ModE), which is the term used to categorise English after c.1500. The ME period thus corresponds roughly with the centuries which lie between the Norman Conquest of 1066 and William Caxton's introduction of printing in 1475. All three periods can be further subdivided chronologically; thus ME is sometimes divided into Early ME (EME) and Late ME (LME), dividing roughly in the middle of the fourteenth century correlating with the approximate date for the birth of Chaucer (c.1340). These historical states of the language may be contrasted with Present-Day English (PDE). A chronological table appears as Figure 1.1.

Figure 1.1

Old English (Anglo-Saxon)	up to c.1100
Middle English	c.1100–c.1500
Early Middle English	c.1100–c.1340
Late Middle English	c.1340–c.1500
Modern English	from c.1500
Present-Day English	

ME is, of course, descended from OE, but it differs from it in a number of ways. Contact with other languages from the end of the OE period onwards, notably with Old Norse (the language of Viking invaders) and with varieties of French, affected the status and appearance of English in a very profound way. At the end of the ME period, the status of the English language changed again, and this change led in turn to changes in linguistic transmission and structure which are sufficient for scholars to distinguish a new language-state, that is ModE.

Of course, it is important to remember that the transitions from OE to ME, and from ME to ModE, were gradual ones. People did not shift from one language-state to another overnight. But it is generally accepted by scholars that there are certain common characteristics of the varieties of ME which distinguish them from earlier and later states of the language. We will be discussing these common characteristics later in this book.

1.2 How to use this book

There is no single correct way to work with this book. We assume that most of you will be studying with teachers, all of whom will have (quite rightly) their own views as to what is the correct way to learn about ME. However, we are also aware that many of you will be working more or less by yourselves, and that is why we have supplied some suggestions for further reading in the Recommendations for readings at the end of each chapter.

However, we envisage most students using the book alongside a good collection of ME texts, moving between text and discussion. We are strongly of the opinion that anyone hoping to understand how ME works has to spend a good deal of time reading ME. A small collection of annotated illustrative texts has been included as an Appendix, but you should supplement these texts with your own reading; again we make some suggestions in the Recommendations for reading.

The body of this book is organised into three unequal parts, each of them corresponding to a distinct phase of study. In Part I we try to give you a broad-brush account of ME: its historical setting; how we know about it; how its appearance relates to its social functions during the Middle Ages; and its general linguistic characteristics.

In Part II, these linguistic characteristics are studied in greater depth, in terms of the 'levels of language': *meaning* (*semantics*), *grammar*, *lexicon* and *transmission* (*speech* and *writing*). Meaning is expressed linguistically through the grammar and lexicon of a language. The lexicon (or vocabulary) of a language is its wordstock, whereas grammar is to do with the way in which words are put together to form sentences.

In turn, the grammar and lexicon of a language are transmitted from language-users to other language-users through speech or through writing, which is a comparatively recent development in human history.

These various levels of language are presented in two ways in Part II. First, they are described synchronically, that is at a single moment in time. The form of ME used here is the one with which most of you will be to some degree familiar already, that is Chaucerian English of the kind used in London *c.*1400, which is used as a convenient point of reference throughout. *This section of each chapter may be regarded as core information.* Secondly, this Chaucerian usage is regularly placed within two contexts: *diachronic*, in which it is compared to earlier and later states of the language, including earlier and later varieties of ME, and *diatopic*, that is in relation to the kinds of English used in other parts of the country.

It should of course be emphasised that this privileging of Chaucerian usage is essentially a matter of convenience for modern readers, and does not necessarily reflect any special status which was accorded to Chaucer's English in the poet's own lifetime. The evidence suggests that London English did not become sociolinguistically privileged until some considerable time after Chaucer's death in 1400.

In Part III (the final chapter of the book) we move from description to explanation, focusing selectively on those characteristics of ME which point forward to ModE or back to OE. In this part of the book, we also discuss how the study of ME enables us to engage with larger questions to do with linguistic change and textual issues. The book is, therefore, designed as a progressive course in the study of ME, moving from basic to more advanced notions.

1.3 A note about technical terms

At this point it is perhaps worth raising the question of descriptive terminology. Without using descriptive terms, any discussion about language is impossible. But we are aware that many readers of this book will be a little apprehensive about engaging with some of the necessary technicalities involved in learning about any language.

We have tried to overcome this problem by using only terminology which is in very common agreed use, and by providing concise definitions at strategic points throughout the book; these definitions are specifically flagged in the thematic Index. Useful standard reference-books are cited in the Recommendations for reading below; students will also find it handy to look at other books in this series for fuller accounts.

Recommendations for reading

It is important to see ME within its larger historical context, and students are recommended, before engaging with the detail of ME, to read a good narrative history. The following are recommended:

Barber (1993) is a revised and updated version of the author's *The Story of Language* (1964). It is a clear and useful single-volume account, perhaps the best now available for the beginning student.

Baugh and Cable (1993) is probably the most widely used single-volume history, even though in parts it is somewhat outdated in light of modern research; the first version, by Baugh alone, dates from 1951. A new edition is in press (2002).

Blake (1996) takes a novel approach to the history of English, focusing on the evolution of standard varieties. There are many good things in this book, but its somewhat unusual orientation makes it perhaps not wholly appropriate for beginners.

Graddol *et al.* (1997) is a good introductory textbook, organised around topics in the history of English. It was originally designed for the Open University, and is admirably accessible. It is perhaps best used not in a linear way but as a source-book for seminar discussion.

Millward (1989) is perhaps the best single-volume history to have emerged in the USA. It is highly readable and full of entertaining anecdotes; it also quite gently introduces students to theoretical notions at a fairly early stage. A limitation for European readers is that it uses US linguistic conventions, and readers used to the conventions of the International Phonetic Alphabet (IPA) may be occasionally confused.

Smith (1999), which deals with Old, Middle and Early Modern English, might be seen as a prequel to the current book. Necessarily there is some overlap between the two, but the earlier book is really designed for beginning students in English historical linguistics across the early period, whereas the current publication is for those intending further work focusing on ME.

The following general historical books may prove useful for more advanced students:

The multi-volume *Cambridge History of English* (CHEL) is invaluable, though the level of difficulty (and of controversy) in its content varies. It is not a series for beginners. One of its great strengths – openness to varying points of view – is of course also potentially a weakness, in that individual authors have developed distinctive orientations which do not necessarily cohere as a whole. It is also a little weak on the 'external' history of the language, where Baugh and Cable (1993) remains superior. Nevertheless, there is an immense amount of learning contained in it, and no student of English historical linguistics can ignore it.

Lass (1987) is an important and highly stimulating account, but its orientation is perhaps too controversial to make it a book for beginners; it is perhaps best seen as a follow-up to Barber (1993).

Smith (1996) is designed as a bridge between basic philological work and a broader understanding of the kinds of research question with which English historical linguistics deals.

Strang (1970) remains one of the most radical – and stimulating – approaches to the history of English yet written, although it needs updating in the light of new research. The main complaint levelled at the book is that it works backwards in time, from Present-Day English to Proto-Germanic; it is also somewhat densely written and laid out. These problems are counterbalanced by the level of sophistication achieved, and the range of issues covered. It should perhaps not be used by beginners, though more advanced students should certainly read it.

Wyld (1921) is of course now an elderly book, and in many ways it has been superseded. But Wyld's contribution to the historical study of English has been undervalued in the past, and the amount of detail contained in the book remains impressive. More advanced students will gain something from it. A later book by the same author (Wyld 1936) is, for its time, equally impressive. Wyld was almost alone in his generation as seeing the history of English as *not* simply the march towards standardisation.

On general linguistic terminology, and on overall linguistic orientation, several books could be recommended; the following suggestions are only a very preliminary guide. Apart from those in the ETOTEL series, the following may be recommended:

Gimson (1994) is a standard phonetics textbook, with some historical material. Leech *et al.* (1982) and Greenbaum and Quirk (1990) are clearly written and well organised outlines of the principles of modern English grammar. Waldron (1979) remains a classic survey of lexicology in relation to semantic theory.

Students will also need access to a good ME dictionary. The two principal scholarly dictionaries relevant for ME, the *Oxford English Dictionary* and the *Middle English Dictionary*, are available in printed form and also (by subscription) on-line. Most major university libraries will have the OED and the MED available in both forms, since they are crucial research tools. All the readers and editions referred to at the end of chapter 2 have useful glossaries, such as Davis's in Bennett and Smithers (1974), which is an outstanding piece of etymological scholarship. Perhaps the most useful self-standing small dictionary for the beginning student is Davis *et al.* (1979); this book provides a complete glossary for Chaucer's works, but obviously can be used profitably for the study of other writers.

For OE background, see Hogg (2002) and also Mitchell and Robinson 1997 (a new edition is about to appear).

2 What did Middle English look like?

2.1 Introduction

The discussion so far has been somewhat abstract. To make it more concrete, we need to look at some ME. Figure 2.1 provides four texts of *The Lord's Prayer*, in OE, ME, EModE and PDE respectively.

Figure 2.1

OE (West Saxon dialect, late ninth century)
þū ūre fæder, þe eart on heofonum, sīe þīn nama ȝehālgod. Cume þīn rīce. Sīe þīn pylla on eorþan spā spā on heofonum. Syle ūs tōdæȝ ūrne dæȝhpāmlican hlāf. And forȝief ūs ūre ȝyltas spā spā pē forȝiefaþ þǣm þe pið ūs aȝyltaþ. And ne lǣd þū nū ūs on costnunge, ac ālīes ūs fram yfele.

ME (Central Midlands, c. 1380)
Oure fadir, þat art in heuenys, halewid be þi name. þi kyngdom come to. Be þi wile don ase in heuene and in erþe. ȝiue to us þis day oure breed ouer oþer substaunse. And forȝiue to us oure dettes, as and we forȝiuen to oure dettouris. And leede us not into temptaciouns, but delyuere us from yuel.

EModE (Book of Common Prayer, 1549)
Our Father, which art in heaven, Hallowed be thy Name. Thy kingdom come. Thy will be done, in earth as it is in heaven. Give us this day our daily bread. And forgive us our trespasses, As we forgive them that trespass against us. And lead us not into temptation; But deliver us from evil.

PDE (Alternative Service Book)
Our Father in heaven, your name be hallowed; your kingdom come, your will be done, on earth as in heaven. Give us today our daily bread. Forgive us our sins, as we have forgiven those who have sinned against us. And do not bring us to the time of trial, but save us from evil.

An analysis of these different versions of the same text quickly demonstrates the differences between the four kinds of English. Some differences are very obvious, such as the use of certain special letters which are no longer used: þ (OE and ME) and ð (OE) for PDE **th**; the use of ȝ in OE and of ȝ in ME; the use of p (OE) for PDE **w**; and the use of æ as a common vowel-symbol in OE. It is a convention in OE studies, moreover, to mark long vowels with a macron, for example ē. And some uses are obviously archaic for the time when they were written, such as the use of the archaic word **hallowed**, and the form of the verb **come** in the PDE version (for the more usual PDE MAY [YOUR KINGDOM] COME).

Other differences are more subtle. The OE text has different *inflexions* (special endings on words) to indicate the relationships between words, such as **heofon-um, eorþ-an, dæȝhpāmlic-an, ȝylt-as, costnung-e** and **yfel-e**. Inflexions also appear in the later forms of the language, but the range of differences is much more restricted; in the PDE version, for instance, the only inflexion used on most nouns is **-s**, to signal plurality or possession (although you are probably aware of irregular usages, such as **-en** in **children**). The ME version has a vocabulary distinct from OE, with words derived from French and Latin, such as **substaunse, dettes, temptaciouns, delyuere**. In addition, the ME text uses **u** (often corresponding to later English **v** in medial position) where OE has **f**, for example **forȝiue** in place of **forȝief.**

Even in this short passage of text, therefore, it is possible to find linguistic features which demonstrate major differences between ME and earlier and later states of the language. In the rest of this chapter, a longer passage of ME, taken from the writings of Geoffrey Chaucer, will be subjected to systematic analysis, giving you at least a broad understanding of the main distinguishing characteristics of Chaucer's variety of ME. Later in this chapter there will be some discussion of the evidential basis for ME.

2.2 A passage from *The Canterbury Tales*

Geoffrey Chaucer was born *c.*1340, and died in 1400. We know a lot about him, because he played a prominent role in the service of Richard II. Chaucer began his career as a page in the entourage of a noblewoman. He fought as a soldier in the Hundred Years' War between England and France, and was captured and subsequently ransomed. He then took a series of posts in the medieval equivalent of the civil service; he was also at various times a member of parliament. His services were such that, at the end of his career, he was awarded a substantial pension and was buried in Westminster Abbey. He seems to have been politically adept, surviving political upheavals which brought about the execution of contemporaries such as his admirer Thomas Usk (beheaded 1388), and the dethronement of Richard II. Although his family seems to have originated in northern England, Chaucer lived for most of his life in London, where he had a substantial house over one of the city's main gates.

Chaucer's burial-place at Westminster Abbey later became the nucleus for what is now 'Poets' Corner', and it is as a poet that he is now chiefly remembered, as the author of 'dream-visions' such as *The Book of the Duchess* and *The Parliament of Fowls*, of his verse tragedy *Troilus and Criseyde* and, above all, of his ambitious collection of stories, *The Canterbury Tales*, which rivals in achievement *The Decameron* by his near-contemporary, the Italian writer Boccaccio. Chaucer seems to have composed most of the *Tales* during the 1390s; the cycle was incomplete at his death. Chaucer's poetry, for which he is now best known, seems to have been an activity undertaken in his spare time, although it was written, it seems, for court audiences, including royalty; there are only a few sporadic references to it by contemporaries (notably by the French poet Eustache Deschamps, who refers to Chaucer as **le grant translateur**).

Chaucer's writings come down to us in medieval manuscripts, that is in texts written by hand for the most part on animal skin (usually referred to as parchment or vellum); more versatile paper became common in England only during the fifteenth century. The 'best' manuscripts of Chaucer – that is, those closest to the presumed authorial original – were copied by a group of scribes working as individual artisans in the area around St Paul's Cathedral in London. Thus, what we think of as 'Chaucer's English' is in some senses really 'the English of Chaucer's scribes'.

Perhaps the best-known manuscript of *The Canterbury Tales*, and the basis of most modern editions, is the Ellesmere Manuscript, once the property of the Earl of Ellesmere (hence its name) but now in the Huntington Library in San Marino, California. The passage below, from the prologue of the *Miller's Tale*, follows the Ellesmere text. The passage introduces us to Nicholas, the anti-hero of the poem. Nicholas is a **poure scoler** (an impoverished student) who, a graduate with the degree of MA, is interested in **astrologye**. The narrator, the Miller, finds the technical terminology of astrology (**conclusiouns, interrogaciouns, houres**), supported by appropriate technology (**almageste, augrim stones, astrelabie**) baffling; after putting forward these terms in a complex and confusing succession of subordinate clauses and phrases he dismisses them with **I may nat rekene hem alle.** Nicholas's other interests are more social: **deerne loue.** Nicholas has all the attributes required of the successful 'courtly lover' of the later Middle Ages, being **sleigh, priuee, lyk a mayden meke for to see** and as **sweete as is the roote/ Of lycorys.** These two interests will be brought together in the tale which appears in Figure 2.2.

Figure 2.2

Words and phrases which might confuse modern readers are italicised in the text, and have been glossed in the right-hand margin.

Whilom ther was dwellynge at *Oxenford*	once; Oxford
A riche *gnof,* that *gestes heeld to bord,*	churl; took in paying guests
And of his craft he was a carpenter.	
With hym ther was dwellynge a poure scoler,	[line 3190]
Hadde *lerned art,* but al his *fantasye*	was a Master of Arts; desire
Was turned for to lerne astrologye,	
And *koude a certeyn of conclusiouns,*	knew a number of formulas
To *demen by interrogaciouns,*	answer questions
If that men asked hym *in certein houres*	concerning predictions
Whan that men sholde haue droghte or elles *shoures*	showers
Or if men asked hym what sholde bifalle	[line 3197]
Of every thyng; *I may nat rekene hem alle.*	I cannot count them all
This clerk was cleped *hende* Nicholas.	noble
Of *deerne loue* he koude and of *solas*;	secret love; sexual pleasure
And *therto* he was *sleigh* and *ful priuee,*	concerning that; clever; very discreet
And lyk a mayden meke for to see.	
A chambre hadde he in that hostelrye	[line 3203]
Allone, withouten any compaignye,	
Ful fetisly ydight with *herbes swoote*;	very elegantly furnished; sweet herbs
And he hymself as sweete as is the roote	
Of *lycorys,* or any *cetewale.*	licorice; zedoary (a spice)
His *Almageste,* and bookes grete and smale,	(See Note 1 below)

His *astrelabie, longynge for* his art,	astrolabe (astrological intrument); belonging to
His *augrym stones layen faire apart,*	(See Note 2 below)
On shelves *couched* at his beddes heed;	arranged
His *presse* ycouered with a *faldyng reed*;	cupboard; red coarse cloth
And *al aboue* ther lay a gay *sautrie,*	on top of everything; psaltery (= harp)
On which he made a-nyghtes melodie	[line 3214]
So swetely that all the chambre rong;	
And *angelus ad virginem* he song;	(See Note 3 below)
And after that he song the *Kynges Noote.*	(See Note 4 below)
Ful often blessed was his myrie throte.	
And thus this sweete clerk his tyme spente,	
After his freendes fyndyng and his rente.	(See Note 5 below)

Notes
1. The **Almageste** is a treatise on astronomy by the Greek philosopher Ptolemy. It was known to antiquity as 'megiste', that is 'greatest (work)'. It was transmitted to medieval Europe by Arabic scholars, who referred to it as 'al majisti': hence the title given here.
2. **Augrym stones** 'algorismic stones' were cubes marked with Arabic numerals and used for making calculations; 'algorism' is Arabic for arithmetic. The **stones**, being valuable, are **layen faire part**, that is set apart in a safe place.
3. **Angelus ad virginem** is a hymn on the Annunciation.
4. 'The King's Song' has not been identified.
5. 'And thus this pleasant scholar spent his time, depending on financial support from his friends and his own income.'

2.3 Linguistic analysis

We might now proceed to analyse the language of the passage in Figure 2.2, in terms of transmission (spelling and pronunciation), grammar and vocabulary.

2.3.1 Transmission

The spelling of the Ellesmere manuscript differs in some respects from that of PDE, but there are many similarities; the use of **u** for **v** in, for example, **aboue** is only a minor irritation for the modern reader. However, the pronunciation of the passage, insofar as we can reconstruct it, was very different. ME scribes do not generally seem to have used 'silent' letters. Thus, for example, **gestes** was pronounced [gɛstəs],

hende was pronounced [hɛndə], **gnof** was pronounced [gnɔf] and the initial consonant in **whilom, whan** was still probably pronounced distinctly from that in **with, was** ([ʍ, w] respectively). This last distinction, still commonly made in Scots and Scottish English, was dying out in dialects to the south of London but – although some modern scholars dispute this – there is evidence that Chaucer sustained it. Above all, the long vowels of ME had not undergone the 'Great Vowel Shift', a change whereby long vowels in stressed syllables were 'raised' or (if close already) diphthongised. Thus **bookes** was pronounced [boːkəs], not (as in PDE) [bʊks], and **sweete** was pronounced [sweːtə], not [swiːt].

Since this passage is taken from a poem it is possible to say something about stress-patterns. Chaucer was one of the first English poets to write in 'iambic pentameter', a five-stress/ten-syllable measure from which he deviated for poetical effect. Chaucer's use of the iambic pentameter will be discussed further below, especially in Chapter 7.

2.3.2 Grammar

The grammar of the passage shows many similarities with PDE grammar, but there are some differences. Postmodifying adjectives, a characteristic which may derive from French, appear in the phrases **herbes swoote** SWEET HERBS and **faldyng reed** RED COARSE CLOTH. Subordinate clauses are marked a little differently, with the occasional use of what we would regard as a redundant subordinating conjunction **that**: for example, **If _that_ men asked**; the use of **that** obviously had, within the pentameter frame, metrical advantages. In line 3191, the subordinating element is omitted: **Hadde lerned art** appears where in PDE the pronoun WHO would be used, that is _WHO_ HAD TAKEN AN ARTS DEGREE. The 'auxiliary' verbs **sholde, may** and so on had a lexical force in ME; in PDE the verbs MUST, CAN would be used; **koude** (cf. PDE COULD) is used lexically to mean KNEW in **koude a certein of conclusiouns** and **Of deerne loue he koude**. The pronoun system is different from that of PDE, for example **hem** THEM. Verb inflexions vary a little from those of PDE, such as the **-en** suffix in **layen** SET APART.

2.3.3 Vocabulary

The passage contains words derived from OE (such as **was, heeld, craft**) and the languages with which ME had come into contact (for example **carpenter** from French), but some words (such as **hende** NOBLE, **fetisly** ELEGANTLY) have died out and others have changed their meaning, such as **solas**, cf. PDE SOLACE, which seems to have had a clear sexual connotation in ME. The adjective SWEET appears as **sweete** and **swoote**; the latter form has died out since Chaucer's time.

The points just made are few, but enough has been said, perhaps, to illustrate in a preliminary way major differences between ME and earlier and later states of the language. These differences will be discussed in greater detail in Part II of this book.

2.4 Evidence for Middle English

As we just saw, our primary evidence for ME is supplied by *scribes*, who copied the great corpus – many thousands – of manuscripts which survive from the period. In the remainder of this chapter, we will be looking in more detail at the evidence for ME as supplied by scribes; we will also be looking at how modern scholars have worked with this evidence to help us understand ME texts.

Human beings have changed a great deal in social organisation and living conditions since the Middle Ages, but it is reasonable to suppose that medieval linguistic behaviour is governed by the same principles as that of the present day. Many of the most important advances in historical linguistics have come about through applying insights derived from the study of modern languages to older language-states.

However, students of historical linguistics cannot easily adopt all the investigative methodologies appropriate for the study of modern languages. Thus, for instance, a modern sociolinguistic or dialectological survey entails the collection and analysis of a corpus of data, often in machine-readable form. A carefully chosen sample of informants, selected on the basis of their assignation to a particular social group or geographical area, are asked to undertake a range of linguistic tasks, such as reading a word-list or taking part in a cunningly structured conversation, and their responses are recorded in an appropriately organised way. Linguists can also interrogate their informants to elicit further information or to clarify points. Statistical analysis of the results may then follow.

Fairly obviously, such a methodology is not really possible for historical work without considerable refinement. Linguistic historians working on earlier states of the language depend in the last analysis on written data until the appearance of mechanical techniques of recording at the end of the nineteenth century.

For the OE and ME periods, the main sources of information are literary and documentary manuscripts written by medieval scribes, supplemented from the end of the period by early printed books. There are comparatively few manuscripts containing OE, but there are thousands of manuscripts surviving from the ME period. Most of these manuscripts are now stored in great academic libraries, such as (in the UK) the British Library in London, the Bodleian Library in Oxford and the National Library of Scotland in Edinburgh, or (in the USA) the Huntington Library in California and the Pierpont Morgan Library in New York. Such manuscripts have been acquired over many years from private owners, though some, such as the Royal Collection in the British Library, derive from Henry VIII's acquisitions in the sixteenth century when the monasteries were suppressed. The evidence from manuscripts and early printed books is supplemented to a limited extent by inscriptions on stone, wood, metal (including coins) or bone, and (more importantly) by place-names.

Clearly, historical linguists working with such materials cannot choose their informants for their social class or geographical setting, and those informants cannot be literally interrogated for further information; manuscripts survive for all sorts of reasons, and the scribes who wrote them are long dead. Moreover, complex questions of context and trans-mission surround this material: did scribes copy exactly what they saw before them, or did they intervene, to a greater or lesser extent? If they did not understand what they were trying to copy, did they change it? Did they try to improve what they saw? Above all, we have no clear way of distinguishing social class. The 'lowest' medieval classes were illiter-ate, as were many women of all social classes, and the 'highest' frequently did not use English at all, but preferred French and Latin. Even when – as rarely happens – we know the names of medieval scribes, we very rarely know anything about them and their social backgrounds.

It is therefore very important not to draw linguistic conclusions from textual data without first subjecting the texts to careful examination. Texts are never simply illustrative of past states of the language, for every text has a special context which conditions its content.

2.5 Two illustrations

Two illustrations of this point are offered here; our first comes once more from the writings of Chaucer. The scribe of the Ellesmere Manuscript of *The Canterbury Tales* almost certainly also copied another manuscript of the same work; this second version, the Hengwrt Manuscript, is now in the National Library of Wales at Aberystwyth. The following passage contains parallel sections from both the Ellesmere and the Hengwrt texts, in which the original (as opposed to modern editorial) punctuation of the manuscripts has been retained. Modern lineation has been added, however, to aid references. A translation is not offered here, for reasons which will become clear at the end of the chapter.[1]

Hengwrt Manuscript

Here bigynneth the prologe of the tale of the wyf of Bathe

Experience , thogh noon Auctoritee
Were in this world , is right ynogh for me
To speke of wo , that is in mariage
For lordynges , sith þat I twelf yeer was of age   5
Thonked be god , that is eterne on lyue
Housbondes atte chirche dore , I haue had fyue
If I so ofte , myghte han wedded be
And alle were worthy men , in hir degree
But me was told certeyn , noght longe agon is   10
That sith þat Crist ne wente neuere but onys
To weddyng in the Cane of Galilee
That by the same ensample , taughte he me
That I ne sholde , wedded be but ones
Herke eek , lo , which a sharp word for the nones   15
Bisyde a welle , Ihesus , god and man
Spak , in repreeue of the Samaritan
Thow hast yhad , fyue housbondes quod he
And that ilke man , which that now hath thee
Is nat thyn housbonde , thus he seyde certeyn   20
What that he mente ther by , I kan nat seyn
But þat I axe , why þat the fifthe man
Was noon housbonde , to the Samaritan
How manye , myghte she han in mariage
Yet herde I neuere , tellen in myn age   25
Vp on this nombre , diffynycioun
Men may dyuyne , and glosen vp & doun
But wel I woot expres , with outen lye
God bad vs , for to wexe and multiplye
That gentil text kan I wel vnderstonde   30
Eek wel I woot he seyde þat myn housbonde
Sholde lete , fader and moder and take to me
But of no nombre , mencioun made he
Of Bigamye , or of Octogamye
Why sholde men thanne speke of it vileynye   35
Lo here , the wise kyng daun Salomon
I trowe , he hadde wyues many oon
As wolde god , it leueful were to me
To be refresshed , half so ofte as he
Which yifte of god hadde he , for alle hise wyuys   40

No man hath swich , that in this world alyue is
God woot , this noble king as to my wit
The firste nyght hadde many a murye fit
With ech of hem , so wel was hym on lyue
Blessed be god , that I haue wedded fyue   45
Wel come the sixte , whan þat euere he shal
For sith I wol nat kepe me , chaast in al
Whan myn housbonde , is fro the world agon
Som cristen man , shal wedde me anon
For thanne thapostle seith , þat I am free   50
To wedde a goddes half , where it liketh me
He seith , that to be wedded is no synne
Bet is to be wedded , than to brynne
What rekketh me , theigh folk , seye vileynye
Of shrewed Lameth , and his bigamye   55
I woot wel , Abraham was an holy man
And Iacob eek as fer as euere I kan
And ech of hem , hadde wyues mo than two
And many another , holy man also

Ellesmere Manuscript

The Prologe of the wyues tale of Bathe

Experience , though noon Auctoritee
Were in this world , were right ynogh to me
To speke of wo , that is in mariage
For lordynges , sith I . xij . yeer was of Age
Ythonked be god , that is eterne on lyue   5
Housbondes at chirche dore I haue had fyue
For I so ofte , haue ywedded bee
And alle , were worthy men in hir degree
But me was toold certeyn nat longe agoon is
That sith that Crist ne wente neuere but onis   10
To weddyng in the Cane of Galilee
By the same ensample , thoughte me
That I ne sholde , wedded be but ones
Herkne eek , which a sharp word for the nones
Biside a welle Iesus god and man   15
Spak , in repreeue of the Samaritan
Thou hast yhad , fyue housbondes quod he
And that man , the which þat hath now thee
Is noght thyn housbonde , thus seyde he certeyn
What that he mente ther by , I kan nat seyn   20
But þat I axe , why that the fifthe man
Was noon housbonde to the samaritan

How manye , myghte she haue in mariage
Yet herde I neuere tellen in myn age
Vp on this nombre diffinicioun   25
Men may deuyne , and glosen vp and doun
But wel I woot expres with oute lye
God bad vs , for to wexe and multiplye
That gentil text kan I vnderstonde
Eek wel I woot he seyde myn housbonde   30
Sholde lete fader and mooder and take me
But of no nombre , mencioun made he
Of bigamye , or of Octogamye
Why sholde men , speke of it vileynye
Lo heere and , the wise kyng daun Salomon   35
I trowe , he hadde wyues , mo than oon
As wolde god , it were leueful vn to me
To be refresshed , half so ofte as he
Which yifte of god , hadde he , for alle hise wyuys
No man hath swich , þat in this world alyue is   40
God woot , this noble kyng , as to my wit
The firste nyght had many a myrie fit
With ech of hem , so wel was hym on lyue
Yblessed be god , that I haue wedded fyue
Welcome the sixte , whan euere he shal   45
For sothe , I wol nat kepe me chaast in al
Whan myn housbonde , is fro the world ygon
Som cristen man , shal wedde me anon
For thanne , thapostle seith , I am free
To wedde a goddes half wher it liketh me   50
He seith , to be wedded , is no synne
Bet is , to be wedded , than to brynne
What rekketh me , thogh folk seye vileynye
Of shrewed Lameth , and of bigamye
I woot wel , Abraham , was an hooly man   55
And Iacob eek , as ferforth as I kan
And ech of hem , hadde wyues mo than two
And many another man also

Despite the fact that both the Ellesmere and the Hengwrt manuscripts were almost certainly copied by a single scribe there are a number of differences between them. Substantive differences, such as the switch in tenses at line 2 and the use of **for** or **to** in the same line, are likely to be due to differences in the exemplars used for the copying of the two manuscripts.

However other differences are likely to be the result of the scribe's own linguistic behaviour, which tolerated a degree of variation. For

instance the scribe appears to have used three different forms for PDE
THOUGH: **thogh**, **though** and **theigh**. The first two forms, derived
from Old Norse **þó**, are common in both manuscripts, while the latter
form, derived from OE **þeah**, is found only in the Hengwrt manuscript.
The scribe also had two spellings of the word NOT: **nat** and **noght**, both
of which are used frequently throughout both manuscripts. The presence of two different spellings of the word MERRY, **murye** and **myrye**,
displays the variety of usages found within the London dialect during
this period. The two passages also show differences in the use of capital
letters, as found in the spellings of **age/Age** and **samaritan/Samaritan**
in lines 4 and 22; the PDE practice did not become established until the
eighteenth century.

There are also morphological differences between the texts, as may be
seen by a comparison of the forms of the past participle. The Hengwrt
manuscript has forms without the y- prefix, while the Ellesmere manuscript has a number of instances with y-, such as **Thonked/Ythonked**
(line 5), **wedded/ywedded** (line 7), **blessed/yblessed** (line 44). Differences in the use of **that** may also be found in the conjunctions in these
passages, e.g. **sith þat/sith** (line 4), reflecting a variation that is also
found in Chaucer's own usage which he commonly exploited for
metrical purposes. A similar kind of variation is found in the form of
relative pronoun in this passage, which appears as **which** in line 18 of the
Hengwrt manuscript, and as **the which** in the Ellesmere manuscript.
Differences in word order may represent different scribal preferences, or
may simply derive from the different copytext used for the two manuscripts, for example **now hath thee/hath now thee** (line 18).

The second illustration comes from the EME period (that is between
1100 and *c.*1340). Towards the end of the twelfth century, a poet, possibly called Nicholas of Guildford, wrote *The Owl and the Nightingale*. In
this poem, the contentiousness of human beings is satirised through
burlesque: an Owl and a Nightingale use techniques derived from
medieval lawsuits to mock each other's natural attributes. The text
survives in two manuscripts by different scribes: MS Cotton Caligula
A.ix, now in the British Library in London, and MS Jesus 29, part of the
Jesus College collection currently stored in the Bodleian Library in
Oxford. The Caligula text is generally felt to be the 'better', that is closer
to the presumed authorial original. Yet its scribe, oddly, has two distinct
spelling-systems, as illustrated in the following passages (A, B). Passage
A comes from early in the poem; the Nightingale is attacking the Owl
for her unnatural appearance. In Passage B, from towards the end of the
poem, the Owl laments that **riche men** POWERFUL MEN neglect
Master Nicholas.

Passage A (lines 75–8)

þin eʒene boþ colblake & brode.
Riʒt swo ho weren ipeint mid wode.
þu starest so þu wille abiten.
al þat þu mist mid cliure smiten./

[Translation: Your eyes are coal-black and broad, just as if they were painted with woad; you glare as if you wish to bite everything that you could strike down with your claws.]

Passage B (lines 1775–8)

wið heore cunne heo beoþ mildre
an ʒeueþ rente litle childre.
swo heore wit hi demþ adwole.
þᵗ euer abid maistre nichole.

[Translation: With their kindred they are more merciful and they give income(s) to little children; thus their intelligence judges them in error, in that Master Nicholas is always kept waiting.]

There are a number of interesting points to be made about the language of this text, but for our purposes only one is necessary: the two spellings for ARE, boþ (in Passage A) and beoþ (in Passage B). The scribe distinguishes the systems quite carefully; spelling-system I (that is the system of Passage A) appears in lines 1–901, 961–1183, and spelling-system II (the system of Passage B) appears in lines 902–960, 1184–end. Plainly the scribe is reflecting differences in the text from which he is copying, which was probably copied by two different scribes; equally plainly he does not feel able to impose one consistent usage over the complete text.

Many reasons have been offered for the practice of the Caligula scribe, but perhaps the most plausible is that the scribe was trained to write in Latin, and was thus accustomed to copy texts letter-by-letter – for changing a letter in an orthographically fixed language, such as Latin, could confuse readers more thoroughly than in English, where spelling did not become focused (let alone fixed) until the fifteenth century.

2.6 Editing Middle English

So far we have concentrated on looking at ME texts in their manuscript contexts. This approach has many advantages, since it demonstrates the differences between ME and PDE, but it also presents certain challenges in terms of ease of understanding (as will have been clear to you).

Most of the Illustrative Texts in the Appendix are therefore edited in accordance with modern practice, that is using PDE conventions of punctuation.

We will not be taking editorial issues much further at this stage (but see Chapter 7 below). However, it is perhaps worth looking a little at punctuation since it is a comparatively neglected area of linguistic enquiry. Modern punctuation is grammatical, that is it is a visual cue, designed to help the reader understand the grammatical structure of the text being read. Thus punctuation marks sentences, clauses and so on. Medieval punctuation – when it was used at all, for some scribes do not bother with it – is rhetorical; that is, it flags pauses for breath or emphasis in order to assist those reading the text aloud to others. Obviously there is an overlap between grammatical and rhetorical punctuation, but the difference is basic, and it correlates with the shift from the prototypically oral culture of the Middle Ages to the prototypically literate culture of the present day.

It is not, of course, possible for us to recreate medieval oral culture; we are modern people, used to modern conventions, and even when we read medieval texts we will be reading them in modern ways. So it is therefore legitimate for us to present medieval texts using modern conventions, as long as we are aware that there is a difference between them.

Modern conventions of punctuation also help us when we wish to translate ME into PDE. Translation is a basic skill for anyone wanting to work on ME, and it is important that you learn to do this competently; the activity of translating formally, especially at the beginning stages of study, forces you to confront differences of usage and work out the linguistic structure of the texts you are encountering. For that reason we suggest some translation exercises at the end of this chapter. Of course, such exercises are only a beginning; you will need to exercise your skills in translation over a much wider range of texts than those offered here. (See further the Recommendations for reading for Chapter 2 below.)

Exercises

The passage below contains the same Chaucerian text as on pp. 15–17 above, but using modern conventions of punctuation. Attempt a translation of this passage into PDE prose, using present-day grammar, vocabulary and conventions of punctuation. You may find it helpful to consult a modern edition (e.g. Benson *et al.* 1986) or translation.

Hengwrt MS

Here bigynneth the prologe of the tale of the Wyf of Bathe.

'Experience, thogh noon auctoritee
Were in this world, is right ynogh for me
To speke of wo that is in mariage;
For, lordynges, sith þat I twelf yeer was of age,
Thonked be God that is eterne on lyue,
Housbondes atte chirche dore I haue had fyue-
If I so ofte myghte han wedded be-
And alle were worthy men in hir degree.
But me was told, certeyn, noght longe agon is,
That sith þat Crist ne wente neuere but onys
To weddyng, in the Cane of Galilee,
That by the same ensample taughte he me
That I ne sholde wedded be but ones.
Herke eek, lo, which a sharp word for the nones,
Bisyde a welle, Ihesus, God and man
Spak in repreeue of the Samaritan:
"Thow hast yhad fyue housbondes," quod he,
"And that ilke man which that now hath thee
Is nat thyn housbonde," thus he seyde certeyn.
What that he mente ther by, I kan nat seyn;
But þat I axe, why þat the fifthe man
Was noon housbonde to the Samaritan?
How manye myghte she han in mariage?
Yet herde I neuere tellen in myn age
Vp on this nombre diffynycioun.
Men may dyuyne and glosen, vp & doun,
But wel I woot, expres, with outen lye,
God bad vs for to wexe and multiplye;
That gentil text kan I wel vnderstonde.
Eek wel I woot, he seyde þat myn housbonde
Sholde lete fader and moder and take to me.
But of no nombre mencioun made he,
Of bigamye, or of octogamye;
Why sholde men thanne speke of it vileynye?
Lo, here, the wise kyng, daun Salomon;
I trowe he hadde wyues many oon.
As wolde god it leueful were to me
To be refresshed half so ofte as he!
Which yifte of god hadde he for alle hise wyuys!
No man hath swich that in this world alyue is.
God woot, this noble king, as to my wit,
The firste nyght hadde many a murye fit

With ech of hem, so wel was hym on lyue.
Blessed be God that I haue wedded fyue!
Wel come the sixte, whan þat euere he shal.
For sith, I wol nat kepe me chaast in al.
Whan myn housbonde is fro the world agon,
Som cristen man shal wedde me anon,
For thanne th'apostle seith þat I am free
To wedde, a Goddes half, where it liketh me.
He seith that to be wedded is no synne;
Bet is to be wedded than to brynne.
What rekketh me, theigh folk seye vileynye
Of shrewed Lameth and his bigamye?
I woot wel Abraham was an holy man,
And Iacob eek, as fer as euere I kan;
And ech of hem hadde wyues mo than two,
And many another holy man also.'

Recommendations for reading

The best way of learning about ME is to read a lot of ME, and there are numerous readers and editions designed for the beginning student. The following is a selection of such resources. Unfortunately, several collections are out of print, but library copies can be consulted and second-hand copies can still be found. EME is particularly poorly served by major publishers.

Beginning students may also find it helpful at the outset to read ME texts in translation. Still the best translation of *The Canterbury Tales* is Coghill's verse rendering (1952) which, though not a substitute for the real thing, does give beginners an immediate flavour of Chaucer's achievement.

Bennett and Smithers (1974) is the best scholarly collection of EME texts yet produced. The literary and linguistic commentaries are excellent, but demand a high degree of philological knowledge and sophistication. The glossary, by Davis, is masterly.

Benson *et al.* (1986) is the standard edition of Chaucer's works. It is primarily designed for literary students, though it does include a very useful linguistic discussion. The texts themselves have been thoroughly edited to make them accessible to modern students, however, and the process of editing has sometimes obscured interesting linguistic details.

Burnley (1992) is one of the best resources available for the historical study of English, being a collection of well-chosen and carefully annotated texts designed to illustrate various stages in the language's evolution; it should be used alongside a good narrative history. There are some excellent selections from ME.

Burrow and Turville-Petre (1997) is skewed towards literary interests, but the linguistic apparatus is admirably clear and well presented, albeit in terms of traditional grammar; our book may be seen as complementary and supplementary to their work rather than as a replacement. The selection of texts is good, with excellent commentaries, though it is much stronger on later ME than on Early ME. The latest edition contains fairly extensive selections from Chaucer's writings.

Dickins and Wilson (1952) has been largely superseded by Bennett and Smithers, but it contains several interesting texts not found in the later collection.

Hall (1921) was a pioneering collection of EME texts, and remains useful for advanced students. It contains texts not found in later readers.

Jones (1972) offered beginning students an outline of ME grammar from a contemporary theoretical-linguistic perspective; it offers an interesting synthesis between some modern linguistic ideas and more traditional philological perspectives.

Mossé (1959) combines a grammatical account with a useful reader. For many years, Mossé was the only large-scale survey of ME for beginning students. Although it has in some ways been superseded by Burrow and Turville-Petre (1997), its linguistic (as opposed to literary) focus means that it remains useful for those students whose interests are primarily in English historical linguistics.

Sisam (1921), although also old-fashioned in its presentation and in some of its introductory material, remains a useful reader for later ME, and makes a useful companion to Hall.

As well as the readers above, it is perhaps appropriate at this stage to flag some useful grammatical surveys designed as introductions (other than Mossé (1959) and Burrow and Turville-Petre (1997)). The three best general books in the field are all largely restricted to transmission and morphology: Brunner (1963), Fisiak (1964) and Wright & Wright (1928). All these books have distinctive virtues; in many ways the last, though the oldest, is the most user-friendly for a modern reader. Although similarly restricted in scope and focusing on Chaucerian usage, Sandved (1985) is invaluable and authoritative. Smith (1999) might be used as a prequel to the current volume.

More advanced students will need to work with the editions published by the Early English Text Society (EETS). EETS was founded in the middle of the nineteenth century, primarily to provide quotations for the *New English Dictionary* (later the OED), but it developed to become the main publisher of OE and ME literary and non-literary texts, with one or more publications appearing every year. EETS editions have varied in orientation and appearance since the foundation of the series. The earliest editions, in the nineteenth and early twentieth centuries, were usually 'diplomatic', that is they were transliterations of particular manuscripts reproduced in printed form. More recent EETS editions tend to be 'critical' editions, attempting to reflect presumed authorial intentions, although it is usual for these editions to be accompanied by detailed descriptive and interpretative introductions which supply details of the individual peculiarities of manuscripts and indications of where editorial emendations have been carried out (see further Chapter 7 below).

The publishing programme of EETS is often committed for many years in advance, and other useful supplementary series have appeared. Of these perhaps the most accessible yet scholarly are Middle English Texts, which is still active, and the Clarendon Medieval and Tudor Series, which is now unhappily defunct (although second-hand copies can still be found). Major academic publishers also continue to produce individual editions of important ME texts outside the standard series, such as Davis (1971–6).

A recent welcome development is the appearance of electronic editions, available either on disk or (much more commonly) online. Students of Chaucer will find invaluable *The Canterbury Tales* Project's CD of *The Wife of Bath's Prologue and Tale* (see for details <http://www.cta.dmu.ac.uk/projects/ctp/>). However, by far the most useful resource currently available is the *Middle English Compendium*, available from <http://ets.umdl.umich.edu/m/med/>. The Compendium, which is being continually updated, is available by subscription; it can be accessed from most major university libraries. An advantage is that subscribers to the Compendium also have access to the *Middle English Dictionary* online. SEENET (the Society for Early English and Norse Electronic Texts) will become an important publisher in the near future. For other online links, see the comprehensive (and regularly updated) list maintained by the STELLA project at the University of Glasgow: <http://www.arts.gla.ac.uk/SESLL/STELLA/links.htm>.

There are also spoken-word performances. The best-known, and probably the most accessible, are the tapes produced by the Chaucer Studio. On a smaller scale, a CD, *The Sounds of Early English* (2002), to accompany Smith 1999, is obtainable from the STELLA Project,

University of Glasgow, Glasgow G12 8QQ, Scotland, UK.

Students interested in editorial procedures may find it useful to consult McCarren and Moffat (1998), which may be regarded as a standard handbook for anyone setting out to create an edition of an ME text. This book also includes a very useful list of printed facsimiles of ME manuscripts, by R. Beadle (pp. 319–31); in our experience students gain a lot from looking (even in reproduction) at the manuscript-evidence for ME.

Notes

1. Although they are the most authoritative manuscripts of the *Tales* – that is they seem to reproduce a text very close, in substantive terms, to what Chaucer actually wrote – neither the Hengwrt nor the Ellesmere manuscript represents Chaucer's own usage. There is, however, some evidence that the Hengwrt manuscript reproduces Chaucer's linguistic practice a little more accurately; see further Chapter 7 below.

3 Middle English in use

3.1 Introduction

So far, our discussion has been textual, that is we have been concerned with the appearance of ME, i.e. what it looked like. However, in order to understand how ME got to appear as it does, some contextualisation is needed. In Chapter 3, we will analyse the *functions* of ME, and show how these functions constrain the forms which ME took. We will investigate two things: who used ME, and what did they use ME for? We will also investigate the formal implications of these functions in terms of dialect and standardisation during the ME period.

3.2 Who used Middle English?

On the eve of the Norman Conquest, written and spoken English – that is, OE – was widely used throughout the Anglo-Saxon kingdom. In some parts of the East and North this variety was much influenced by varieties of Norse (the language of the Viking invaders), and in one or two western areas of what is present-day England, such as Cornwall and parts of Herefordshire, some people continued to use varieties of Celtic. But otherwise English was used in both speech and writing throughout what is now present-day England. The Anglo-Saxon nobility spoke English habitually, and the Anglo-Saxon state used written English extensively to record transactions and legal decisions. The written English most generally in use was Classical Late West Saxon, based on the usage of Wessex, the most powerful of the Anglo-Saxon kingdoms, which was centred on the city of Winchester, in southern England.

The Conquest changed this situation. The bulk of the population immediately after 1066 – approximately four million people, according to some estimates, most densely clustered in the southern half of England – continued to speak English, and written OE, notably the great prose homilies of Ælfric and Wulfstan, continued to be copied for at least a century after the Conquest, especially in the English West Midlands. However, the new ruling élite spoke Norman French (which became Anglo-Norman), the variety of French current in Normandy, and the introduction of continental documentary practices meant that Latin – the international language of law and learning – gradually replaced English as the medium of legal record. The *Domesday Book* of 1087, William the Conqueror's most distinctive administrative innovation, was written in Latin.

It is perhaps worth recalling at this point that such a multilingual society as post-Conquest England is not as curious at it might seem from a modern, Anglophone perspective. English is now an international language, spoken by some seven hundred million speakers worldwide as a first language, and by many more as a second language. In the Middle Ages, however, English was a marginal language in Western European terms; in some ways, its position was roughly equivalent to that of present-day Dutch or Finnish in terms of numbers of speakers. If English-speaking people did not want to be cut off from the rest of the known world, they needed to understand other languages.

Although the relationships between English, French and Latin changed in detail, the functional configuration just outlined remained essentially the same until towards the end of the EME period, that is up to *c.*1340. The nobility seems to have become primarily English-speaking comparatively quickly, a situation which was encouraged by King John's loss of lands in France at the beginning of the thirteenth century. Anglo-Norman, it is true, continued to be used in Parliamentary debates until the middle of the fourteenth century, and in some poetry after that date.

However, the appearance of books for the aristocracy on how to speak French, such as Walter of Bibbesworth's *Treatise* from the middle of the thirteenth century, suggests that English is the mother tongue but that French was a necessary accomplishment for cultivated discourse; this 'cultivated' French was Central French, not Anglo-Norman, and was evidently adopted because of the cultural ascendancy of Central French in the later Middle Ages. Robert of Gloucester's *Chronicle*, which dates from roughly the same time as Walter's *Treatise*, makes the point – but, significantly, does so in English: **Bot a man conne Frenss, me telth of him lute** FOR UNLESS A MAN KNOWS FRENCH HE IS THOUGHT OF LITTLE ACCOUNT.

In the written mode, Latin, and later French, had national documentary functions; both languages, for instance, were used for *Magna Carta* in 1215, and the various offices of state continued to use Latin well into the fifteenth century. A good deal of English was written – there is more written English surviving in manuscripts from the two centuries after the Conquest than in all the Anglo-Saxon centuries put together – but the language seems in general to have had a local, parochial function: English was used, for example, for the medieval equivalent of primary education, in the small classrooms of parish priests, or for writing texts designed for a local readership.

There were of course important local variations in this overall picture, which reflect varying social conditions relating to the wealth or otherwise of the area in question. In some parts of the country such as the North and the far South-West, where land-quality (the basis of medieval wealth) was poorer, vernacular literacy seems to have disappeared for much of the EME period. On the other hand, wealthier areas, such as East Anglia, the South-East or the South-West Midlands, sustained local literacy in the vernacular long after the Conquest. However, the English texts produced during the EME period seem in general to have been composed with a very particular, local readership in mind. Although there are a couple of occasions when English was used nationally, notably Henry III's *Proclamation* of 1258 which was issued in English as well as in French and (possibly) Latin, these occasions are exceptions to the general pattern.

Only in the fourteenth century did this situation begin to change, again in relation to social developments; it is for this reason that 1340 is generally chosen by scholars as a rough dividing date for EME and LME. The *Domesday Book* reveals that the land, the basis of medieval economic and political power, may have rested on the back of the peasantry, but was controlled by a relatively small class of landlords, consisting of the King, his magnates and leading churchmen and ecclesiastical institutions; this structure persisted even after the Dissolution of the Monasteries by Henry VIII in the sixteenth century.

However, there were fluctuations and signs of new developments. The slump in population (from six to four million) following the Black Death in the fourteenth century meant social turbulence, a labour shortage and a consequent increase in prosperity for the remaining lower-class population, who could demand higher wages. The Peasants' Revolt of 1381, a direct response to a crude incomes policy known as the Statute of Labourers, is an important straw in the wind. Contemporary writers, as may be expected, reflect intimately the social concerns of their time. The name of the eponymous hero of Langland's philosophical poem, Piers Plowman, was adopted as a battle cry by the peasants in their Revolt, while Gower, in his Latin poem *Vox Clamantis*, mocks the Revolt's leadership.

Social fluidity encouraged the growth of towns and the appearance of a bourgeoisie – the word indicates in its etymology the key role of urbanisation – in the shape of an emerging royal bureaucracy and a rising mercantile class. The rise in the size and importance of London is the most distinctive feature of late medieval English society, but similar growth has also been noted in the population of other towns, such as York, Norwich, Oxford and Gloucester. Towns in the Middle Ages provided trading opportunities, being centres for the markets and fairs which were essential for a developing economy; they also made possible the development of craft-skills. London, as seat of government and the country's premier trading port, attracted immigrants from further and further afield during the course of the period, especially as agrarian development increased the population beyond that which could be supported on the land using medieval agricultural practices. Modern demographic research (Burnley 1983: 112–13) has reconstructed the pattern of immigration into the capital during the thirteenth and fourteenth centuries; archaeological evidence has confirmed how London was at the centre of contemporary road- and water-borne communication.

The bourgeoisie was Anglophone, and its sons were taught in grammar schools, in English. John Trevisa recorded at the end of the fourteenth century how innovative schoolmasters such as John Cornwal and Richard Pencrych taught their pupils in English, not French,

> **so that now, the yer of oure Lord a thousand thre hondred foure score and fyue, of the secunde kyng Richard after the Conquest nyne, in al the gramerscoles of Engelond childern leueth Frensch, and construeth and lurneth in Englysch ...**
>
> (quoted in Sisam 1921: 149)

By the end of the Middle Ages, therefore, French had become marginalised in England as a second, 'high-status' language, used rather as it was in nineteenth-century Russia.

The importance of the vernacular was reinforced by two key extra-linguistic developments. Printing, brought to England by William Caxton at the end of the fifteenth century, succeeded because it met the rising demand for texts to which the old scribal system could not respond; and the Reformation made vernacular literacy a religious requirement – a prerequisite for reading the new vernacular Bibles. The 'triumph of English', sometimes ascribed to the literary efflorescence of the late sixteenth century, has its roots at least a hundred years earlier.

3.3 For what was Middle English used?

During the transition from OE to ME, roughly between 1100 and 1250, some literary works carried on Anglo-Saxon traditions: the *Peterborough Chronicle*, for instance, was a continuation of the *Anglo-Saxon Chronicle*, begun in the ninth century. However, continental influences also left their mark; although Laȝamon's *Brut* attempted, in antiquarian fashion, to reproduce aspects of Anglo-Saxon epic, it derived much of its content from Wace's Anglo-Norman *Roman de Brut*; and although *Ancrene Wisse* and associated texts derived much of their technique from native homiletic traditions they nevertheless demonstrate an intimate knowledge of continental exegetical technique and rhetorical practices. From the middle of the thirteenth century onwards, the range of text-types represented in ME literature is much extended, from romances such as *Havelok the Dane* or *Floris and Blauncheflour*, to the burlesque-satire *The Owl and the Nightingale*, the version of the beast-epic known as *The Fox and the Wolf*, and the tradition of short 'lyric' verse represented in MS London, British Library, Harley 2253; all these texts represent the conscious adoption of French/Anglo-Norman or Latin genres.

However, the great flowering of ME literature took place from the second half of the fourteenth century. The appearance of major vernacular writers from the end of the fourteenth century and into the fifteenth is intimately connected to the rise in the status of English associated with the appearance of a distinct bourgeois class. It was now possible to be eloquent in English. Something similar had happened to Italian a century before; indeed, contemporaries drew parallels between the rise of English poetry and the appearance of the great Italian poets Dante, Petrarch and Boccaccio. It is no accident that Geoffrey Chaucer – a royal bureaucrat, as it happens – chose to write in English for his mixed audience of courtiers and civil servants (the two categories tended to overlap). That his choice was a conscious one is indicated by the fact that Chaucer's friend and contemporary John Gower wrote extensively in Latin (*Vox Clamantis*) and French (*Le Miroir de l'Homme*) as well as in English (the *Confessio Amantis*). Chaucer could have written in French or Latin instead of English – he translated freely from both languages, and also from Italian – but he chose not to. Parliament – Chaucer was at times during his career an MP as well as a civil servant – debated in English from 1362, and state documents in English began to appear commonly from the second quarter of the fifteenth century.

Many traditions of writing in English may be noted from this period. A 'courtly' tradition of rhyming verse modelled on French and Italian literature, for instance, forms one important strand, exemplified by the romances of the Auchinleck Manuscript, and subsequently by Geoffrey Chaucer – author of *The Canterbury Tales* and *Troilus and Criseyde* – and his friend John Gower (author of the *Confessio Amantis*) and their disciples, such as Thomas Usk, Thomas Hoccleve, and John Lydgate. Such verse is characterised by the use of French-derived metrical forms, such as the decasyllabic iambic pentameter, and it also uses end-rhyme. During the fifteenth century, courtly verse became highly mannered, as poets demonstrated their skill through the employment of elaborate, Latinate diction – so-called 'aureate' verse.

Of equal sophistication, but ultimately to be supplanted by verse of the Chaucerian type, is the poetry of the so-called 'alliterative revival', which derived, with much modification, from Anglo-Saxon verse-tradition but in content looked to continental models, such as *Sir Gawain and the Green Knight*, or *William of Palerne*. Such verse lasted longest in the Northern and Western parts of England, where more conservative cultures dominated. Late ME alliterative poetry is sometimes known as 'pure-stress' verse since there is no close correlation between the length of the line and the number of syllables; cohesion is supplied by alliteration between verse-units and the special poetic diction used derives from OE usage.

A tradition of vernacular devotion saw poetic expression in William Langland's English alliterative philosophical poem *Piers Plowman* and in the prose associated with the Oxford theologian and 'premature Protestant' John Wycliffe. Native traditions of chronicle-prose are sustained in the writings of Thomas Malory; though translated from **the Frenche booke**, Malory's Arthurian cycle is expressed in the so-called 'paratactic' style, whereby clauses are placed in parallel, subordination is avoided and thus the causal relationships between events are left to readers to reconstruct. By contrast, Caxton, in his own prose, develops a usage – the so-called 'trailing-style', with much use of subordinate clauses – which derives directly from contemporary French models.

3.4 The dialects of Middle English

The functions of English, which changed over time, have implications for the written representation of the language. In Anglo-Saxon times, as we have seen, Classical Late West Saxon became in some senses a 'standard' language, since it appeared in texts copied outside Wessex, the area where this dialect originated. 'Standard' is in some ways an unfortunate term; it is probably more accurate to describe this variety of OE as a focused usage in the written mode which, although never as far as is known codified, was selected, elaborated and accepted for employment outside its area of origin. There is of course no evidence that it correlated with any prestigious form of speech; the adoption of West Saxon (hence WS) correlated with an emerging national function for the written mode.

The terminology just used derives from a formulation made first by Einar Haugen (1966):

A usage can be *selected* for some reason;
A usage may be *codified* and thus fixed (for example by an Academy, as in seventeenth-century France, or simply by means of an educational system);
A usage may be *elaborated*, in that it becomes the usage available for every linguistic function;
A usage may be ultimately *accepted*, as the only usage acceptable in the usage of powerful members of the society in question.

Classical Late WS lost most of its elaborated functions in the transition from Anglo-Saxon to Norman government consequent upon the events of 1066; the revival of Latin learning on the continent of Europe and the arrival of a new French-speaking aristocracy in England meant that English became a vernacular without any national function. This restriction of the function of English persisted, even though, as we have already noted, there is good evidence that much of the Norman-descended aristocratic class in England quite rapidly learnt English and used it in everyday speech.

As a result, when it was written, English after the Conquest began to exhibit marked dialectal diversity in the written mode as Latin and French took on the documentary and more broadly literary functions hitherto met by 'standard OE'. As we have seen, written English remained widely used in writing as well as speech. However, this development seems again to have been essentially local; English had a local function. When people wished to use written language for communication beyond their own localities they used the international languages: Latin and French.

Since the vernacular was in general parochially focused rather than regionally or nationally focused, wide variation in the written mode of English became developed. Since the function of written English had become particular and local, written and (perhaps even more importantly) designed for reading only within a limited area, it was therefore open to modification to reflect spoken-language changes peculiar to the individual dialect-areas. Indeed, it would make sense to modify inherited spelling-conventions for local use, since that would make easier the teaching of reading and writing on a 'phonic' basis.

As a result of the development of these parochial spelling-practices, the ME period is, notoriously, the time when linguistic variation is fully reflected in the written mode. Thus the *Linguistic Atlas of Late Mediaeval English* (LALME: the authoritative survey of late ME dialects) records no fewer than five hundred ways of spelling the item THROUGH in use during the period 1350–1450, for example

throgh, thorw, þorow,
thurhgh, yruȝ, dorwgh,
yora, trowffe, ȝurch, trghug

(evidence from LALME, volume IV). ME has therefore been described as '*par excellence* , the dialectal phase of English' (Strang 1970: 224), in that, during the ME period, dialectal variation is fully expressed in the written as well as in the spoken modes.

Despite this plethora of evidence for contemporary linguistic variation, however, it was until comparatively recently scholarly practice to confine the discussion of ME dialects to a rather small set of texts considered to be of first-class evidential value, that is authorial holographs, which are supposed to give precise information about the language of a (comparatively) fully contextualised individual. During the ME period, such texts are few: Dan Michel's *Ayenbite of Inwyt* (Canterbury, 1340) is one such, as are the holograph writings of the poet and scribe Thomas Hoccleve (early fifteenth century) or much of the fascinating fifteenth-century collection of papers and letters collected by and for the Paston family of Norfolk. To these might be added the English poetry of John Gower, William Langland and possibly even Geoffrey Chaucer himself, all of whose usages may be reconstructed from the evidence of manuscripts copied around or just after the time of the poets' deaths.

However, the completion of LALME in 1986 meant a massive addition to the body of localised and localisable texts for the period 1300/1350 to 1450/1500, and hence a liberation from the restricted corpus hitherto studied. The focus of LALME is on individual scribal usage represented in medieval manuscripts; thus scribes are granted equal importance to authors in terms of their status as linguistic informants. Moreover, the written language is regarded as an object of interest in its own right rather than as indirect evidence for the spoken mode. The research which produced LALME will be described at greater length below. LALME, in combination with its successor projects (the *Linguistic Atlas of Early Middle English* and the *Atlas of Older Scots*) has in short revolutionised ME studies. LALME and its successors are above all an enabling project; the identification of localised and localisable texts makes it possible for scholars to produce fuller grammatical descriptions across the diatopic range than have hitherto been achievable. Such work is already under way in a number of centres.

3.5 Written standardisation

We have seen that towards the end of the ME period, English was developing at the end of the Middle Ages as an 'elaborated' language, available across the country for use in a range of functions. As English took on these national functions, there is evidence from at least the fifteenth century onwards of the emergence of sociolinguistic variation in the use of English. In other words, it became possible to write and speak English in 'more' or 'less' proper ways. As French ceased to be used as a prestigious spoken language, prestigious forms of English emerged, studded with loanwords from French, used to mark social difference; with the rise of humanism in the fifteenth and sixteenth centuries, Latin vocabulary was also transferred wholesale into the English lexicon.

This development has implications for the representation of dialect variation in writing towards the end of the ME period. Texts covered in LALME date from between 1300 and 1500; earlier texts were included in the Southern part of the survey, and later ones from the Northern part. The reason for this diatopic divergence is to do with the standardisation of the written mode, which took place earlier in the South than in the North, and which obscured the earlier pattern of richly recorded dialectal variation. By the sixteenth century, in England at least, the public written mode of the vernacular had become standardised – focused – in a way which points forward to the fixed and educationally enforced standard of PD written English. The use of printing for reproducing English texts from the end of the fifteenth century provided prescriptive norms for contemporary manuscript-usage.

The standardisation of English correlates with the functional extension of the vernacular back into national life beyond the parochial. John Fisher has gone so far as to express the view that precise spelling-forms were adopted as the result of a particular royal initiative on the part of Henry V (see, for example, Fisher 1984, 1996). However, Fisher's views, although they derive in part from insights developed during the creation of LALME, have been challenged by the LALME team (see notably Benskin 1992). The standardisation of spelling seems to have been a by-product of the general elaboration of English, and not the result of a centrally controlled codification.

As a result of work pursued under the aegis of LALME, it is possible to trace the stages of standardisation in ME more precisely. M. L.

Samuels in 1963 offered what has become the seminal account of the evolution of 'Types' of what he called 'incipient standard' during the fourteenth and fifteenth centuries:

Type I: Central Midlands Standard ('Wycliffite')
Type II: Earlier fourteenth-century London ('Auchinleck')
Type III: Later fourteenth-/early fifteenth-century London ('Ellesmere')
Type IV: Post-1430 London ('Chancery'/'King's English')

These types represent, within the cline of ME usages, focused varieties found in several manuscripts, characterised by the prototypical appearance of particular forms. It is important not to overstate their cultural hegemony; the Types represent foci within the range of late ME written usage rather than fixed sets of shibboleths. Prototypical forms, not all of which co-occur in every text belonging to the Type in question, are:

Type I: **sich** SUCH, **mych** MUCH, **ony** ANY, **silf** SELF, **stide** STEAD, **ʒouun** GIVEN, **siʒ** SAW
Type II: **werld** WORLD, **þat ilch(e)** THAT VERY, **no(i)þer** NEITHER, **þei(ʒ)** THOUGH, **þai/hij** THEY
Type III: **world**, **thilke/that ilk(e)** THAT VERY, **neither** NEITHER, **though** THOUGH, **they** THEY, **yaf** GAVE, **nat** NOT, **swich(e)** SUCH, **bot** BUT, **hir(e)** THEIR, **thise** THESE
Type IV: **gaf** GAVE, **not** NOT, **but** BUT, **such(e)** SUCH, **theyre** THEIR, **thes(e)** THESE, **thorough/þorowe** THROUGH, **shulde** SHOULD

Types II through IV represent varieties of London English in the fourteenth and fifteenth centuries; Type IV is, very broadly speaking, the ancestor of modern English spelling. Texts which are generally taken to represent each Type are given in brackets above after each Type: thus 'Auchinleck' flags the use of Type II by Scribe I of the Auchinleck manuscript of romances; 'Ellesmere' is of course the Ellesmere manuscript of *The Canterbury Tales*; and 'Chancery English' (perhaps more properly 'King's English') refers to the usage of a cluster of fifteenth-century government documents.

Type I, in use from the middle of the fourteenth century to the middle of the fifteenth, is rather different from Types II–IV. This type appears in many manuscripts associated with Wycliffe and his followers, and also in certain scientific texts such as medicas. Texts in Type I use a mixture of forms common in Central Midland counties in Middle English times; it is thus sometimes referred to as Central Midlands Standard.

More recently – as indicated on p. 34 above – M. Benskin has offered (e.g. 1992) what is arguably the most convincing account of the process, as a prolegomenon to his forthcoming extended survey of the subject.

Benskin argues that the standardisation of English spelling during the fifteenth and sixteenth centuries was driven by what might be termed 'communicative pressures'. The evidence seems to indicate that the reduction of the exotic range of spelling-possibilities in English took place as a communicatively driven response to the set of functions which English developed during the course of the fifteenth century, and which also manifested itself in the great humanistic programme of translation into English during the sixteenth century. As the English language gradually ceased to be the medium of merely parochial literacy and began to take on national functions in succession to Latin and French, so the richly diverse spelling-systems of ME became inconvenient, and more exotic spellings were purged, leaving a 'colourless' *lingua franca* behind. At a later stage, a London-focused spelling-system was adopted as the basis of present-day usage. In other words, once English developed a national function, the disadvantages of written variation began to outweigh the advantages, and standardisation of the written mode resulted.

3.6 The standardisation of speech

Whereas the evidence for the standardisation of writing is fairly clear (even if its interpretation is controversial), evidence for the standardisation of speech in late ME is of very uncertain quality. In the *Reeve's Tale*, Chaucer attempted to represent Northern speech in his characterisation of two students, thus:

> 'Symond', quod John, 'by God, nede has na peer.
> Hym boes serue hymselue that has na swayn,
> Or elles he is a fool, as clerkes sayn.
> Oure manciple, I hope he wil be deed,
> Swa werkes ay the wanges in his heed.'

In this passage, verbal inflexions in **-s** (cf. Chaucerian **-th**), such as **has**, **boes** BEHOVES and **werkes** are Northern features, as is some of the dialect vocabulary, for example **wanges** TEETH or (more subtly) the meaning of **hope** (in Northern ME, THINK rather than HOPE). **Swa** for Southern ME **so** is also a marked North/South distinction.

However, Chaucer's humour seems to be based upon the oddness of people from different parts of the country rather than from the sense of a standardised spoken language; indeed, the two Northerners seem to be of higher social class than the Cambridgeshire miller they fool. A rather better example dates from the generation after Chaucer, in the fifteenth century: the use of a **Southren tothe** by the comic sheepstealer Mak

in the Wakefield (Yorkshire) *Second Shepherds' Play* (Cawley 1958: 48).
(Italicised words and phrases are glossed at the end of the passage.)

2 *Pastor.*	Mak, where has thou gone? Tell vs *tythyng.*	
3 *Pastor.*	Is he commen? Then *ylkon* take hede to his *thyng.*	
Mak.	What! *ich* be a yoman, I tell you, of the kyng,	201
	The self and the some, *sond* from a greatt lordyng,	
	And sich.	
	Fy on you! Goyth hence	
	Out of my presence!	205
	I must haue reuerence.	
	Why, who be ich?	
1 *Pastor.*	Why make ye it so *qwaynt?* Mak, ye do *wrang.*	
2 *Pastor.*	Bot, Mak, *lyst ye saynt?* I trow that ye *lang.*	
3 *Pastor.*	*I trow the schrew can paynt, the dewyll myght hym hang!*	
Mak.	Ich shall make complaynt, and make you all to *thwang*	211
	At a worde,	
	And tell euyn how ye doth.	
1 *Pastor.*	Bot, Mak, is that sothe?	
	Now take outt that Sothren tothe,	
	And sett in a *torde*!	

tythyng NEWS
ylkon EACH ONE
thyng THINGS
ich I (pronoun)
sond MESSENGER
qwaynt CUNNING
wrang WRONG
lyst ye saynt? DO YOU WANT TO PLAY THE SAINT?
lang LONG (TO DO SO; verb)
I trow the schrew can paynt, the dewyll myght hym hang! I BELIEVE
THE RASCAL TALKS DECEPTIVELY, THE DEVIL COULD HANG
HIM!
thwang BE FLOGGED
torde TURD

In this passage, the usual verbal inflexions of the North (in -s) are
abandoned in favour of -th endings, such as **goyth** and **doth**. Mak also
uses a Southern first-person pronoun, **ich**; interestingly, this form is
not that found in the 'incipient written standard' of the period, Type IV,
and this indicates that a clear model for standardised usage had not yet
been established. The key factor is Southern-ness; Mak's affectation of
Southern dialect features of grammar, and of French-derived vocabulary
(such as **presence** and **reuerence**) seems to correlate with the claim

he makes that he is a **yoman ... of the kyng**. Mak's pretensions to Southern-ness, and his correlation of Southern-ness with courtliness, would seem to be the earliest example of something which was much more widely commented on in the sixteenth century, for example George Puttenham's comment (*The Arte of English Poesie*, 1589). Puttenham describes how the accomplished poet should adopt the usage of **the better brought vp sort**:

> ... ye shall therfore take the vsuall speach of the Court, and that of London and the shires lying about London within lx. myles, and not much aboue.

Such clear evidence is lacking for the fourteenth and fifteenth centuries; although there are hints that a prestigious form of speech was available in the late ME period, there is no definite statement other than hints of the kind offered by the *Second Shepherds' Play*.

Exercises

Questions for review

The following questions are designed to help you review issues raised in this chapter. They can also be used to help focus discussion in seminars.

1. Give an account of the changing relationships between Latin, French and English during the ME period.

2. 'The standardisation of English spelling relates directly to the elaborated status of the English language.' Discuss.

3. Give an account of Samuels's four 'Types' of incipient standard varieties of English (see Samuels 1963).

4. In the *Wakefield Second Shepherds' Play*, the character Mak is described as having a **southren tothe**. What is the significance of this description for our understanding of the evolution of standardised spoken English?

Recommendations for reading

Most of the issues raised in this chapter are discussed in the standard histories of English, for which see Chapter 1. Strang (1970) is perhaps the most comprehensive discussion to date, in the context of a single-volume general history, although students should also consult the account in CHEL volume II; full references are given in Smith (1996), especially chapters 4 and 5.

On the extralinguistic functions of ME, perhaps the best introduction is Clanchy (1993), which focuses on the period of transition from OE to ME. Clanchy is a documentary historian, and his work is concerned with broad issues of literacy rather than the detail of linguistic behaviour. Beginning students may also find useful the account in Smith (1991), while more advanced students might consult chapters 4 and 5 in Smith (1996), which contains full references.

ME is, as has been stated, '*par excellence*, the age of written dialects', and dialectology is therefore of central concern to all students of ME. The dialectology of ME has been revolutionised by the publication of LALME (1986), and the introduction to Volume I of LALME is, for advanced students, one of the best introductions to ME linguistic studies yet written. Advanced students will also find useful the collection of important papers brought together in Laing (1989).

Most of the comprehensive histories of the language contain discussions of the rise of written standard English, but students should also consult the seminal papers of Samuels (1963 [reprinted with corrections 1989], 1981) and Benskin (1992). Fisher's extensive writings on standardisation (e.g. 1984, 1996) derive in part from Samuels' work, but have been severely criticised; a new comprehensive discussion, by Benskin, is currently in progress.

4 Spellings and sounds

4.1 Some preliminaries: the relationship between speech and writing

In Chapter 1, it may be recalled, the relationship between levels of language was identified as follows: meaning (semantics) is expressed through grammar and lexicon, and grammar and lexicon are transmitted through speech and writing. This relationship may be expressed in diagrammatic form (see Figure 4.1). It will be clear from this diagram that there are special relationships between lexicon and grammar, both of which express meaning, and between speech and writing, both of which transmit lexicon and grammar. Issues relating to lexicon and grammar will be pursued in Chapters 5 and 6; in this chapter, the focus is on transmission, that is on speech and writing.

Before we turn to the details of the ME system, it is important to clarify the relationship between speech and writing in general terms. Speech is clearly much older than writing. Indeed, it seems likely that Neanderthalers, who lived 500,000 years ago, could speak, though – given the physical differences in their vocal tracts – their sound-systems must have been very different from anything now known. Writing-systems are much more recent, and are recorded only from the last 4,000 years or so. It is worth recalling that many peoples never developed such systems for their languages, and it is quite possible for societies of considerable sophistication to function without them. For instance, the Inca empire in Peru communicated over immense distances using the *quipu*, a system of knotted cords used as mnemonics to aid the oral transmission of messages, but there was no written language as we understand it. Nevertheless, many societies have developed special symbolic systems for communicative purposes, using tools (for example, chisels, pens, ink) applied to stone, clay tablets, parchment, paper and so on.

Broadly, there are two kinds of writing-system in existence: ***phonographic*** and ***logographic***. In logographic systems, such as Chinese, spoken

Figure 4.1

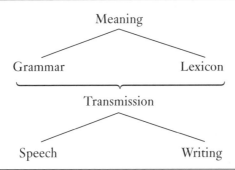

words are represented by pictures, to a greater or lesser degree of conventionalisation. In phonographic systems, written symbols correspond to individual sounds or sound-clusters. The International Phonetic Alphabet is a phonographic system.

The distinction between logographic and phonographic systems seems clear-cut, but is in practice less so. Until the invention of mechanical recording at the end of the nineteenth century, it was not possible to capture speech in permanent form; writing is designed as a comparatively permanent record of utterances. Writing has therefore an inbuilt conservatism, which means that it is slow to represent linguistic change; it thus often lags behind spoken usage, and becomes less phonographically accurate as a result. Moreover, since writing is often designed for communication beyond the immediate speech-community it serves, it quickly develops a degree of conventionalisation designed to cater for different readerships who possess different phonological systems. The result is that a system which may be primarily phonographic develops some logographic and conventionalised aspects.

Such tendencies may be demonstrated by examples from PDE. Arguably logographs are symbols such as '&' and '+'. More subtly, the word **knight**, for instance, used to be pronounced [knɪxt] during the ME period; however, sound-changes since the end of the fifteenth century mean that the symbols <k> and <gh> are now 'silent'. <gh>, in the sequence <igh>, has developed a diacritic function in PDE, flagging a diphthongal pronunciation of the preceding <i>. Another example is to do with the letter <u> in **cut** or **put**. In present-day Southern English dialects, the vowels in these two words are now distinct: [ʌ] and [ʊ]. However, the older pronunciation made no difference in the vowel in these words, much as is the case in present-day Northern English accents. The writing-system is conservative, and does not distinguish the two.

Thus, although English remains an essentially phonographic writing-system, it has over many years of use developed certain conventionalised features. It is for this reason that present-day children learning to read English begin with 'phonics' (like C - A - T = **cat**, for instance) but then proceed to 'look-and-say', whereby the word is 'learnt' as a symbolic whole (**knight**, for example).

In general terms, this relationship between speech and writing has long been understood. Greek and Roman linguists actually devised a special way of categorising these relationships in a phonographic system: the so-called 'doctrine of *littera*'. According to this categorisation, the letter (*littera*) consisted of a written manifestation (the *figura*) and a spoken manifestation (the *potestas*). More recently, linguists, aware of the systematic character of the two modes, have developed other ways of categorising speech and writing, using the terms *phoneme* and *allophone* (for speech), and *grapheme* and *allograph* (for writing).

Phonemes and graphemes may be defined briefly as the minimally different units of speech and writing enabling meaning-distinctions to be made. Thus the sounds /b/ and /p/ are phonemes, distinguishing the meaning of the words /bat/ and /pat/, while the letters <b> and <p> are graphemes, distinguishing the meaning of the words <bat> and <pat>. It is conventional to place phonemes in slash-brackets, thus /.../, and graphemes in angle-brackets, thus <...>.

Allophones and allographs may be defined as the realisations of individual phonemes and graphemes. Thus, for instance, [ɬ] and [l] are allophones of /l/; to replace one with the other in realising the initial consonant in /lap/ does not change the meaning of the word even though the two realisations sound rather different. It is conventional to place allophones in square-brackets, thus [...].

Allographs are realisations of graphemes; for instance, the realisation of <a> may vary from font to font, thus << a a **a** a **a** >> and so on. There does not seem to be a generally accepted way of denoting allographs formally, perhaps because linguists (as opposed to paleographers or students of typography) have not categorised them very often. We will discuss allographs very rarely here, but when we do we will mark them by a double angle-bracket, thus <<...>>.

4.2 Reconstructing ME pronunciation

In the previous section, we established a model for describing the relationship between speech and writing. This model derives from observation of present-day languages, where it is possible to have direct access to both modes: we can hear (and now record in electronic form) speech, and we can see writing. How can we use this model for a past state of the language where there is no direct access to the spoken mode? Reconstructing the sound-systems of past states of a language is a complex matter, and depends on bringing together a number of different types of evidence. Our discussion of the ME sound-system will be based on the following kinds of evidence:

1. Evidence arrived at through *comparative reconstruction*, whereby other languages, and later states of the same language, are used to reconstruct the sound-system of ancestral forms of the language. This technique is based on a basic 'genetic' axiom, which is that related languages or dialects share a common ancestry; by comparing these languages or dialects it is possible to work out what that ancestor sounded like. The process of comparison takes place through the anaysis of *cognates*, that is words deriving from a common ancestor (cf. Latin *co* + *gnātus* 'born together'). For instance, Germanic languages such as Dutch, German, Swedish – and English – belong to the larger Indo-European 'family' of languages. All the Germanic languages have an initial fricative in words like **father** or **fish**, cf. present-day German **Vater**, **Fisch**, where cognate words in the other Indo-European languages tend to have a plosive, such as Latin **pater**, **piscis**.

2. Evidence arrived at though *internal reconstruction*, whereby later residual elements in a language demonstrate earlier usage. For instance, there is a PDE difference between the final consonant in **house** (noun) and **house** (verb); in the former the consonant is voiceless [s], in the latter it is voiced [z]. We know that in OE, the verb had inflexional endings, for example **hūsian** (infinitive), cf. the noun **hūs**. Examination of occurrences of [z] in PDE words descended from OE shows that such forms emerged from intervocalic environments; [s] appears in other environments. It thus seems likely that in OE, [s] and [z] were allophones of the same phoneme. In PDE, of course, /s/ and /z/ are distinct phonemes, as in the distinct pronunciations of **house** (noun, verb); such 'minimal pairs', as they are called, came into English not only with the loss of inflexions but also through borrowing from other languages, notably French, cf. **cease** or **seize**, both of which are French loanwords.

3. Evidence arrived at through *the analysis of verse*. Verse in the Middle Ages is a linguistically patterned form of art, depending on parallelism and regularity in the spoken mode, for example through metre and rhythm, rhyme and alliteration. It is thus possible to use verse for reconstructive purposes. For instance, the evidence is that Chaucer wrote in

iambic pentameter, a metrical type which was dominant in English verse from the end of the fourteenth century onwards (indeed, Chaucer was one of the first poets to use it). Some literary critics have expressed uncertainty about the significance of the -e spelling which is found in many manuscripts of Chaucer's verse, in forms like **gode** (as well as **god**) for GOOD. Metrical analysis shows, however, that the -e spelling was regularly pronounced in particular grammatical environments.

4. Finally, there is evidence from *the analysis of spelling*. Languages which use phonographic writing-systems are based ultimately upon a mapping between phonemes and graphemes. (A writing-system which mapped allophones would be highly inefficient, since every writer would need to develop his or her own symbolic system – which would defeat the purposes of communication.) It is, therefore, in principle possible, when comparing spelling to other sources of evidence, to establish how that mapping works.

To exemplify how the analysis of spelling is undertaken, we will look again at the history of the English fricatives. In PDE, we distinguish the phonemes /v/ and /f/, cf. the minimal pair **vine**, **fine**. However, the evidence is that, in OE, [v] and [f] were allophones of the same phoneme; [v] was used intervocalically and [f] was used elsewhere. If [v] and [f] are allophones of the same phoneme, and if graphemes map onto phonemes, then we should expect [v] and [f] to be symbolised in writing in the same way. Furthermore, in OE, <f> is used for the labio-dental fricative, whether voiced or voiceless, cf. **yfel** EVIL beside **fisc** FISH. The regular graphemic distinction between <v> and <f> had to wait until ME times; the transfer to ME of loanwords from French introduced a minimally-distinctive contrast between /f/ and /v/. A graphemic distinction in the written representation of the two phonemes is therefore to be expected, and that is what is found, for example **vine**, **fine**, using <v> for the voiced sound and <f> for the voiceless.[1]

These preliminary remarks provide the necessary underpinning for the rest of the chapter. In what follows, an attempt has been made to distinguish between basic and more advanced information. The discussion on pp. 44–6 may be regarded as an outline introduction to ME transmission, with an outline on pp. 46–50 of one (well-known) variety: Chaucerian usage. The material on pp. 50–64 is for the more advanced student, and can safely be left aside by the beginner.

4.3 Middle English sounds and spellings: an outline history

In PDE, there are many sound-systems (*accents*) currently in use, for example Northern English, London English, Irish English, American English and so on. Similarly, there were many accents of OE and ME, albeit geographically restricted to parts of the British Isles. However, in PDE, some of these accents have become 'prestigious', that is they are habitually used by speakers of high status in their societies. In England, this accent is called 'Received Pronunciation' or 'RP'; to use RP is to flag one's social status in relation to others. As was discussed in Chapter 3, there is no evidence for such prestigious accents until the very end of the ME period.

Whereas PDE accents vary, written variation is much rarer. Normative writing-systems are taught in schools, and failure to use them correlates with social failure. That there are a few rather trivial differences between British/Canadian and US/Australian usage, such as **favour/favor**, does not invalidate the general point.

The history of writing-systems during the OE and ME periods is much more complex, and was discussed briefly in Chapter 3; the discussion in this chapter builds upon that foundation. For much of the OE period, writing seems to have been an art confined to a few people, and rather little evidence remains. Although it is conventional to say that OE has four dialects (WS, Old Kentish, Old Mercian and Old Northumbrian) the reality is that, for much of the period, we have evidence for spelling-systems from only a few provincial centres in these four areas. Only towards the end of the OE period does writing seem to have become more widespread; as the kingdom of Wessex dominated late Anglo-Saxon polity, it is not surprising that Late West Saxon, the language of Wessex, became the prestigious form of writing in English. Thus Northumbrians and Mercians seem to have used the WS writing-system even though their spoken accents must have diverged markedly from WS speech. After the Norman Conquest, as was discussed in Chapters 1 and 3, English ceased to have a national function; documentary functions were taken over by Latin, and many cultural functions were taken over by varieties of French.

However, as we also saw in Chapters 1 and 3, English texts continued to be copied after the Conquest. Moreover, new texts in English were also composed, increasingly so as the ME period developed. At first, such texts were written in Late WS, but, as Anglo-Saxon traditions died out, scribes began to develop local writing-systems, reworking conventions not only derived from Anglo-Saxon tradition but also Latin and French. At least one daring experimentalist, Orm, used a few letter-forms which he seems to have invented himself. These local systems, though deriving from inherited systems, were (very broadly) designed to reflect a local phonology with a local graphology.

PDE spelling has to cater for a whole range of accents, since it has a national function, and thus (as we have seen) is both phonographic and logographic; many of the problems which PDE orthography presents for both native and non-native learners are to do with this compromise. However, written ME, since it did not have a national function, could be expressed in local spelling-systems which were much more phonographic. ME readers, who seem to have been taught to read wholly by the 'phonic' method, would not have needed to worry about logographic forms since the spelling they encountered would have been designed to reflect their own accent. As a result, as was discussed in Chapter 3, ME is the period when accentual (and other) variation is expressed in the written mode more thoroughly than ever since. Towards the end of the ME period, however, English began to take on national functions once again; as we saw in Chapter 3, standardised systems, based upon London usage, emerged.

The remainder of this chapter falls into two parts. In the next section, a detailed description is offered of one ME system of transmission: the sound-system of Geoffrey Chaucer, and the spelling-system we find in the best manuscripts of his poetry. The choice of Chaucerian usage for special study is severely practical: it is likely that most readers of this book will have first encountered ME through reading Chaucer, and it is for that reason that it has been selected as a reference-point.[2, 3] Once this point of reference has been established, the remaining section in the chapter contains detailed accounts of the origins and development of sound- and spelling-systems found in various parts of the country at different times in the ME period.

4.4 Chaucerian transmission

Chaucer's *sound-system* can be organised into the following categories: *vowels in stressed syllables* (short, long, diphthongal), *vowels of unstressed syllables* and *consonants*. For each category, an inventory of phonemes will be offered in what follows, with comments on the lexical distribution of these phonemes and discussion (insofar as it is possible) on allophonic realisations.

The Chaucerian (that is 'Ellesmere') *spelling-system* can also be treated in an organised way. Chaucerian spellings reflect, very broadly, phonemic patterns; thus spellings will be discussed here in parallel with their corresponding sounds. However, there are some purely graphological matters which should be dealt with at the outset:

1. *OE runic <þ> 'thorn'* was retained in many ME written varieties

Figure 4.2

Old English figura	potestas	Middle English figura
<ᵹ>	[g]	<g>
<ᵹ>	[j]	<ȝ>
<ᵹ>	[x]	<ȝ>
<s>	[z]	<ȝ>

to reflect dental fricatives (both voiced and voiceless), but it tends to be replaced by <th> as the ME period progresses. It is found rarely in the Ellesmere text, and there largely only in some determiners (such as þe, þat THE, THAT).

2. OE scribes used <ᵹ> as the *figura* for /j, x, g/. Modern editors tend to replace it with <g>. The present-day letter <g> was known in Anglo-Saxon times, but used for copying Latin; in the transition from OE to ME, however, <ᵹ> (later <ȝ>) was regularly used for /j, x/ while <g> was used for /g/.

By Chaucer's time, <ȝ>, known as 'yogh', commonly represented /x/ and /j/, though it was gradually being replaced by <y> initially and <gh> medially. It was also used sporadically for /w/ and even for /z/ – in the latter case because OE <ᵹ> and Old French <z> were by this time written identically, as <<ȝ>>. The letter <ȝ> is not found in the Ellesmere manuscript of *The Canterbury Tales*, but is common in other important early Chaucerian manuscripts (see Figure 4.2).

3. <u, v> were used interchangeably to represent both vowel [ʊ] and consonant [v], with <v> generally being used initially, <u> elsewhere.

4. <y> was used interchangeably with <i>, especially in environments where contemporary handwriting could be confusing, such as before or after <m, n, u>; all these letters could be written using the 'minim' stroke: <<ɪɪɪ, ɪɪ, ɪɪ>>. <o> was used for <u> in similar environments. This practice accounts for the PDE spellings **come** (cf. OE **cuman**) and **love** (cf. OE **lufu**), which could potentially appear as <<cuɪɪe>> and <<luɪɪe>> in ME.

5. In many varieties of ME, including that exemplified by the Ellesmere manuscript, <e>, <o> and sometimes <a> could be doubled to indicate

Figure 4.3

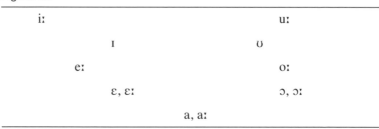

'length'; cf. **good** GOOD, **fleen** FLEE, **taak** TAKE. <o(o)> also appeared in London ME for words which had ā in OE, such as **sto(o)n** STONE (OE **stān**), **ho(o)m** HOME (OE **hām**).

As in OE, *stressed monophthongal vowels* fell into two major classes: *long* and *short*. In OE, there seems to have been no qualitative distinction between long and short vowels; the distinction was wholly one of quantity. However, there is indirect evidence that the long and short vowels of OE developed qualitative as well as quantitative distinctions during the transition to ME, so that the short vowels were more open in quality than their long equivalents. By about 1400, London English seems to have had something like the following inventory of monophthongal vowel-sounds: /iː, ɪ, eː, ɛː, ɛ, aː, a, ɔː, ɔ, oː, uː, ʊ/ (see Figure 4.3).[4]

The *short vowels* [ɪ, ɛ, a, ɔ, ʊ], were generally spelt <i/y, e, a, o, u> respectively. Those forms where an <o> was used for <u> in minim environments, such as PDE **love, come**, generally occur in present-day southern English dialects with the pronunciation [ʌ]; the general ME pronunciation, /ʊ/, is retained in PD Northern English accents.

The *long vowels* [iː, eː, ɛː, aː, ɔː, oː, uː], were generally spelt <i/y/ij, e/ee, e/ee, a/aa, o/oo, o/oo, ou/ow> respectively. Here are some examples, with equivalent present-day pronunciations, for the most part as in Received Pronunciation and General American. In some cases, marked with a double asterisk **, the present-day pronunciation given is that found in Modern Scots, which has not developed the slightly confusing diphthongal sounds found in southern English prestigious accents.

ME	PDE	PDE example	ME example
[iː]	[aɪ]	LIFE	[liːf] **lyf, lif**
[eː]	[iː]	MEET	[meːtən] **meten**
[ɛː]	[iː]	MEAT	[mɛːtə] **mete**
[aː]	[eː]**	NAME, TAKE	[naːmə, taːk] **name, taak**
[uː]	[aʊ]	HOW, TOWN	[huː, tuːn] **how, toun**
[oː]	[uː]	MOOD	[moːd] **mo(o)d**
[ɔː]	[oː]**	BOAT, HOME	[bɔːt, hɔːm] **bo(o)t, ho(o)m**

The regular distinctions between ME and PDE pronunciations of long vowels may be noted. The raisings and diphthongisations which produced the PDE system, known as the 'Great Vowel Shift', took place at the beginning of the EModE period; it has been argued that they are the result of sociolinguistic interaction in late medieval/Early Tudor London.

In the *vowels of unstressed syllables*, the qualitative distinctions which existed in OE were already becoming obscured in late Anglo-Saxon times. This pattern continued in ME: Chaucer's unstressed vowel-sounds seem to have been [ə, ɪ]. Both were usually spelt <e, i/y> in the Ellesmere manuscript, such as -e in **olde** or -y- in **sweryng**.

The major difference between OE and ME vowel-systems was in *diphthongs*. The OE diphthongs monophthongised and merged with other sounds during the transition from OE to ME, and new diphthongs had emerged in the system through vocalisations of consonants and borrowings from French. Chaucer's system seems to have been somewhat as follows:

[aɪ]	<ai, ay, ei, ey> as in **day**, **grey** and so on
[ɔɪ]	<oi, oy> as in **joye** JOY, **poynt** POINT[5]
[aʊ]	<au> as in **saugh** SAW (verb)
[ɔʊ]	<ow> as in **knowe(n)** KNOW
[ɪʊ]	<ew> as in **newe** NEW, **lewed** IGNORANT (cf. PDE **lewd**)[6]

The *consonant-system* of Chaucerian English was much the same as that found in the best-known 'reference accents' of PDE: Received Pronunciation (RP) in England and General American (GenAm) in the USA. The inventory of consonant-sounds in Chaucerian English seems to have been only a little different from that of PDE RP: /p, b, t, d, k, g, tʃ, dʒ, f, v, θ, ð, s, z, ʃ, h, m, n, l, r, w, ʍ, j/ were all phonemic in ME. The major differences between ME and PDE usages are as follows:

1. Chaucerian English does not seem to have had any 'silent' letters. Thus **sweete**, **knyf** were pronounced [swe:tə, kni:f] respectively.

2. <gh> was pronounced [x], as in **knyght** [knɪxt]. The usual PDE pronunciation of <gh>, that is 'silent <gh>', appears from the fifteenth century onwards. The pronunciation with [f] in ENOUGH, ROUGH and so on began to appear from the fifteenth century, but spellings such as **boft** BOUGHT, **dafter** DAUGHTER still appear in the eighteenth century, showing that the present-day distribution of pronunciations had not become settled even by that date. The pronunciation /rux/ ROUGH was still common in eighteenth-century Scots.

3. **Nacioun** NATION, **sure** and so on were pronounced with /sj/ rather than with PDE [ʃ].

4. Initial <w, k, g> were all pronounced in Chaucer's language in words like **write(n)**, **gnawe(n)**, **kne(e)** KNEE. It seems likely that their employment reflects contemporary secondary articulations of the consonant. For example, <wr> possibly indicates the pronunciation of [r] with lip-rounding.

5. /ʍ, w/ seem to have remained distinct phonemes in Chaucer's language: thus **wyn** WINE [wiːn], **while** WHILE [ʍiːl]. However, the beginnings of the present-day southern English pronunciation, which has merged the two sounds on /w/, is indicated in some late ME dialects to the south of London, such as **wan** WHEN.

6. The PDE sound [ŋ] is phonemic in RP but not in present-day Northern English accents. Thus **sin**, **sing** form a minimal pair in RP /sɪn, sɪŋ/ SIN, SING, but in Northern English [ŋ] is an allophone of /n/, cf. [sɪn, sɪŋg]. /ŋ/ was not in Chaucer's phonemic inventory, and thus his usage for this item was comparable with that of present-day Northern English.

4.5 Middle English sound-systems

We might now move to a more detailed discussion of the origins of the various ME sound-systems. Just like PDE, ME had a wide variety of accents. Traditionally, ME dialects have been divided into five geographical areas: the North, the West and East Midlands, the South-East and the South, in accordance with the map given in Figure 4.4. Such labels are in many ways unsatisfactory. However, such a broad-brush set of distinctions as 'North', 'West' and so on may be allowable at this initial stage, and it is generally accepted by scholars that these divisions do reflect distinctive clusterings of accents around prototypical cores.

Even so, it is important to grasp at this stage that the boundaries between dialect-areas are fuzzy. For this reason the map in Figure 4.4 indicates where accents are to be found, but does not draw clear-cut boundaries between them. Recent work on ME dialectology has shown that – like PDE dialects – ME dialects are not a set of discrete usages but a continuum of overlapping phenomena. No one could deny that there are very distinct differences between, for example, Northern and Southern English, or between 'GenAm' and 'RP', but precisely where, geographically, this difference becomes salient is hard to define in clear-

Figure 4.4 Schematic map of the dialects of Middle English.

cut, 'either/or' terms. Indeed, it seems fairly clear that any such attempt is fundamentally misconceived; natural languages simply do not work in this way. Moreover, ME varied extensively diachronically as well as diatopically. All systems during the course of the ME period underwent considerable changes – generally at different speeds in different parts of the country, with different outcomes. ME sound-systems derive from the variety of accents which existed in Anglo-Saxon England, including not only OE but also varieties of Old Norse. There was also a degree of later influence from varieties of French.

As discussed in the companion volume on OE, it should be noted that the evidence for non-WS dialects in OE is comparatively slight. Three attested OE dialects are conventionally recorded (other than WS): Old Northumbrian and Old Mercian (often classed together as Old Anglian), and Old Kentish. However, there are known to have been other (non-attested) OE dialects, such as East Saxon, and those non-West Saxon texts which do survive are generally acknowledged to give only a partial picture of the kinds of variation to be found within the dialects they represent.

The remainder of this section is divided into three sub-sections: (1) Syllables and stress, (2) Consonants and (3) Vowels.

4.5.1 Syllables and stress

A syllable in English consists of vowels and any surrounding consonants; thus a word like **book** is made up of one syllable, and a word like **booklet** is made up of two syllables. Syllables in English consist of an optional onset (consonantal), a compulsory peak (a vowel) and an optional coda (consonantal). Thus permissible syllable-shapes in English are: CV, CVC, V and VC. Syllable-boundaries are sometimes problematic, since the coda for one syllable may also be acting as the onset for the next.

Syllables may be stressed and unstressed: that is, they may be more or less prominent when pronounced. Thus, in the word **booklet**, the syllable represented in writing as **book-** is more prominent than the syllable represented by **-let**: **book-** is stressed, **-let** is unstressed. Prominence in PDE is achieved by a mixture of length, loudness and pitch.

Stress has implications for the phonetic quality of segments. Thus the two words **catastrophe** and **catastrophic**, though obviously etymologically related, contain quite different sequences of vowels simply because the pattern of stressing is quite different.

Most English words are stressed according to the Germanic stress-rule, whereby the first syllable of the stem is stressed, for example héaven, shówing and so on. This was the case in ME. Loan-words are generally subjected to this pattern (such as sólid), though there may be some delay in their assimilation (for example, garage; many older English speakers and most Americans pronounce this word with stress on the second syllable, garáge, whereas younger British speakers almost invariably stress the first syllable, gárage). Such mixed patterns seem to have existed in ME.

In polysyllabic words, a special stress-pattern existed, known as the *Countertonic Principle*, that is the 'balancing' of the main stress; this pattern appeared in native words such as ótherwìse, líkelihòod. The Countertonic Principle reflects a balancing pattern relating to the wider stress-pattern, whereby there is a regular alternation between stress and non-stress; within a polysyllabic (that is, more than disyllabic) lexeme one of these was less prominent than the other and thus stressed as 'secondary'. Thus there was a secondary stress two syllables later.

The Countertonic Principle is also found in French words, for example còuntenánce; however, in French the secondary stress generally appears before the primary stress. When words were borrowed into English from French before 1500 they were gradually subjected to imposition of native patterns: for example náture (native) vs. natúre (French) (disyllables); cóuntenànce (native) vs. còuntenánce (French).

English speakers naturally tended to prefer the native pattern, thus oríginàl. The result of the Countertonic Principle working in both English and French is that the stressing of polysyllables in English became a mixture of Romance and Germanic patterns.[7]

4.5.2 Consonants

The main developments in consonants between OE and ME were as follows:

(a) *Phonemicisation of voiced and voiceless fricatives* has already been discussed (see p. 44). Three pairs of forms are usually included in this discussion: [v, f], [z, s] and [ð, θ]. In OE, these were pairs of allophones, in complementary distribution: voiceless forms appeared word-initially and word-finally, while voiced forms appeared intervocalically. In PDE the sounds are all distinct phonemes. This change seems to have taken place in the ME period, caused in part, it seems, by contact with French, from which were introduced into English such pairs of loan-words as vine/fine, seal/zeal. However, there were native sources of voiced word-initial forms. In Southern accents, initial voicing of fricatives seems to have been widespread, and this seems to be the source of the distinction between PDE **fox, vixen** (cf. OE **fox, fyxen**). The loss of inflexional endings (see p. 8) meant that other forms in contrastive distribution arose, such as **reeve, reef** (cf. OE **gerēfa**, ON **rif**). A good illustration of the process is the contrast between the PDE pronunciation of **house** as a noun (with a voiceless word-final consonant) and as a verb (with a voiced word-final consonant); the distinction derives from the OE pair **hūs** (noun)/**hūsian** (verb) where the distribution of voiced and voiceless sounds was in complementary distribution.[8]

(b) *Norse supplied certain consonant-clusters*, such as /sk/ in **skyrte** SKIRT. This cluster had existed in prehistoric OE, but underwent a sound-change to [ʃ]. When, at the end of the OE period, the Norse form was borrowed into English, it developed a distinct meaning from its OE cognate **scyrte** SHIRT.

(c) *Loss of phonemic long consonants*: OE distinguished short and long consonants, cf. **man** ONE (pronoun), **mann** MAN (noun). During the transition from OE to ME the distinction broke down.

(d) *Loss of h in <hl>, <hn>, <hr>*: There is some controversy about this development, which had taken place by *c.*1200 at the latest, thus EME **lauerd** (OE **hlāford** LORD), **nesche** (OE **hnesc** SOFT), **ringe** (OE **hring** RING). The prevailing view of modern scholars is that <h> in OE seems to have represented a velar fricative, probably [x], and that the clusters <hl, hn, hr> represent /xl, xn, xr/ respectively (Hogg 1992: 39–40). The cluster **hw**, however, remained in many dialects, though with various spellings; see p. 62 below.

(e) *Three more minor changes* were: firstly, vocalisation of voiced velar fricatives in the environment of a preceding [l, r], for example OE **swelgan** SWALLOW (verb); secondly, loss of /w/ in the environment of a preceding [s, t] and a following back vowel, for example PDE SWORD (cf. OE **sweord**) beside PDE SWIFT; and thirdly, the OE prefix **ge-** was 'weakened', becoming **i-, y-** in southern dialects of ME; in Midland and Northern dialects, it disappeared altogether.

(f) Some OE consonants were vocalised after monophthongs to produce *new diphthongs*, such as **dai** DAY (cf. WS **dæg**). These developments are discussed further on p. 58.

Figure 4.5

i, iː, y, yː	u, uː
e, eː	o, oː
æ, æː ɑ, ɑː	

4.5.3 Vowels

As we saw on p. 52, vowels follow distinct patterns of development depending on whether they appear in stressed or unstressed syllables. Vowels in stressed syllables are known as *stressed vowels* while vowels in unstressed syllables are known as *unstressed vowels*. It is usual to discuss the history of *stressed vowels* in terms of *qualitative* and *quantitative* developments. Qualitative developments are to do with questions of vowel-height, frontness or backness, roundedness and so on; quantititative developments are to do with length and shortness.

It is also usual to discuss ME vowels as 'reflexes' of WS vowels, in terms of both spelling and pronunciation, since WS is by far the best-attested OE variety. This practice is, of course, purely for convenience, given that most ME vowel-systems, including Chaucer's, descend from non-WS systems. However, as was indicated on p. 26 and p. 45, these non-WS systems are only fragmentarily attested in Anglo-Saxon times.

Bearing this caveat in mind, it is useful to recall the WS monoph-thongal vowel-system. The inventory in Figure 4.5 is accepted by most scholars.

This system is roughly that of the ninth century, that is the period of King Alfred. Notable characteristics of the system are its three heights, and the quantitative (not qualitative) distinction between short and long vowels.[9]

Now, as we have seen (p. 48), Chaucer's system had a general qualitative distinction between short and long vowels. How this distinction arose is a matter of scholarly controversy, which will not be pursued in this book; however, there is some evidence for the dating of the change (see further p. 59 below). The resulting system is generally accepted to be as in Figure 4.6.[10]

The reflexes of certain WS vowels in stressed syllables vary diatopically in ME. The following are the most salient variations:

(a) WS y, ȳ is reflected in spelling as <u, uy> in southern and western texts, as <e> in the South-East, and as <i, y> elsewhere: for example **hull, hell, hyll/hill** HILL; **fure, fere, fire/fyre** FIRE (cf. WS **hyll, fȳr**).

Figure 4.6

iː		uː
ɪ		ʊ
eː		oː
ɛ, ɛː		ɔ, ɔː
	a, aː	

Figure 4.7

	WS	Old Anglian	Old Kentish
ǣ¹:	ǣ	ē	ē
ǣ²:	ǣ	ǣ	ē

Figure 4.8

	SW	M, N	SE
ǣ¹:	/ɛː/	/eː/	/eː/
ǣ²:	/ɛː/	/ɛː/	/eː/

It is usual for scholars to correlate these spellings with the pronunciations [uː/ʊ, eː/ɛ, iː/ɪ] respectively.

(b) WS **æ** is reflected in spelling as <e> in the West Midlands, and as <a> elsewhere: for example **dei, dai** DAY (WS **dæg**); in the spoken language the distinction would seem to be between [ɛ, a] respectively. WS **a** is reflected in spelling as <a> in most ME varieties, also with the sound-value [a]. However, <o> appears in the environment of <n, m> in the WM dialect of ME, as in **mon** MAN (cf. WS **mann**), with the presumed sound-value [ɔ].

(c) WS **ǣ**: Unless subject to quantitative changes, ME reflexes of WS **ǣ** appear in spelling as <e>, for example **strete** ROAD (cf. WS **strǣt**). However, there seem to have been some differences in the pronunciation of <e> (WS **ǣ**) in the different ME accents. The ME distribution of reflexes of **ǣ** corresponds to dialectal differences in OE. In WS, **ǣ** had two sources: Proto-Germanic **ǣ** and pre-OE **ā** (Proto-Germanic **ai**) with 'i-mutation'; these are known as $\bar{æ}^1$ and $\bar{æ}^2$ respectively. The OE pattern, using philological notation, was as in Figure 4.7.

ME reflexes of WS $\bar{æ}^1$ and $\bar{æ}^2$, all spelt <e>, may be correlated with OE dialect-distinctions as in Figure 4.8.

In Essex, WS $\bar{æ}^1$ and $\bar{æ}^2$ are reflected in spelling as <a>, presumably to be pronounced /aː/ for example **strate**, a characteristic which seems to reflect the (unattested) East Saxon accent of OE. Since both $\bar{æ}^1$ and $\bar{æ}^2$ are spelt <e> in ME, the only ways of detecting which is being used are (1) by rhymes, and (2) by forms which had undergone quantitative shortening; see further p. 59 below.

(d) The reflex of WS $\bar{a}$ was spelt <a> in the North but <o> everywhere else. It is conventional to correlate the <o>-spellings with a rounded ME /ɔː/; in the North, OE $\bar{a}$ seems in the spoken mode to have undergone a fronting of /aː/ > /ɑː/, cf. PDE/PD Scots **home/hame**. WS $\bar{o}$ was fronted to /øː/ in Northern dialects of ME, with spellings such as <ui>, cf. Older (and present-day) Scots **guid**. The Northern developments of these vowels, it has been suggested, derive from interaction with Old Norse – a plausible suggestion, given the close geographical correspondence between the dialectal distribution of these forms and the pattern of Norse settlement as revealed through Norse place-names. There was, of course, a substantial Norse element in the ME lexicon, and some forms sustain Norse vowel-pronunciations, generally merging with OE patterns; thus Northern ME **fra** FRO(M) derives its front-vowel pronunciation from its Norse ancestry (cf. present-day Scots **frae**).

The system of diphthongs in OE has attracted a good deal of scholarly controversy (Hogg 1992: 16–20), but is of secondary importance for the student of ME. The traditional view is that late WS had two sets of diphthongs: **ea** and **ēa**, **eo** and **ēo**, held to represent the pronunciations [æə, æːə, eə, eːə] respectively; these were all 'falling' diphthongs (that is the first element of the diphthong was stressed). All these WS diphthongs of the OE period became monophthongs during the transition to ME, as follows: [æə] merged with WS [æ], [æːə] merged with WS [æː] and [eə, eːə] became [ø, øː]. Of course many non-WS varieties of OE had a distribution of diphthongs which differed from WS, for example WS **eald** OLD appeared for Old Anglian **ald**. Moreover, some late WS developments in certain phonetic environments confuse the pattern just given; thus so-called 'late WS smoothing' yielded **seh** SAW (= verb; cf. early WS **seah**), which subsequently became ME **seigh** and so on. Chaucerian **saugh** derives from the Anglian form **sæh**. These OE differences have obvious implications for the distribution of forms in ME.[11]

New diphthongs arose during the transition from OE to ME from vocalisations of OE **w**, **g**, **h**, such as ME **dai** DAY (cf. WS **dæg**), **drawe(n)** DRAW (= verb; cf. WS **dragan**), **spewe(n)** SPEW (cf. WS **speowian**), **saugh** SAW (with diphthongisation of Old Anglian **æ** in the environment of a following velar fricative). Loans from ON shared in these developments, for example **main** STRENGTH. French loanwords supplied the inventory with the two new diphthongs **ui**, **oi** /ʊɪ, ɔɪ/, as in, for example, **puint** POINT, **royal** ROYAL. Both diphthongs could be spelt <oi>, and there is some evidence that all items with /ʊɪ/ could be pronounced /ɔɪ/ and vice versa (see Dobson 1968: 811: 'The important principle that all words which have ME **ui** were in English capable, from their first adoption, of a variant with ME **oi** has not been clearly recognized.'). The coalescence of the two sounds on **oi** /ɔɪ/ to produce the PDE pattern took place during the EModE period.

The relevant *quantitative developments of stressed vowels* between OE and ME are as follows. (a) and (b) below took place before the end of the OE period; (c) began after the year 1200. These changes all derive from attempts to sustain what is known as 'isochronicity', that is regular intervals between stressed syllables. We know from the analysis of OE verse that stressed syllables were generally 'long'. That is to say, their rhyming component consisted of a long vowel followed by a single consonant (VVC), for example **stān** STONE, or a short vowel followed by two consonants (VCC), for example **storm** STORM. By a process known as '*resolution*', the sequence 'short vowel – single consonant – long vowel' (VCV) seems also to have been regarded as an acceptable equivalent to the long syllable, for example **nama** NAME. (For detailed discussion of (a) and (b) below, and for the basis of the argument just presented, see Hogg 1992: 210–14.)

(a) Late OE: *Lengthening before Voiced Homorganic Consonant Groups*, such as OE **cild** CHILD, late OE **cīld**, OE **bindan** BIND, EME **bīnden**, OE **lang** LONG, late OE **lāng**. 'Homorganic consonant groups' are clusters of consonants made using the same vocal organs, that is the same place of articulation; l and d, for instance, are both made using the tip of the tongue and the alveolar ridge. It seems that such clusters, when *both* consonants were voiced (that is sharing the same manner of articulation), became perceived as a single consonant, and the preceding vowel was therefore lengthened in order to preserve isochronicity, thus VCC > *VC > VVC. Homorganic lengthening failed when the consonant cluster consisted of three consonants, cf. OE and late OE **cildru** CHILDREN; there are also sporadic instances where the lengthening failed anyway (cf. the PDE distinction between WIND (noun) and WIND (verb), OE **wind, windan**, though this may be a disambiguating choice to avoid confusion between the two words).

(b) Late OE: *Shortening before non-Homorganic Consonant Groups*, for example late OE **cepte** (< **cēpte**) KEPT, **wifmann** (< **wīfmann**) WOMAN. This process would seem to be the reverse of (1), and probably arose through the reassignment of the consonant beginning the second syllable to the end of the preceding syllable; a non-homorganic double-consonant cluster resulted, and the stressed syllable became 'over-long', that is VVCC. Interesting variation within the paradigm resulted, such as the PDE distinction between KEEP (cf. OE **cēpan**) and KEPT (cf. late OE **cepte**).

(c) Early ME: *ME Open Syllable Lengthening* (MEOSL). Early in the thirteenth century the short vowels **a, e** and **o** [a, ɛ, ɔ] were lengthened in so-called 'open syllables' of disyllabic words, for example OE **beran** > ME **bēre(n)** BEAR (= verb), OE **macian** > ME **māken** MAKE, OE **þrote** > ME **thrōte** THROAT. The development seems to have taken place a little earlier in Northern ME. Later, in the late thirteenth (Northern) and fourteenth (Southern) centuries, **i** and **u** [ɪ, ʊ] also underwent lengthening to [eː, oː] respectively, for example OE **wicu** > ME **weke** WEEK, OE **wudu** > ME **wode** WOOD; lengthening to [eː, oː] indicates an earlier lowering of the OE short vowels. The effect was limited in the North, since by this time disyllabic words were fewer as a result of earlier loss of the 'final -e' inflexion. MEOSL developed as the unstressed vowels began to lose metrical 'weight', that is VCV > VCv (= defective) > VvCv (= compensated). There is some evidence that MEOSL took some time to affect the phonological structure of English, and that though the change may be dated to the early thirteenth century it was still working its way through the phonological structure of the language in Chaucer's time (see further Dobson 1962; also see Smith 1996: 96–8 and references there cited).[12, 13]

Unstressed vowels (that is the vowels of unstressed syllables) were less differentiated in ME than they were in OE, largely because of the large-scale loss and/or obscuration of inflexions (see Chapter 6). Where such vowels remained, they were in general pronounced /ə/ and spelt <e>. The only exceptions seem to have been /ɪ/ in **-isshe**, for example (as in **heuenysshe** HEAVENLY), /ɔ/ in **bishop** and so on, /ʊ/ in **buxum** OBEDIENT and so on, and some vowels in words which had secondary stress in OE, such as OE **-dōm** – although these last seem to have been subject to reduction to /ə/ during the OE period. In some dialects, mostly Northern, /ɪ/ seems to have been more common, for example **bokis** BOOKS; in Western dialects, /ʊ/ appears, for example **oþus** OATHS. Certain French vowels continued to be differentiated as long as the syllables in which they occurred received secondary stress, for example **hónòur, géntìl**. In earlier loans from French, initial unstressed vowels were often omitted, for example **stat** from OF **estat** STATE, **crown** from OF **corone** CROWN.

4.6 Middle English writing-systems

The system of the Ellesmere manuscript was described on pp. 46–50 above. In this section the origins of various letter forms are discussed, and some historical background is offered.

In Anglo-Saxon times, English and Latin were written in distinct versions of the 'insular script'. The two versions differed graphetically, notably in the form of the letter <g>, which appears as <<ʒ>> in vernacular texts but as <<g>> in Latin. During the transition from OE to ME, Latin and French practices of spelling began to leak into the copying of English.

The most salient developments in ME *consonant*-symbols are the following:

(a) In late OE, <c> was generally used to represent [k] and [tʃ]. The distinction in sound was, during the 'pre-OE' period, environmentally conditioned; [c] (which later developed as [tʃ]) appeared in the environment of following front vowels, and [k] before back vowels and consonants, for example **cild** CHILD, **cēosan** CHOOSE, **cū** COW, **clif** CLIFF. Subsequent sound-changes disturbed this pattern, and [k]-pronunciations thus began to appear before front as well as back vowels, for example **cyning** KING, **cēne** KEEN. To distinguish these sounds, <k>, a minor variable in the Latin alphabet, was adopted. The letter <k> was used rarely in vernacular script during the Anglo-Saxon period, but became much more widespread after the Norman Conquest, probably encouraged by the Northern French practice of using <k> for [k] in the environment of a following front vowel while retaining <c> for use before consonants and back vowels.

In Northern French varieties, <c> was used to represent two sounds: [ts] and [k]. In EME, <c> was sometimes used for OE <ts>, for example **milce** MERCY (cf. OE **miltse**). However, by the end of the thirteenth century, a sound-change [ts] > [s] took place in French. The result of this change was that, in French, <c> and <s> became alternative graphs corresponding to spoken /s/. In English, <c> was then not only used in French loanwords (such as **city**) but was also extended to native forms such as **mice** (cf. OE **mȳs**).

The OE cluster <cw> was displaced by <qu, qw>; thus OE **cwic** LIVING, **cwēn** QUEEN become PDE QUICK, QUEEN. Forms with <qu> appear sporadically in early OE texts, but are otherwise rare; occurrences in English only become common from the thirteenth century. The usage derives from Latin practice, subsequently passed on to French – although in PD French the <qu>-spelling corresponds to spoken [k].

(b) In OE, <ȝ> was used as the written correlate of the sounds [j, g]; <ȝ> also appeared in the combination <cȝ>, which represented [dʒ]. As with OE <c>, the distribution of [j, g] was environmentally conditioned: [g] appeared initially before back vowels and in the combination [ng]; in other initial positions <ȝ> represented [j].

During the transition from OE to EME, <g>, hitherto restricted to use in Latin scripts, began to be used for [g], leaving <ȝ> (which began to be written <<ȝ>>) available to represent [j] initially, and [x] elsewhere. In ME alphabets, <ȝ> is referred to as 'yogh'. From the thirteenth century onwards, <ȝ> is recessive, being replaced by <y> and <gh>. During the ME period it was frequently written in a manner indistinguishable from <z>; see (3) below. <cȝ> was replaced by <gg>.

(c) In PDE handwriting, <z> can appear as <<z>> ('figure-2 zed/zee') and <<ȝ>> ('figure-3 zed/zee'). The letter <z> seems to have had a marginal status in most (though not all) languages which have used and still use a Latin-derived alphabet. In Roman handwriting and inscriptions the letter is generally realised in its figure-2 <<z>> form; it sporadically appears in OE in place of the cluster <ts>, for example **bezt** (beside **betst**) BEST.

During the ME period, <z> was more commonly employed than it seems to have been in OE. In ME it was realised, as in PDE, in two ways: a figure-2 type <<z>> and a figure-3 type <<ȝ>>. Both <<z>> and <<ȝ>> for <z> appear in French scripts from the twelfth and thirteenth centuries. <<ȝ>> seems to have been the more common realisation, judging from the standard authorities, whereas <<z>> seems to have become more rarely used as time passed. <<ȝ>> appears to have been customary by the fourteenth century.

The French <<ȝ>>-type realisation of <z> closely resembles in form the ME development of the OE letter <ȝ> 'yogh', and the native- and French-derived forms of 'yogh' and <z> came to be written identically, as <<ʒ>>, by many ME scribes. This practice is exemplified by forms such as **boʒeʒ** BOUGHS in MS London, British Library, Cotton Nero A.x where the first <<ʒ>> is <ʒ> and the second <<ʒ>> is <z>. Since the context usually made it clear which letter was intended, ambiguity as to the 'phonic' correlate of the letter in question rarely arose in most dialect-areas.

(d) In OE, <h> was used as the written equivalent of [h, x], initially and medially/finally respectively. It occurred also in clusters no longer found in late ME or PDE, for example initially before <l, n, r>, as in **hlāford** LORD. During the transition to ME, <h> was dropped from such clusters; in medial and final positions it tended to be replaced by <ʒ> and <gh>, for example **seigh/saugh** SAW (= verb; cf. OE **seah**).

<h> also gradually developed a role as a diacritic, in the PDE groups <ch, wh, sh, th>. The OE equivalents of these letter-clusters were <c, hw, sc, þ/ð> respectively. During the EME period, and for some time into the ME period, intermediate forms are also found, such as <ss, sʒ, sch> for PDE <sh>. There is even the form <x> found in East Anglian texts in place of PDE <sh>, for example **xal** SHALL, though this usage is restricted to only a few words and may indicate a distinct pronunciation.

<th> gained ground only slowly; although the form was found in the very earliest OE texts, it was soon replaced by <þ> 'thorn' and <ð> 'edh'. Edh ceased to be used comparatively early in the ME period, but the runic letter thorn survived for some time in ME, although it was often (especially in Northern ME) realised in writing in a way indistinguishable from <y>, namely <<y>>. In the form <<y>>, it was retained as a convention in early printed books in a few lexical items, for example <<ye>> for THE.

As just stated, the PDE reflex of OE <hw> is <wh>, but other spellings in ME, such as Northern (and Scots) <qu(h)-> and Southern <w-> are also found. These forms may indicate distinct pronunciations; certainly the evidence of PDE varieties is that present-day Scots distinguishes 'OE **hw**-words' (with /ʍ/) from 'OE **w**-words' (with /w/), whereas present-day Southern varieties tend to reflect both OE sounds in /w/.

(e) In almost all OE texts, <w> was represented by the runic letter 'wynn' <ƿ>, although it has become conventional for Anglo-Saxon scholars not to use wynn in modern editions. Wynn could, of course, easily be confused with other letters (such as <y>), and EME scribes adopted various devices to distinguish the two letters, for example by placing a dot over <y>. Eventually, <w>, which was available in French scripts, took over.

<w> also appears in the OE clusters <wr> and <wl>. The latter gradually disappeared during the late ME period, but the former has been retained into PDE, though not pronounced in 'standard' varieties; cf. silent <w> in PDE ANSWER, SWORD and so on.[15]

(f) Consonantal <v> in initial position first appears in EME texts, chiefly in words derived from Latin and French; it was then transferred to vocabulary derived from OE. The development related to the appearance of the new phonemic distinction between /f, v/: see p. 53 above.

(g) <j> was originally a 'long-tailed' version of <i>, used in Latin in final position, for example in inflexions as in **filij** SON (genitive), or in numerals such as **viij** EIGHT. This practice was adopted in ME. The PDE use of <j> was only finally established in the EModE period.

The most salient developments in ME *vowel*-symbols were as follows:

(a) OE <æ> disappeared early in the ME period, being replaced variously by <a, e, ea> and so on. As was discussed on p. 57 above, the OE digraphs <ea, eo, ie> seem to have represented diphthongal pronunciations; as these pronunciations changed, the old digraphs began to take on new functions. Thus <eo>, for instance, was retained in ME West-Midland texts as a spelling for the monophthongs [ø, øː].

(b) OE <y> signified a close rounded front vowel, /y/. In late WS <y> began to be used as an alternative graph for <i>, and this practice became usual in ME, especially in minim environments (see p. 47 above). Where the vowel remained rounded in the spoken mode, as seems to have been the case in Western texts, <u, ue> were commonly employed.

(c) OE **u** appears in many EME texts as <u>, as in OE. In later ME, especially in Southern texts, reflexes of OE **ū** are frequently spelt <ou, ow>, for example **þou** THOU, **now**; this usage derives from OF practice, where it begins to appear from the thirteenth century (Pope 1934: 278).

(d) Long vowels were variously flagged in ME. In Northern varieties (including Scots), <i> was used as a diacritic, for example **guid** GOOD. Doubling of letters was widely adopted, even to flag 'long **a**': thus Chaucerian texts frequently have <aa> in **caas** CASE. Since -**e** was still employed in many dialects as an inflectional marker, it was not used – as it is in PDE – to flag the 'length' of the preceding vowel until compara-tively late in the ME period. However, as we might expect given the early loss of inflexional -e in these varieties, it occurs fairly early in Northern ME and in Scots, as an alternative to the use of <i>, for example **gude** GOOD, **fude** FOOD.

Finally, ME scribes used many *marks of abbreviation*. Abbreviations are generally expanded by modern editors of ME texts, often 'silently' (that is, without marking them for modern readers). This practice is defensible if the intended readers are primarily literary students, but less so for those interested in language. The most common ME abbreviations are: **-n, -m**, as in **nacioū**; **-e**, as in **lettrᵉ**; **-at**, as in **þᵗ**; **-er**, as in **bettʋ**; **-us**, as in **þ⁹**.

Exercises

Questions for review

1. Define the notion 'phonemicisation', and illustrate the process from the history of ME.

2. 'The analysis of writing-systems is a crucial piece of evidence for the reconstruction of sound-changes in ME.' Discuss.

3. 'It is fundamental to the history of English vowels that the long and short vowels were practically identical in quality till about 1200, and that afterwards they became distinguished by the short sounds becoming more open ... than the long sounds to which they had previously corre-sponded' (A. Campbell, *Old English Grammar*, 1959: 14, note 2). Discuss.

4. Give an account of the quantitative changes in stressed vowels which took place in the Late OE and EME periods. Can you suggest any reasons for these changes?

Other questions

1. Provide a phonemic transcription, in Chaucerian ME, of the follow-ing passage from Chaucer's *Pardoner's Tale*. There are interpretative notes at the side to help you.

> **But, sires, now wol I telle forth my tale.**
> **Thise *riotoures* thre of whiche I telle,**   debauchers
> **Longe *erst er prime* rong of any belle,**   before the
>   first hour

Were set hem in a tauerne to drynke,
And as they sat, they herde a belle clynke   5
Biforn a *cors, was* caried to his graue.   corpse [who]
                                     was ...
That oon of hem *gan callen* to his knaue: called
'Go *bet*,' quod he, 'and *axe* redily   quickly; ask
What cors is this that passeth heer *forby*;   past
And looke that thou reporte his name weel.'   10
'Sire', quod this *boy, 'it nedeth neuer-a-deel*;   servant; it's
                                     not at all
It was me toold er ye cam heer two houres.   needed
He was, pardee, an old *felawe* of youres,
And sodaynly he was *yslayn* tonyght,   14 slain
Fordronke, as he sat on his bench *vpright*.   very drunk;
                                     straight

2. Write notes on the history of the pronunciation of the following words from the late OE period to PDE. OE forms appear in the WS variety.

cild CHILD   **nama** NAME

Recommendations for reading

General issues to do with the relation of writing to speech are discussed in Samuels (1972: chapter 1), Smith (1996: chapter 2) and, comprehensively, in Sampson (1985). Questions of change are addressed, with references, by Smith (1996: chapters 4–5); at a higher theoretical level, students might find Samuels (1972: chapters 3–4) of value. Very important research on writing systems with special reference to ME is currently being undertaken by M. Benskin; for a preliminary statement of some of the issues, see Benskin (1982). Discussions of the transmission of ME appear in all the standard handbooks cited at the beginning of Part I, for example Brunner (1963), Fisiak (1964), Smith (1999), Wright & Wright (1928). Sandved (1985), though restricted to discussion of Chaucerian usage, is invaluable and authoritative. There are also more advanced accounts, of which the most important are:

Comprehensive surveys of English historical phonology, in English, are Prins (1972) and Jones (1989). Prins' book is the more conventional, and perhaps the more useful for the beginning student; Jones' book, which is couched in the framework of dependency phonology, is more innovatory and more challenging for beginners. Both books contain full discussions of ME.

Jordan (1974) was originally published in 1925, and it has remained essentially the same through subsequent revisions. The edition cited is the English translation and revision published by E. Crook; this is a useful version of Jordan's classic work, but there are problems in the translation and the updating was only sporadically carried through. Although Jordan's study is now outdated in the light of LALME (1986), it remains the only survey dedicated to ME phonology and attempting comprehensiveness. On unstressed vowels, see Minkova (1991).

LALME (1986), although primarily a dialectological survey, includes a mass of information about transmission which makes an essential starting-point for any new study of the structure of ME sound- and spelling-systems.

There are of course numerous surveys of English historical phonology in other languages, notably German. Of these by far the most important is Luick (1964).

Notes

1. The account of the emergence of the /v/–/f/ distinction just given is the standard account, and holds in general terms. There is, however, some evidence for an alternative origin for the distinction. In Southern dialects, initial fricatives seem to have been voiced in native words well before the ME period, and some forms with such voicing clearly derive from a dialect 'mixture'; cf. the PDE pair FOX, VIXEN, which share the same root (cf. OE **fox**, **fyxen**). Furthermore, the form **hliuade** TOWERED, with an example of **u** for **v** (cf. WS **hlifode**, infinitive **hlifian**, and also p. 47 above) in the OE poem *Beowulf* does seem to be an indication, in the written mode, of intervocalic voicing. However, such spellings are rare before the ME period.

2. It should perhaps be emphasised again that Chaucerian usage was not, for the poet's contemporaries, in any sense a 'standard' form of the language, to be imitated outside London – although there is some evidence that a few spellings characteristic of the Ellesmere MS of *The Canterbury Tales*, for example, were imitated sporadically after Chaucer's death as a special 'poetical' language.

3. The term 'Chaucerian usage' will be adopted in what follows, for the sake of simplicity, to refer to both Chaucer's own sound-system and the spelling of the 'best manuscripts'. However, strictly speaking such a term is inaccurate; we have no certain direct evidence as to Chaucer's own spelling, although it is possible to be fairly certain about Chaucer's pronunciation. A reconstruction of Chaucerian orthography by M. L. Samuels (1983), which correlates with the spellings of the possibly Chaucerian *The Equatorie of the Planetis*, continues to be hotly debated by scholars; see Horobin forthcoming for an up-to-date summary of the discussion.

The controversy which this suggestion has engendered means that it is in-appropriate to offer Samuels' reconstruction as the basis for discussion. In any case, it does not differ very significantly from the usage of, for instance, the Ellesmere and Hengwrt manuscripts of *The Canterbury Tales*. These manuscripts may be taken as a convenient orthographic reference-point since their usage has been generally adopted by modern editors of the *Tales*. When spelling-systems alone are being discussed, we have tried to refer consistently to 'Ellesmere usage'.

4. Since only some distinctions between short and long vowels (such as /ɔ, ɔː/) were, strictly speaking, phonemic, there is a notational problem; should the diacritic 'ː' be used to distinguish /i, ɪ/ when they are already distinct qualita-tively? However, it is convenient in historical work to keep 'long' and 'short' vowels distinct notationally. We shall therefore continue to use the diacritic 'ː' to mark long vowels while acknowledging the theoretical problem.

5. Some contemporaries of Chaucer distinguished [ɔɪ] <oi, oy>, for example, **joye** JOY and [ʊɪ] <oi, oy>, for example **poynt** POINT, but Chaucer rhymes the two. The existence of two distinct diphthongs in ME is well-attested, but there is controversy about their distribution within the lexicon. Some words, derived from Latin/Germanic **au** before **j**, or earlier French **ei**, had only **oi**, for example **joy, royal**; other words varied between **oi** and **ui**, for example **boil**.

6. It is possible that some words in Chaucerian English seem to have been pronounced with [ɛʊ] rather than [ɪʊ]: **lewed** IGNORANT, **fewe** FEW, **shewe(n)** SHOW (cf. EModE **shew**) and **beautee** BEAUTY. However, the evidence of later rhymes is that [ɛʊ] merged with [ɪʊ] and shared in its development.

7. Of course, the process of assimilation of French loanwords to English stress-patterns did not take place overnight, and there is good evidence that both 'English' and 'French' pronunciations could appear side by side. Chaucer joked about this practice when he wrote **Diuerse folk diversely they seyde** (*Reeve's Tale* 3857; see also *Merchant's Tale* 1469, *Squire's Tale* 202).

8. The /v, f/ distinction seems to be the most significant of the three develop-ments. The [ð, θ] phonemicisation remains somewhat anomalous in English; minimal pairs are few (for example **thy, thigh**). The distinction seems to have arisen as the result of factors to do with stress, whereby 'function' words like **the, these, this** and so on developed voiced initial fricatives whereas 'lexical' words like **thing, thought, thank** retain the voiceless sound. It is perhaps no coincidence that there is no orthographic distinction between the two: <th> represents both voiced and voiceless sounds. The [z, s] phonemic distinction is similarly marginal; there are few minimal pairs with initial fricatives other than **seal, zeal**, and the forms which arise from inflexional loss are also few. Sporadic uncertainty about the status of <z> (cf. **criticise, criticize**) is also suggestive.

9. Textbooks frequently refer to this system using 'philological' symbols:

i, ī, y, ȳ, u, ū, e, ē, o, ō, æ, ǣ, a, ā. The philological system has many practical advantages, in that it enables scholars to track sound-changes more easily. The disadvantages of this system are that it makes the spoken/written confusion easier, and also allows uncertainty about a given sound's phonological status. It will be adopted sparingly here.

10. In older textbooks, special 'philological' symbols are sometimes used for /eː, ɛː, oː, ɔː/, namely ē̞, ę̄, ō̞, ǭ respectively. It should be noted that there remain many controversial issues relating to Chaucer's phonological inventory, for example the qualitative relationship between /ɛ, ɔ/ and /ɛː, ɔː/, the phonological status of /aː/ and so on. It is not proposed to pursue these issues further here, other than to draw them to students' attention.

11. Early WS had a third pair of diphthongs, ie and īe. Late WS reflexes of such 'OE ie, īe words' (for example **gieldan** PAY, **gīet** YET, **dierne** SECRET, **hīeran** HEAR) generally have y, ȳ in their stead, and share in the ME development of the stressed vowels in original 'y, ȳ -words' found in all OE dialects, including WS (for example **hyll** HILL, **fȳr** FIRE). Of course, this merger was restricted to the Southern dialect area during the ME period. A few seem to have developed presumed unrounded reflexes, such as i, ī. It should be noted that some scholars hold that ie, īe were not given a diphthongal pronunciation in WS; for details of this controversy and more examples, see Hogg 1992: 194–9.

12. The later lengthening of i, u in MEOSL conditions has been variously explained. A recent plausible suggestion, for which there is some modern experimental evidence, has been that close vowels have an inbuilt tendency to resist lengthening; see Jones 1989: 114 and references there cited, and also Smith 1996: 97.

13. The lower quality of ME short as opposed to long vowels, in comparison with the relationship between OE short and long vowels, seems to be indicated by the different outcomes of lengthening-processes. Whereas vowels undergoing Homorganic Lengthening seem to retain their quality (such as **cild** > **cīld** CHILD), vowels undergoing MEOSL seem to be 'lowered' (such as OE **wicu** > ME **wēke** WEEK). See Campbell 1959: 14, note 2.

14. Orm, the author of *The Ormulum*, seems to have been the deviser of a special form of the letter <g>, <ᵹ>, which he used to distinguish /g/ from /ȝ, ᵹᵹ/, spelt <ȝ, gg> respectively; see p. 165 below.

15. Oddly, a version of <w>, <uu>, had already been used in some of the earliest OE texts, and was transmitted by Northumbrian scribes to parts of the continent of Europe, notably Germany. It was replaced by wynn in later OE.

5 The lexicon

5.1 Some preliminaries: the word and its structure

Most readers are able to recognise *words* in English since they are clearly marked in our writing system. Words have various forms, such as noun, adjective, verb, adverb, pronoun and so on. They function within phrases; thus a phrase can be composed of a noun with an accompanying adjective, such as GOOD GIRLS. The set of words found in a particular language makes up its *vocabulary* or *lexicon*. Along with grammar, the lexicon expresses meaning; grammar and lexicon are transmitted by means of speech or writing. Grammar and lexicon therefore have a close relationship within the linguistic system, and it is important to be aware that words may be defined not only by what they mean but also by what they do, that is how they function grammatically.[1]

There is a category of analysis below the word: the *morpheme*. The morpheme is often defined as the minimal unit of grammatical analysis. It is probably easiest to demonstrate what a morpheme is by example. Thus, in the sentence THE KIND GIRLS WERE GIVING BOOKS TO ALL THEIR FRIENDS, there are ten words, but fourteen morphemes. This can be demonstrated if we separate each morpheme with a hyphen (-): THE-KIND-GIRL-S-WERE-GIV-ING-BOOK-S-TO-ALL-THEIR-FRIEND-S.

These morphemes cannot be placed in any order to produce acceptable English sentences. Some permutations are acceptable ('well-formed') in PDE, for example THE-BOOKS-WERE-BE-ING-GIV-EN-BY-THE-KIND-GIRLS-TO-ALL-THEIR-FRIEND-S, but other combinations are not, such as *BOOK-THE-S-ING-WERE-BE-EN-GIV-THE-BY-KIND-S-GIRL-ALL-TO-FRIEND-THEIR-S. Thus GIRL, BOOK, FRIEND and so on are potentially mobile or *free*, and can be employed in many positions, whereas -S and -ING above are immobile or *bound* morphemes, that is they must be attached to some other element to produce a 'block' within the sentence. Moreover, the ordering of elements within the block is stable, in the sense that -S and -ING have to follow, not precede, the element to which they are attached: thus GIRL-S and GIV-ING are acceptable, but not *S-BOOK or *ING-GIV. Finally, it is not acceptable to interrupt these blocks by interposing other elements, for example *FRIEND-THE-S. These stable, uninterruptible blocks, made up from a free morpheme and (optionally) bound morphemes, may be termed words. The two kinds of morpheme have traditionally been discussed in other ways, that is in terms of *stems* and *affixes*; these terms may be taken to be synonymous with free and bound morphemes respectively.[2]

Students may also encounter another term in word-studies: the *lexeme*. A lexeme is the overall term for words which are related in *paradigmatic* terms, that is which vary inflexionally; thus SING, SANG, SUNG are members of one lexeme, BOTTLE, BOTTLES are members of another, and so on. The notion of the lexeme will be referred to occasionally later in this book.

The definition of 'word' offered above is a formal one, in that it relates to the grammatical role of the category in question and its structural characteristics. However, another, older definition is that words map onto *concepts*. There are several theoretical problems with this definition, but it has its uses. Lexicography would be hard-pressed without the ability to map word onto definition and children's language-learning would be impossible, for children build up their lexicons by isolating individual words and attaching them to individual concepts. This dual definition of the notion 'word', formal and conceptual, will be assumed in what follows.

This chapter is organised a little differently from the others, in that the discussion of Chaucerian usage is located towards the end; this is because Chaucer's lexicon really needs to be seen in its diachronic setting before any meaningful discussion can be had.

5.2 The origins of ME vocabulary

The English lexicon in Chaucer's time consisted of a mixture of forms inherited from OE and forms 'borrowed' from languages with which ME came into contact.[3, 4] New forms were also derived from processes of word-formation: *compounding* and *affixation*.

5.2.1 Inheritance and borrowing

The core lexicon of ME and PDE – that is, the set of words which have the most widespread currency – derives from OE and the bulk of the OE lexicon was, in turn, inherited from Proto-Germanic. This last component included words which have no cognate in the other Indo-European languages, and which presumably either entered Germanic through early contact with non-Indo-European languages now extinct, or are forms whose cognates have simply not survived in those languages, for example wīf WOMAN, drincan DRINK (cf. Present-Day French la femme WOMAN, boire DRINK).

Some elements of OE vocabulary, however, did derive from contact with other Indo-European languages, whereby a foreign word would be adopted and modified to comply with OE structures. A number of languages did leave their mark on the OE lexicon, notably Greek and Latin. A few Greek words are found in all the Germanic languages, and may have come into Germanic directly through contact between Greek and Proto-Germanic. However, all such words were also borrowed into Latin, and it is therefore quite possible that these words entered Germanic through contact with Latin. Examples of such words in their OE forms are dēofol DEVIL, engel ANGEL, cirice CHURCH. It may be observed that, unsurprisingly, many Latin loanwords are to do with Roman technology or with the spread of the Christian religion.

However, OE seems to have been relatively inhospitable to words from other languages; by contrast, a characteristic feature of ME is its habit of borrowing from other languages to increase its wordstock. There seem to have been three reasons for this hospitality towards loanwords during the ME period: (1) there was large-scale contact between English-speakers and users of other languages, notably varieties of Norse and French; (2) the 'Latin renaissance' of the twelfth century meant widespread use of Latin for documentary purposes, and thus the potential for greater 'leakage' from Latin into ME; and (3) since ME was a much less inflected language than OE (see p. 8), it was easier to adapt words from foreign languages to cohere with the syntactic structures of the borrowing language.

It should be noted that the general effect of loanwords was to increase the size of English vocabulary; PDE now has (in comparison with OE, and also some modern Western European languages) a very large lexicon. This development is largely the result of interaction with Norse, Latin and French, much of it during the ME period. Words inherited from OE form the bulk of the 'basic' vocabulary of PDE, though many OE words were lost during the ME period, frequently being fully replaced by loans, for example OE earm POOR. Some OE items are now only retained in dialects, for instance attorc(r)op, which has generally been replaced in PD standard usage by SPIDER but is still attested in the PDE dialect of Lancashire.

As will be clear from the preceding discussion, there are three main sources of loanwords into English during the ME period: Norse, Latin and French. Many *Norse* words were actually borrowed into the spoken mode during the OE period but had been 'hidden' by the standardised written record and only appeared in ME times. Only a very few Norse-derived words are recorded in OE texts, and these belong to very specialised registers of language, for example **griþ** TRUCE, **liþsmenn** SAILORS, **ūtlaga** OUTLAW. Most loanwords from Norse which are found in PDE but date from the ME period express very common concepts, cf. PDE BAG, BULL, CAST, DWELL, EGG, ROOT, UGLY, WINDOW, WING, and it is noticeable that Norse seems to have supplied English with such basic features as the third person plural pronoun, THEY/THEM/THEIR. Some, though not all, of these forms are found in Chaucerian English; Chaucer still uses **ei** (from OE) rather than Norse-derived EGG, and he uses only the nominative form of the Norse-derived third-person plural pronoun (**they** beside OE-derived **hem, here**).

The intimate relationship between English and Norse is further demonstrated by the subtle interaction which, most probably, underlies the emergence of the PDE pronoun SHE. This development is further discussed in Chapter 7; at this stage it suffices to indicate that the PDE form seems to derive from a blend of OE **hēo** with a Norse-type pronunciation, ***hjō**, which subsequently developed into ME **scho** (Northern) and **sche** (Southern).

Interestingly, some Norse words which had cognates in OE developed distinct meanings when borrowed into English. A good example of this process is provided by the history of the PDE forms SHIRT, SKIRT, which derive from the cognates **scyrte** (OE) and **skyrta** (ON) respectively. Although the words originally referred to the same item of clothing, they developed distinct meanings within English, probably because of slightly different fashions of dress in English and Norse cultures. Thus the distinction in meaning demonstrates the truth of Leonard Bloomfield's dictum, 'Where a speaker knows two rival forms, they differ in connotation, since he has heard them from different persons and under different circumstances' (Bloomfield 1935: 394).

A number of *Latin* words came directly into English during the ME period, largely as learned words carried over in the translation of Latin texts, for example **testament, omnipotent**, although some may have come into English through French, such as **purgatorie**. Through Latin also came words from more exotic languages, such as Arabic (such as **saffron, cider**). The following words may also have been taken into English via Latin, though they may also have come via French: **jubilee,** cider (Hebrew), **sable** (Slavic), **coach** (Hungarian). However, the great wave of Latin borrowings into English takes place from the fifteenth century onwards, with the first, late medieval stirrings of what developed into 'renaissance humanism'. The first wave of this development is associated with the appearance of so-called *aureate diction* during the fifteenth century, that is at the end of the ME period. Aureate vocabulary is derived largely from Latin, although some words have a French basis; it was devised as a 'high' or 'elevated' poetic diction used for special ceremonial or religious occasions.

Perhaps the best-known practitioner of aureate diction in the late ME period was the poet John Lydgate (*c*.1370–1449/1450), monk of Bury St Edmunds, court poet and self-styled disciple of Chaucer. Something of the flavour of Lydgate's aureate verse may be captured in the following extract from his *A Balade in Commendation of Our Lady* (a poem, incidentally, where Lydgate calls for aid from the **auriat lycour** of the muse Clio – Lydgate seems to have been the first English writer to use the term 'aureate'). Lydgate bases his imagery on the Latin Vulgate Bible, the Latin religious writings of St Bernard, and – notably in this passage – the *Anticlaudianus* of the twelfth-century philosopher and Latin writer Alan of Lille. Thus the Virgin Mary is depicted as **a closid gardeyn** ENCLOSED GARDEN (an image derived from the Biblical Song of Songs), **free of weedes wicke** EVIL WEEDS, **a cristallyn welle** CRYSTAL SPRING, **a fructif olyue** FRUITFUL OLIVE-TREE, **a redolent cedyr** FRAGRANT CEDAR, and **a lantyrn of light**; the poet begs the Virgin to be **oure lyfis leche** OUR LIFE'S DOCTOR.

> O closid gardeyn, al void of weedes wicke,
> Cristallyn welle, of clennesse cler consigned,
> Fructif olyue of foilys faire and thicke,
> And redolent cedyr, most derworthly ydynged,
> Remembyr of pecchouris vnto thee assigned,
> Or þe wyckid fend his wrath vpon vs wreche,
> Lantyrn of light, be þu oure lyfis leche.
>
> (cited from Norton-Smith 1966: 26, lines 36–42)

In some ways, aureate diction prefigures the *inkhorn terms* of the Elizabethan period, in that it transfers obscure Latin vocabulary to the vernacular in order to impress; but in other ways aureate diction is conservative, being an attempt to transfer the grandiloquence of the Latin church liturgy to the vernacular (see further Norton-Smith 1966: 192–5).

By far the largest number of words borrowed into English during the

ME period are taken from varieties of *French*. The only French loanword
found in manuscripts older than 1066 is **prūd** PROUD and its derivatives
(such as **prȳt** PRIDE); most borrowings from French take place in
the centuries after the Norman Conquest. Up to the thirteenth century,
such borrowings were rather few and reflected the role of French as
the language of the ruling class (cf. PDE JUSTICE, OBEDIENCE,
MASTERY, PRISON, SERVICE, all of which are first found in English
during the early ME period). Most of these words were adopted from
Norman French (NF), sometimes demonstrated by the distinctive form
of the adopted word in PDE compared with its present-day standard
French cognate, for example WAR (ME and NF **werre**): present-day
standard French **guerre**, CARPENTER (ME and NF **carpenter**):
present-day standard French **charpentier**, GLORY (ME and NF
glorie): present-day standard French **gloire**.

However, from the fourteenth century onwards, French words from
Central French dialects enter the language at a great rate, reflecting the
cultural status of Central France. It seems to have become customary for
the higher social classes in England to signal their class-membership
by studding their English with French-derived vocabulary. Chaucer's
lexicon is rich with words derived from French, for example **honour**,
chivalrie, **curteisie**, **compaignye** and **tendre** – all of which have
survived barely changed into PDE. The extent of the impact of French
vocabulary on Chaucer's writing is demonstrated by an analysis of the
following passage, the opening lines of the General Prologue to *The
Canterbury Tales*. Italicised words are derived from French.

> Whan that Aprill with his shoures soote
> The droghte of March hath *perced* to the roote,
> And bathed euery *veyne* in swich *licour*
> Of which *vertu engendred* is the flour;
> Whan Zephirus eek with his sweete breeth
> *Inspired* hath in euery holt and heeth
> The *tendre* croppes, and the yonge sonne
> Hath in the Ram his halue *cours* yronne,
> And smale foweles maken *melodye*,
> That slepen al the nyght with open ye
> (So priketh hem *nature* in hir *corages*);
> Thanne longen folk to goon on *pilgrimages*
> And *palmeres* for to seken *straunge* strondes ...

How far Chaucer was personally responsible for the adoption of
French words in the English language remains a controversial question.
It seems most likely that Chaucer was simply reflecting in his verse the
current usage of his social class; that quotations from Chaucer contain

frequently the earliest citations of words derived from French in the OED is probably simply a result of the skew towards quotations from major authors which is characteristic of that dictionary. Some usages demonstrate the interaction of Norse and French. An interesting case, demonstrating the impact of Norse and also (indirectly) French, is to do with the development of the *phrasal verb*. Phrasal verbs are a characteristic English formation that developed during the ME period; they consist of a verb-particle combination of the model GIVE UP, SIT DOWN and so on. These verbs seem to derive from OE verbs such as **bistandan** STAND BY, but their increase in use during the ME period probably derives from interaction with Norse. Strang (1970: 276) notes that there is a stylistic restriction on the use of phrasal verbs even now: 'The verb-particle combinations seem always to have had the air of colloquiality that still often clings to them'. It is interesting to note, in the light of the discussion so far, that a large number of PDE phrasal verbs have conceptually congruent, but connotatively distinct, non-phrasal verbs which are of greater formality and which derive from French or Latin, for example COME ACROSS: DISCOVER, TAKE OFF: MIMIC, BUTT IN: INTERJECT, LOOK AFTER: SUPERINTEND. Many of these non-phrasal conceptual equivalents are first recorded in ME times.[5]

Other languages had a much smaller impact on ME vocabulary. A few *Celtic* loans are first recorded in ME, but probably were already in spoken English during the Anglo-Saxon period: **bard, clan, crag, glen**. A few forms are possibly (but not certainly) derived from Celtic: **bald, gull** and **hog** are examples. Other lexemes were borrowed into French from Celtic, and were thence transferred to ME, such as **change, garter** and **mutton**.

Low German and *Dutch* had a growing impact on the English lexicon throughout the ME period, as a result of increasing commercial links between England and the great trading ports of the Low Countries, such as Antwerp (now in Belgium). Unsurprisingly, the range of vocabulary is rather limited: **halibut, skipper** and **pump**, for instance, are derived from seafaring connections, while **bung, cork** and **tub** derive from trading-containers. However, a few words, such as **clock, grime, tallow** and **wriggle**, form a set not associated with any specialised register.

5.2.2 Word-formation

Much more than by borrowing, OE increased its wordstock through word-formation, rather as present-day German does (cf. present-day German **Fernsprecher** TELEPHONE, literally 'distant-talker'). Two principal methods were used: *compounding* of words already existing in the language, and *affixation*. Such phenomena are attested in PDE, but they seem to be particularly common in OE. Examples of compounding are: **sciprāp** SHIPROPE, CABLE, **lofgeorn** EAGER FOR PRAISE, **wīdcuþ** WIDELY KNOWN, **blīþemōd** HAPPY IN SPIRIT. Examples of affixation are: **bedǣlan** DEPRIVE (**be** + **dǣlan** = FROM + SHARE), **unfriþ** STRIFE (**un** + **friþ** = UN + PEACE), **cildhād** CHILDHOOD (**cild** + **hād** = CHILD + -HOOD/STATE). A marked feature of OE word-formation was the use of prefixes to extend or develop meaning, for example **brecan** BREAK; **abrecan** DESTROY; **bærnan** BURN; **forbærnan** CONSUME.

It may be noted that in these last examples, the extended forms **abrecan** and **forbærnan** have been replaced in PDE by French-derived vocabulary (DESTROY, CONSUME). It has been suggested that such replacements helped obscure the traditional methods of word-formation and encouraged further simple borrowing. In other words, the more ME borrowed, the less it became accustomed to 'internal' methods of increasing word-stock; the less ME became accustomed to internal methods of increasing word-stock, the more it borrowed.

However, it should be noted that ME continued to use OE strategies of word-formation. The most productive kinds of OE compound nouns continued to appear in ME, with forms such as **bagpipe**, **toadstool**, **nightmare**, **wheelbarrow** (noun + noun); **sweetheart**, **quicksand**, **commonwealth** (adjective + noun). New kinds of combination also appeared: **sunshine** (noun + verb), **hangman** (verb + noun), **runabout** (verb + adverb), **outcast** (adverb + verb).

French usages were also adopted to augment patterns of English word-formation, although not really until the fourteenth and fifteenth centuries; as Strang (1970: 189) puts it, this delay 'illustrates ... how considerable is the time-lag before [the] patterning properties [of form-ative functions] are isolated and exploited'. English borrowed such words as **agreeable**, **profitable** and **reasonable** from French. The suffix -ABLE could be isolated fairly easily in such words, and used to create new ME adjectives, for example **believable**, **knowable**, **unspeakable**, which are recorded in the written mode by 1500. A less productive development was the noun + adjective combination, for example **knight-errant**; but this usage, which goes against the prototypical English phrasal element-order of modifier + headword, has never really developed in the history of the language.

'Clipped' forms of French loanwords are also found, usually alongside full forms with slightly distinct meanings, such as **squire** (cf. French **esquire**), **stress** (cf. **distress**). This pattern arose since ME, like PDE, stressed the first syllables of words; French words with stress on the second syllable, could then be easily misinterpreted (see p. 60 above).

5.3 Some notes on meaning

The meaning of a word is usually defined in terms of *connotation* and *denotation*. The denotation of a word is its core conceptual meaning, while a word's connotations are the web of associations which 'go with' the word; such connotations are especially liable to change through time. Thus, in PDE, WOMANLY is an adjective denoting female-ness and human-ness, but for many English-speakers the adjective retains Victorian associations with passivity and weakness which are fairly deeply embedded in terms of connotation. Denotative change, however, is also common; the history of the meaning of a word such as SILLY (OE sælig), for instance, can be traced continuously over a thousand years by way of its OE meaning (HOLY), through the stages INNOCENT, SIMPLE to its current denotation, STUPID.

A good example of the process, which has excited scholarly controversy, is the ancestor of the PDE taboo-word SHIT (that is EXCREMENT). Interestingly, the early citations of the word indicate that it was acceptable in a number of contexts, including medieval and early renaissance scientific discourse, as in **If he may not schite oones a day, helpe him perto ... with clisterie** (Lanfranc's *Cirurgie, c.* 1400), **An ounce for them that spetteth blode, pysseth blode, or shyteth blode** (*Brunswyke's Distill. Waters,* 1527). The verb is also cited in the courtly romance *Kyng Alisaunder,* which survives in the mid-fourteenth-century Auchinleck Manuscript: **The addres shiteth precious stones** (one of the marvels of the East, according to the author of *Kyng Alisaunder*). The word seems to have developed exclusively low-style connotations only when the French-derived noun **ordure**, which first appears in English in the fourteenth century, was widely adopted towards the end of the fifteenth century.

There are numerous other examples of such differences between ME and PDE. It seems that, as French words were borrowed into English, so they took over some of the semantic 'slots' hitherto occupied by native words. Thus, for instance, **mood** (OE **mōd** SPIRIT) in Chaucerian English is closer in meaning to that of PDE MOOD, since the older meaning had been taken over by a French loanword, namely SPIRIT. **Smear** (from OE **smierwan**) meant ANOINT, SALVE, SMEAR; when the French loan ANOINT was adopted, SMEAR developed connotations of crudeness.

Another example is GANG: ME **gyng**, etymologically related to PDE

GANG, nowadays has generally negative connotations. Thus in standard desk-dictionaries we find definitions such as the following, where the primary meaning is given first:

> A band of roughs or criminals; a number of people or animals (*esp* elk) associating together; a number of labourers working together; a set of boys who habitually play together ... (Chambers 1998)

The word, in the form **gyng/ging** and so on seems to be used in ME to refer fairly neutrally to any group of people; thus, in the ME poem *Pearl*, written in the North-West Midlands towards the end of the fourteenth century, the word is used as a collective noun for the company of 144,000 blessed virgins referred to in the Biblical Book of Revelation. This 'neutral' reading of the word is supported by evidence in OED, such as this early citation from the mid-fourteenth-century romance *Kyng Alisaunder.* **Alisaunder, in the mornyng,/ Quyk hath armed al his ging.** The change in the meaning of the word would seem to be connected in date with the widespread adoption of the French loanword **company**. According to the MED, the first occurrence of the word is in *The Proverbs of Alfred*, in a manuscript dating from *c.*1275 although the text itself dates from a century before. However, the word is rare until the second quarter of the fourteenth century, and in many senses is only found from the fifteenth century onwards.

More subtly, grammatical words such as the ancestors of PDE SHALL/WILL and MAY/MIGHT have distinct meanings in ME even if there is some semantic overlap between them; thus Chaucerian **shal** and **wol** retained strong lexical connotations of obligation and volition respectively, and Chaucerian **may**, **might(e)** are best translated as CAN, COULD respectively. Some evidence for this interpretation of Chaucerian **shal/wol** is given in passages such as the following, where the obligation/volition distinction is crucial to the interpretation of the text. The speaker is Nicholas, the clerk who is attempting to deceive the carpenter in order to seduce the latter's wife. The basis of his deception is through convincing the carpenter of the imminent return of Noah's (**Nowelis**) flood.

> **Werk al by conseil and thou shalt nat rewe,**
> **And if thou werken wolt by good conseil,**
> **I vndertake, withouten mast or seyl**
> **Yet shal I sauen hire and thee and me.**
>
> (*Miller's Tale*, A.3530–3)

D. Burnley finds in these lines 'an instructive variation between **shal** and **wol**, in which the distinction between inevitability and volitional colouring is very clear' (1983: 45). In other words, the carpenter, if he *will* act according to the dictates of Nicholas, *is obliged* not to regret it; and if he *will* act thus, Nicholas *must* save them all from the Flood.

5.4 Word geography

Meanings of words can vary diatopically as well as diachronically. The creation of LALME and the recent completion of the MED will make it possible for new work in the field of word geography, hitherto rather neglected in ME studies. The broad outlines of how the subject might be tackled in the context of ME have been clarified in recent research (see, for instance, McIntosh 1973, Hoad 1994 and Lewis 1994, and references there cited).

One obvious approach to word geography relates to the use of Norse words in place of OE ones for the same referents, for example Northern ME **kirk, stern, slik** instead of OE-derived (and Southern ME) **church, star, such**. It might be noted that the distribution of the **kirk/church** distinction has changed over time; **kirk** has receded to the present Scottish border since ME times. Interestingly, **-kirk** remains widespread in northern England as an element in place-names, for example **Kirkby, Ormskirk** and so on, illustrating the fact that place-names frequently display characteristics which have died out in other dialectal manifestations from the area in question.

Another word-geographical issue is to do with diatopic variation in meaning. There is good evidence that meanings varied diatopically as well as diachronically within the English-speaking area during the ME period. Chaucer himself was clearly aware of this fact, and he demonstrates it in his humorous evocation of Northern speech in the *Reeve's Tale*. The ME verb **hope(n)** seems to have varied in meaning diatopically, in accordance with its derivation from two cognate but semantically distinct verbs. In the North, **hope(n)** derived from Norse **hopa**, meaning THINK, BELIEVE, whereas in Southern ME, the verb derived from OE **hopian** HOPE, EXPECT. As Burnley indicates (1983: 148), Chaucer is probably using wordplay for humorous effect when he makes the young Northern student John in the *Reeve's Tale* say **Oure maunciple I hope he wol be deed**. In Northern ME – John's 'natural' speech – this line could be glossed I BELIEVE OUR MANCIPLE IS DYING; in Southern ME, the line could be glossed (ludicrously) I HOPE OUR MANCIPLE WANTS TO BE DEAD.

5.5 Chaucer's lexicon

The origins of the ME lexicon having been established, Chaucer's usage can be seen in its proper context. In diachronic terms, as we might expect from the discussion above, Chaucer's vocabulary consists of inherited and 'borrowed' forms: words deriving from Chaucer's OE inheritance, and words borrowed from the languages with which English had come into contact (Norse, French, Latin and so on). However, simply tracing the etymological origins of ME vocabulary is not sufficient if our aim is to understand how ME vocabulary was used. In synchronic terms, Chaucer's lexicon, like that of PDE users, reflects a range of registers and styles. In what remains the most important study of this subject, D. Burnley has pointed out (1983: 155) that

> Chaucer's vocabulary ... must not be considered to be monolithic, not even divided into two or three etymologically differentiated blocs. It is better considered as a texture, an 'architecture' of associations, wrought by the social values its users and his audience perceived in it, and by their recognition of properties to verbal contexts, technical discourse, literary genres, or familiar situations.

In other words, Chaucerian vocabulary can – like PDE – be classified in terms of denotation and connotation.

This poetic handling of connotation might be simply demonstrated, using an ME example, through Chaucer's use of the word **sola(a)s**. In PDE, the noun SOLACE may be defined thus: 'consolation, comfort in distress; pleasure, amusement; a source of comfort or pleasure' (Chambers 1998). Citations in the OED from the EModE period onwards indicate that the primary denotation of SOLACE is the first of these definitions: 'consolation', specifically religious.

Chaucer's use of the word suggests that there was in ME a subtly different set of meanings for **solas**. The word appears twice in the *Parson's Tale*, a religious treatise on the Seven Deadly Sins, but in both cases it seems to be used of *non*-religious pleasure. There is no **solas**, we are assured, in hell – the implication being that searching for **solas** might bring us there – and **solas in worldly thynges** is described as **ydel** VAIN. In the *General Prologue*, the Host contrasts tales of **solaas** with tales of **sentence** (that is MORAL INSTRUCTION), and the contrast is made explicit in the *Miller's Tale*:

> **And thus lith Alison and Nicholas,**
> **In bisynesse of myrthe and of solas,**
> **Til that the belle of laudes gan to rynge**
> **And freres in the chauncel gonne synge**

(A.3653–6)

Chaucer uses the word **solas** in many other contexts, but it generally retains its associations with earthly – and specifically sexual – pleasure; rather rarely does the word carry connotations of spiritual consolation, and when it does the effect is ambiguous. A particularly interesting example appears at the beginning of Chaucer's **tragedye**, *Troilus and Criseyde*:

> And preieth for hem that ben in the cas
> Of Troilus, as ye may after here,
> That Loue hem brynge in heuene to solas ...
>
> (I.29–31)

The passage is deeply ambiguous. The Narrator, who describes himself as someone **that God of Loues seruantz serue** (I.15, a parody of the papal title SERVANT OF THE SERVANTS OF GOD), urges his audience to pray for the unhappy Troilus so that he may receive a reward in Love's heaven. But Love's heaven is not to be identified with the Christian heaven, for **this heuene** in III.1251 is identified as Criseyde's embrace.

Citations of the word in other ME texts support this interpretation. **Solas** is to be achieved through sensual pleasures: **Among the men is no solas,/ If that ther be no womman there** (Gower, *Confessio Amantis*); **He was ... of grete Solace in Iaypynge** (*Conquest of Ireland*). And **solas** is regularly contrasted with the **delit** of heaven: **He hase forsaken ... all þe ricchis and solacez of þe werld** (Mandeville); **He amonestis vs to pass fra erthly solace and ȝern anly delit of heuen** (Rolle). The theological point is made explicit in *The Castle of Love*: **Alle ting vnder heuen made was to mannes solace**. In sum, the word **solas**, although the ancestor of PDE SOLACE, has undergone a very definite change of connotative meaning since the end of the fourteenth century.

5.6 Vocabulary and style

Chaucer's handling of vocabulary is intimately connected with *stylistic* choice. Like many medieval theorists on these matters, Chaucer distinguished explicitly between 'high', 'middle' and 'low' styles, a classification which correlates with modern notions of *register*. High style was designed for 'noble' or 'royal' discourse – **as whan that men to kynges write** (*Clerk's Prologue* 18), as Chaucer puts it – whereas low style was appropriate for lowly or coarse subject-matter. Middle style represented a kind of stylistic norm from which high and low styles deviated. Of course, Chaucer was not constrained by this typology of styles – his writing tends to be highly modulated in stylistic terms – but notions of stylistic level were evidently widely shared by contemporaries and underpin many of Chaucer's effects. The most obvious distinguishing feature of style was vocabulary. Certain words were associated with high style; these words are often (though not by any means invariably) derived from French and Latin, since these languages were still, in Chaucer's time, regarded as appropriate for high-status, international discourse. Chaucer and his class probably spoke English habitually, but they were aware of French as an important component of their linguistic heritage and, it seems, they flagged their social distance from 'lower' people by studding their English with French-derived words. It is no coincidence that French and Latin borrowings almost invariably belong to the open word-classes (nouns, lexical verbs, adjectives, adverbs), are salient in semantic terms and receive full-stress in spoken discourse; they are frequently polysyllabic, which again marks them out from the generally monosyllabic character of late ME vocabulary. Native/Norse words tend to be neutral or 'low' in connotation; very common open-class words and the closed-class words of ME are almost entirely derived from OE/ON (the ordinal number 'second' is a notable exception to this rule). Thus words like **effect, egalitee** EQUALITY, **embassadrye** NEGOTIATION, **endamagen** INJURE MATERIALLY, **experience, evidence** and so on, derived from Latin and French, belong to a 'high' – and very specialist – register, whereas words such as **eche** EACH, **ende** END, **ers** ARSE, **eten** EAT, **euer** ALWAYS, **ille** ILL, **take(n)** TAKE, derived from OE or from Norse, are 'middle' (that is neutral) or 'low'.

In the generations after Chaucer, the literary tendency to associate Latin- and French-derived words with high style became even more marked, and was expressed in the emergence of so-called 'aureate' diction – **half-chongyd Latyn**, as a contemporary aptly put it – which is a feature of many fifteenth-century verse-writers such as John Lydgate and William Dunbar, and which must have reflected – however in-directly – a social fact (see p. 73 above). When Chaucer employs a word like **amphibologies** (AMBIGUOUS DISCOURSE), he is using an evident exotic, probably borrowed from Latin via French, and his in-tention is 'to add dignity and ceremony to literary composition' (Burnley 1983: 136). The adoption of such a form is simply an extreme example of what was probably a common everyday practice amongst certain social groups.

The point is confirmed if we examine the fate of two words which were borrowed into English during the fourteenth century: **commence** and **regard**. These words are of course derived from French, but com-parison of their PDE meanings with that of PD French **commencer**,

regarder shows a connotative distinction. PDE and PD French words share conceptual denotations (relating to inception and observation), but differ in connotation; in PDE the two words belong to a distinct 'high' register whereas the French words are – in the context of the French lexicon – stylistically neutral.

It is, however, important to realise that some words derived from French and Latin had, by Chaucer's time, lost their high-style connotations. Thus, in the *Parson's Tale* (860), we are told that the English word for Latin **fructus** is **fruyt**, and in the prologue to the *Second Nun's Tale* (106) we are told that **peple in Englissh is to seye for Greek leos** (cited Burnley 1983: 135). As Burnley points out, both **fruyt** and **peple** are borrowed originally from French, but evidently by Chaucer's time they had lost any connotation of status they might have had earlier in the ME period. This example reminds us that words operate in a synchronic as well as a diachronic context; register rather than etymology is the key point to observe. A comparison of the language of Emily in the *Knight's Tale* with that of Alisoun, the mock-courtly heroine of the *Miller's Tale*, is illuminating in this regard. Both women use words derived from French, but some words are used by Alisoun only when imitating the language appropriate to noble ladies (for example **curteisie**); there are other words with a French etymology (such as **blame**) that she will use in less courtly settings. There is also good evidence that, by Chaucer's day, some French-derived words had become 'debased'. Thus the adjective **gent** NOBLE, commonly used in ME romances dating from the early fourteenth century, is only employed by Chaucer in ironic contexts, for example in Chaucer's parody of 'tail-rhyme romance', *Sir Thopas*.

To exemplify Chaucer's handling of register, and to conclude this chapter, we might examine two passages from his dream-vision poem *The Parlement of Foules*. The *Parlement* – a celebration of St Valentine's day, when, it was believed, birds chose their mates – includes a series of speeches by the birds which are socially differentiated. In the first passage the genteel birds of prey use 'high' language to express high-flown emotion, whereas in the second the humble waterfowl use 'lower', more earthy language. French vocabulary (such as **merci, grace, disobeysaunt, souereyne**) is more common in the first passage, but also occurs in the second (for example **causeles, resoun**); it should also be noted that Chaucer plainly considers it possible to express high emotion in words which derive entirely from OE (**I chese, and chese with wil, and herte, and thought**). Italicised words have been given a marginal gloss.

Passage 1

With hed *enclyned* and with humble cheere		bowed
This royal *tersel* spak, and tariede noght:	415	male eagle
'Unto my soverayn lady, and not my *fere*,		mate
I *chese*, and chese with wil, and herte, and thought,		choose
The *formel* on youre hond, so wel *iwrought*,		female (eagle); made
Whos I am al, and evere wol hire serve,		
Do what *hire lest*, to do me lyve or *sterve*;	420	she may want; die

'Besekynge hire of merci and of grace,		
As she that is my lady sovereyne;		
Or let me deye *present* in this place.		immediately
For certes, longe may I nat lyve in payne,		
For in my herte is *korven* every veyne.	425	cut
Havynge reward only to my trouthe,		
My deere hert, have on my wo som *routhe*.		pity

'And if that I be founde to hyre untrewe,		
Disobeysaunt, or wilful necligent,		
Avauntour, or in proces love a newe,	430	boaster
I preye to yow this be my jugement:		
That with these *foules* I be al torent,		birds
That ilke day that evere she me fynde		
To hir untrewe, or in my gilt unkynde.'		
(414–434)		

Passage 2

'Wel *bourded*', quod the doke, 'by myn hat!		jested
That men shulde loven alwey causeles!	590	
Who can a resoun fynde or wit in that?		
Daunseth he murye that is myrtheles?		
Who shulde reche of that is recheles?'		
'Ye *queke*', seyde the goos, 'ful wel and fayre!		quack!
There been *mo sterres*, God wot, than a payre!'	595	more stars
(589–595)		

Exercises

Questions for review

1. Define and exemplify the linguistic category 'word', with reference to PDE.

2. What are the principal sources of ME vocabulary?

3. Why did English become more hospitable to loanwords during the ME period?

4. 'There is probably nothing so widely misunderstood in the history of English as the true meaning of the influx of French words' (Strang). Discuss.

5. 'Where a speaker knows two rival forms, they differ in connotation, since he has heard them from different persons and under different circumstances' (Bloomfield). Discuss the relevance of this statement for the history of the lexicon in the ME period.

Other questions

1. Look up the following words in the OED and/or MED, and trace their meanings through time with special reference to the ME period:

SILLY   PRESENTLY   NICE   BOY

2. (Attempt this exercise if you have access to the OED and/or the MED online.) Choose any passage from the writings of Geoffrey Chaucer (say ten lines from one of *The Canterbury Tales*). Make a list of the *lexical* (that is open-class words) in the passage, and use the OED and/or MED online to find other citations elsewhere in ME texts. If the ME texts cited appear in the *Middle English Compendium* (the corpus which accompanies the MED online), check the citations in context. Then write an essay on how our understanding of Chaucer's meaning can be enhanced through an analysis of the connotations of ME words. You should establish these connotations through the analysis of other texts from the period.

Recommendations for reading

The lexicon is discussed in all the major handbooks, such as Baugh and Cable (1993), Strang (1970). A very useful study of meaning and changes in meaning is Waldron (1979). Still the standard survey of loanwords is Serjeantson (1935); Cannon (1998) focuses on Chaucer's vocabulary, but is more informed by literary than linguistic theory. Discussion of the structure of the ME lexicon appears in Smith (1996, 1999), with references; by far the most important study in this area is in Samuels (1972:

chapters 4, 5). Explicitly on Chaucer's usage, but with much wider applications and implications, are Burnley (1983), Davis (1974) and Elliott (1974). A classic statement of Chaucer's handling of vocabulary is the essay by E. T. Donaldson, 'The language of popular poetry in the *Miller's Tale*' (in Donaldson 1970: 13–29).

The main resources for the study of the ME lexicon are the historical dictionaries. A useful practical aid for reading Chaucer is Davis *et al.* (1979), which itself derives from the two main resources: the *Oxford English Dictionary* (OED) and the *Middle English Dictionary* (MED). The MED is the primary resource for all students of the ME lexicon; it was completed in 2001 and is now (as the central component of the *Middle English Compendium*) online – a massive extension of its functionality. The OED is also now online, and it seems likely that most scholars will, in time, cease to consult these publications in their inconvenient printed form; certainly it seems likely that new editions of the OED will primarily be published electronically, either on CD or on the Web.

Another important and developing resource is the *Historical Thesaurus of English* (HTE), a notional classification of the English lexicon over time, enabling the structural analysis of meaning-changes in words. The HTE, which includes a substantial component of ME material, is due for publication by 2010 at the latest, although it seems likely that it, too, will be consulted primarily online.

Notes

1. It may be relevant at this stage to flag some of the grammatical terminology used in this book. Words fall into two classes: *open* and *closed*. The open-class word-sets are:

> Nouns (for example GIRL, TABLE, FIRE, THING, RADIANCE, IDEA)
> Lexical Verbs (for example SING, DRIVE, GO, LOVE)
> Adjectives (for example GOOD, BAD, LOVELY, FRIENDLY)
> Adverbs (for example NOW, THEN, CALMLY, ACTUALLY, TODAY)

Open-class word-sets can be joined readily by new coinages, for example SCOOTER (Noun), JIVE (Lexical Verb), HIP (Adjective), GROOVILY (Adverb).

The closed-class word-sets are:

> Determiners (for example THE, A, THIS, THAT, SOME, ANY, ALL)
> Pronouns (for example I, ME, YOU, THEY)
> Prepositions (for example IN, BY, WITH, FROM, TO, FOR)
> Conjunctions (for example AND, BUT, THAT, IF, WHEN, BECAUSE)
> Auxiliary Verbs (for example CAN, MAY, WILL, HAVE, BE)
> Interjections (for example OH, AH)
> Numerals (for example ONE, TWO, FIRST, SECOND)

All these words function within the next element in the grammatical hierarchy: phrases. Prototypically, nouns function as the headwords of noun phrases (for example BOY, GOOD BOYS, THE GOOD BOY) and lexical verbs function as the headwords of verb phrases (for example SINGS, WAS SINGING). Adjectives prototypically function as modifiers of nouns within noun phrases (for example THE GOOD BOY), although they can function as the headwords of adjective phrases (for example GOOD, VERY GOOD in THE BOY IS (VERY) GOOD). Adverbs can function as the headwords or modifiers of adverb phrases (for example CAREFULLY, VERY CAREFULLY), or as modifiers of adjectives within adjective phrases (for example VERY GOOD).

Determiners always act as modifiers to nouns (for example THE MAN), while auxiliary verbs act as modifiers to lexical verbs (for example WAS SINGING). Prepositions can be linked to noun phrases to produce prepositional phrases (IN THE BOOK), while conjunctions prototypically link phrases or clauses together (THE MAN AND THE WOMAN; IF YOU EAT THAT, YOU WILL BE SICK). Pronouns function in place of nouns within noun phrases (for THE WOMAN ATE A BANANA, SHE ATE A BANANA, for example). Numerals prototypically act as modifiers within noun phrases. Interjections (such as OH! ARGH!) form a special category with very special functions. See further pp. 89–90, 120 below.

2. Since students will come across other terminology in the scholarly literature, it is perhaps useful to give some short definitions in this footnote. The basic lexical element in open-class Indo-European words is the *root*, which carries the primary semantic content of the word. The root is generally followed by a *theme*. The function of the theme is a matter of some debate amongst scholars but could well be in origin a kind of grammatical marker, however semantically 'empty' it subsequently became (see Lass 1994: 125n). The theme usually consists of a vowel, but it can also be a consonant. Together, the root and theme make up the *stem* of a word, to which an *ending* may (or may not) be added. Thus, in the reconstructed Proto-Germanic form *stainaz STONE, *stain- is the stem, *-a- is the theme, and *-z is the ending. Roots and themes were carefully distinguished in Proto-Germanic, it seems, but in later dialects (such as OE and ME), many themes have disappeared or have become obscured. They are better preserved in older varieties of Indo-European, such as Latin and Greek; thus in Latin **manus** HAND, **man-** is the root, **-u-** is the theme and **-s** is the ending. An example of a non-vocalic theme is **-in-** in Latin **hominis**, an inflected form of **homo** MAN (= **hom-** + **-in-** + **-is**).

3. Of course, the term 'borrowing' is in a sense not particularly apt since the word usually remains in the parent language; however, it does draw a metaphorical parallel between the development of vocabulary and monetary exchange, which is quite a useful one.

4. *How to recognise loanwords.* There are no hard-and-fast rules for recognising loanwords easily; the following are a few pointers only.

OE and Norse words tend to be part of basic vocabulary, whereas French-and Latin-derived words are, even now, generally used for heightened registers of language. For instance, PDE STAND BY (from OE **bistandan**) might be compared with SUPPORT (from French); in PDE, STAND BY is arguably more colloquial.

Words from Norse often have <k> where PDE has <ch>, and <sk> where PDE has <sh>; compare **kirk/church, mickle/much**; also SKIRT, SHIRT (see p. 72 above).

Words from Norse often have <g> where PDE has <dg> or vowels representing earlier [w] or [j]; compare **brig/bridg, trig/true**.

French words are often polysyllabic. Many have characteristic endings, for example **-able, -age, -ance/y, -ence/y, -ate, -ess, -ory, -ant, -ent, -ician, -ize, -ise, -tion, -(i)o(u)n**, although there is a tendency for these endings to be added to an OE stem (such as PDE KNOWABLE, cf. OE **cnāwan**, French **-able**). Furthermore, words spelt with <c> [s], such as PDE CITY, are generally loans from French, although there are some analogous spellings, for example MICE (cf. OE **mȳs**).

Words containing <oi, oy> are almost all from French.

5. The impact of French on English is largely at the level of vocabulary. It may be significant that, of the phrases recorded by Prins (1952) as showing the influence of French on English phrasing, only about fifteen per cent do not contain French vocabulary, and many of these are late or dubious examples. It may be interesting in this context that French written in England (such as *The Rolls of Parliament*) seems to take on English patterns of syntax as the Middle Ages progress (see Burnley 1983: 236–7, note 10). A few minor examples of French 'influence' on English phrasing are discussed on p. 95 below.

6 Grammar

6.1 Some preliminaries

It may be recalled from Chapter 1 that meaning (semantics) is expressed through grammar and lexicon, and transmitted through speech or writing. The term *grammar* is perhaps the least well-defined of these notions. For some scholars, the term refers to all linguistic categories other than lexicon, including those relating to accent. In this book, however, a more restricted definition of grammar has been adopted: grammar is taken to refer to *syntax* and *morphology*. Syntax is concerned with the ways in which words combine to form phrases, clauses and sentences, for example the relationship between words in such constructions as AMY LOVES BANANAS and WE LOVE BANANAS, where the choice of LOVE or LOVES is determined by the relationship between this word and other words in the construction. Morphology is concerned with word-form, such as the kinds of ending which the form LOVE can adopt, for example LOVES as opposed to LOVED. To sum up, grammar is to do with the ordering of and relationship between elements (syntax) and inflexional variation (morphology). These two kinds of grammatical relations are sometimes referred to as *syntagmatic* and *paradigmatic* respectively.

Three further general aspects of grammar perhaps need definition at this stage (see also pp. 86–7 above):[1]

1. Syntactic categories can be formed into a *hierarchy of grammatical units*. *Sentences* are composed of one or more *clauses*; clauses are composed of one or more *phrases*; phrases are composed of one or more *words*; words are made up of one or more *morphemes* (see p. 69 above).

2. Words are traditionally classified into *parts of speech*. The parts of speech themselves fall into two classes: *open* and *closed*. The open-class set consists of *nouns, lexical verbs, adjectives* and *adverbs*; the closed-

class set consists of *determiners, pronouns, prepositions, conjunctions, interjections, numerals* and *auxiliary verbs.*

3. Grammatical categories have both *function* and *form.* Thus, for instance, a noun can function as the *head* of a *noun phrase;* a noun phrase can function as the *subject* of a clause; and a *subordinate clause* can have an *adverbial* function in a sentence.

This terminology is widely used for the discussion of PDE; it also works well for earlier states of the language. However, there are basic differences between PDE grammar and that of earlier periods, of which the most important is the shift from *synthesis* to *analysis* in expressing grammatical relations. Whereas the relationships within and between phrases and clauses in PDE are largely expressed by word-order, in OE these relationships were expressed to a much greater degree by special endings attached to words (known as *inflexions*). ME occupied an intermediate position on the synthesis/analysis cline, closer to (but still distinct from) PDE. To illustrate this last point, we might compare a few examples in OE, ME and PDE.

The OE inflexional system meant that OE *word-order* was much more flexible than that of PDE. Thus in PDE

1. THE LORD BINDS THE SERVANT

2. THE SERVANT BINDS THE LORD

mean very different things. The word-order indicates the relative functions of the phrases THE LORD and THE SERVANT. Now this was not necessarily the case in OE. Sentence 1 above can be translated into OE as

3. **Se hlāford bint þone cnapan.**

However, it can also be translated as

4. **þone cnapan bint se hlāford.**

5. **Se hlāford þone cnapan bint.**

and so on. In sentences 3–5 above, the phrase **se hlāford**, because it is in the so-called *nominative case*, with a nominative form of the determiner (**se**), is always the subject of the clause in whatever position it appears. And, because it is in the so-called *accusative case*, with an accusative form of the determiner (**þone**) and an accusative inflexion on the accompanying noun (**-an**), **þone cnapan** is always the direct object of the clause. The cases, not the word-order, here determine the relationship between the two phrases. There were conventions in OE that, prototypically, placed the verb phrase in 'second position' (sometimes 'V-2' in the scholarly literature) in main clauses, that is as the second phrase in the clause, but these conventions could easily – more easily than in PDE – be departed from for stylistic effect.

This system did not survive intact into ME. It appears that interaction with Norse encouraged inflexional loss, and the OE conventions of word-order, whereby predicator/object and subject/predicator positioning had become stylistically formalised in particular clause-types, became more fixed to take over the task originally performed by inflexions. The PDE pattern was largely established by the end of the ME period.

Of course, some inflexions still remain in PDE (cf. TOM, TOM'S, PIG, PIG'S, PIGS and so on), and PDE is not as analytic in its grammar as is, for instance, Chinese. There are rather more of these inflexions in ME, for example the retention of adjectival inflexions. Like present-day German, OE distinguished between definite ('weak') and indefinite ('strong') adjectives, for example **se gōda wer** THE GOOD MAN beside **se wer wæs gōd** THE MAN WAS GOOD. Something of this system survived in many varieties of ME, for example the Chaucerian distinction between **the gode man** and **the man was god**. Nothing of this system remains in PDE, except for the odd fossilised use in verse, for example THE DRUNKEN SAILOR.

Thus ME broadly represented an intermediate stage: it is more analytic than OE, but more synthetic than PDE. However, the use of inflexions varied quite markedly in ME, with major diachronic distinctions between Early and Late ME, and with significant diatopic variation. Inflexional innovation seems to have been earlier in the North and North Midlands, and to have been later in the southern dialects; this difference seems to relate to the differing impact of Norse contact in these regions.

These preliminary remarks provide the necessary underpinning for the rest of the chapter. In this chapter, the focus is primarily on Chaucerian usage, simply because this variety is that which is likely to be comparatively familiar for the modern reader; however, information about other varieties is also included.[2]

The remainder of this chapter falls into two parts: *syntax* and inflexional *morphology*.[3] Obviously syntax and morphology are connected, and cross-references will be made throughout.

6.2 Syntax

Three fundamental areas of syntax will be discussed: the **Noun Phrase,** the **Verb Phrase** and **Sentence Structure.** This section deals with the various functions the various forms carry out; for details of forms, constant reference should be made to the morphology section below.

6.2.1 The noun phrase

In PDE, the noun phrase prototypically consists of a *headword* with optional *modifiers,* that is determiners, adjectives and numerals. The headword of a prototypical noun phrase is, as one might expect, a noun; however, within the noun phrase category may also be included phrases where the headword is a pronoun. ME noun phrases are similarly organised. In the following sentences, the italicised groups are noun phrases:

1. *The olde man* loueth *the yonge wyf.*

2. *Sche* loueth *hire housbonde.*

Also within the broad category of noun phrases may be included *prepositional* and *genitive phrases,* where nouns are the prototypical headwords accompanied by prepositions and marked by genitive inflexions respectively. Sentence (3) below contains a prepositional phrase (italicised); sentence (4) contains a genitive phrase (italicised).

3. The knyghte saugh his lady *in the toune.*

4. *The kynges* wyf was ful fre.

Noun phrases in ME, as in PDE, have a range of functions. Prototypically they function as *subjects* and *objects,* but they can also function as *complements.* Genitive phrases prototypically function as *subordinate phrases* within a noun phrase; prepositional phrases can also function as *subordinate phrases,* but prototypically they function as adverbials.

Three further grammatical categories will be discussed in this section: *adjectives, adverbs* and *numerals.* As in PDE, in ME adjectives most commonly modify nouns within noun phrases, but they can also act as headwords within adjective phrases. Adjective phrases are commonly complements, but they can also function as subordinate phrases within a noun phrase. Numerals can act as modifiers within noun phrases; adverbs can act as modifiers within adjective phrases. Adverbs can modify adjectives with adjective phrases; adverb phrases (consisting of one or more adverbs, but with an adverb as a headword) can also, like prepositional phrases, function as adverbials. This configuration was broadly in place in OE, though the formal representation of functions was differently expressed then, that is primarily through inflexions, and only secondarily through element order.

An important syntactic feature in both PDE and ME is *agreement (concord)*. Agreement in ME, as in PDE, was used to track relationships between nouns and pronouns; thus, for example, **sche** points to a feminine referent expressed earlier or later within a piece of discourse. However, in some varieties of ME, agreement also held within the noun phrase, and between noun phrases and adjective phrases. Chaucer's choice of adjectival **-e** in **The gode man** THE GOOD MAN, **The man was god** THE MAN WAS GOOD and **The men weren gode** THE MEN WERE GOOD is determined by noun-adjective agreement (see further pp. 105–6 below).

In ME, there were four inflexional categories relevant for the noun phrase: *case, number, gender* and *person*. These categories had existed in OE; in ME, however, their formal expression, to a greater or lesser extent, developed differently and became – as we would expect – much closer to PDE.

Thus, while there are some paradigmatic differences between ME and PDE nouns, the differences are much more marked between Chaucerian English and OE. In OE, cases were categorised as *nominative, accusative, genitive* and *dative*, correlating with the function of the noun phrase: *nominative* was primarily used to flag subject-function, *accusative* for object-function, *genitive* to indicate possession and *dative* used prototypically in prepositional phrases and in indirect objects. Each case was assigned an inflexional marker, often (though not always) distinctive. In Chaucerian English formal inflexional distinctions between cases were vestigial only.

Thus, in Chaucerian English, nouns were inflected for number (singular/plural), for example **stoon, stoones** STONE, STONES, and for the case of genitive singular (= possessive), for example **kynges** KING'S. No case distinction was made in the plural in Chaucerian English, however, for example **kynges** KINGS, **kynges** KINGS'. As an alternative to the inflected genitive, two other constructions were also used in late ME. One of these is common in PDE: the **of-** construction, using a preposition, cf. PDE THE QUEEN OF ENGLAND beside ENGLAND'S QUEEN. This usage derives from an OE use of **of**, to indicate the material from which something is made (cf. **of treowe** FROM WOOD, OF WOOD), but was doubtless encouraged by the French **de-** construction (cf. **la reine d'Angleterre**). Another, rarer practice was to use a possessive pronoun, as in **The Knyght his Tale** THE KNIGHT'S TALE. An interesting usage is represented by **the dukes doughter of Tyntagelle** THE DUKE OF TINTAGEL'S DAUGHTER, which demonstrates that the -s inflexion was not seen as a separable suffix (as it is in PDE). The example of **of** indicates another characteristic of ME: the use of prepositions. Prepositions are of course commonly used in OE, but in ME they became even more common, taking over many of the functions of the inflexional system.

As in OE and PDE, ME pronouns reflected number, that is singular/plural, for example **sche** SHE, **they** THEY, and case, for example **they/here/hem** THEY/THEIR/THEM. It is noticeable that, unlike nouns, ME and PDE pronouns sustain formal case differences reflecting the OE case-distinctions.[4] The so-called *ethic dative pronoun* used to reinforce a subject-pronoun is fairly common in ME, for example **he wole him no thyng hyde** HE WILL HIDE NOTHING. This usage is archaic in PDE, though was still common in EModE.

Also, as in PDE, ME pronouns are marked by further inflexional categories: person and gender. *Person*, that is First (I, ME and so on, WE, US and so on)/Second (YOU and so on)/Third (HE, SHE, IT, THEY and so on), was formally flagged in Chaucerian pronouns, for example **we, thou, sche** and so on. And, like OE and PDE pronouns, Chaucerian pronouns were formally distinguished on the grounds of *gender*. Singular third-person pronouns were selected on the basis of the sex (that is 'natural gender') of the noun to which they refer. Grammatical gender, a characteristic of OE grammar, is by Chaucer's time no longer a feature of ME.[5] Elements of this system did survive for a while in some varieties of ME, notably in the extreme south of England (such as Kent), but had died out by the late ME period. The system was replaced by the ModE usage, whereby pronoun-assignation was based on real-world knowledge of sexual characteristics.

The regular *relative pronouns* that/þat, (þe/the) which(e) (that) and so on are used in relative clauses, although the relative pronoun is sometimes omitted altogether; furthermore, the present-day distinction between 'human' WHO(M) and 'non-human' WHICH is not regularly made in ME. **This yongeste, which that wente to the toun** THIS YOUNGEST (MAN), WHO WENT TO THE TOWN, beside **if a preest be foul, on whom we truste** ... IF A PRIEST IN WHOM WE TRUST IS FOUL. ... The relative pronoun **which(e)** can be inflected to signal the plurality of its referent, for example **whiche they weren** WHO THEY WERE, beside **which he was** WHO HE WAS. Sporadically **whiche** is used with singular reference when preceded by **the**, for example **the whiche pointz** WHICH POINTS. **Who(m)/whos** are prototypically interrogative pronouns in ME; however, **whom** and **whos** were used occasionally as relative pronouns, although **who** seems not to have been so used.

As was indicated on p. 93, adjectives could be inflexionally marked in some varieties of ME. Thus the form of some monosyllabic adjectives of OE origin is governed by the number of the nouns they modify, for example **old man** OLD MAN, **olde men** OLD MEN. Moreover, as in OE, there are distinct 'strong' and 'weak' adjectival paradigms for such adjectives in Chaucerian English (see pp. 105–6 below), whereby, if the adjective is preceded by the determiners THE, THAT, THIS, THOSE, THESE, the weak form is used. Elsewhere, the strong paradigm was generally used. However, by Chaucer's time the formal distinctiveness of these paradigms was very slight, for example **this olde man** THIS OLD MAN, **this man is old** THIS MAN IS OLD. This distinction seems to have been a feature of formal London usage and had ceased to be observed in Northern ME; in the generation after Chaucer it died out altogether. It should be noted that Chaucer commonly uses a strong form of the adjective after the determiner **a(n)**. This is because **a(n)** was not a determiner in OE, but a numeral **ān** ONE. Thus **an** in **an oold man** simply sustains the inherited strong usage which would have been regular in an OE indefinite noun phrase, such as **eald mann**. Chaucer also uses a weak adjective in vocative constructions, that is when persons are addressed directly, for example **Nay, olde cherl, by God, thou shalt nat so** NO, OLD PEASANT, BY GOD, THOU MUST NOT (DO) SO.

A few adjectives were inflectionally marked in imitation of French usage, for example **weyes espirituels** SPIRITUAL PATHS. It will be observed that in this case, also in imitation of French usage, the adjective follows the noun (this can also occur without marking the adjective for agreement, for example **heestes honurable** HONOURABLE COMMANDMENTS, rhyming with **the firste table**). As in PDE – though rather more commonly – adjectives can be used in ME as the heads of phrases with omission of the noun, for example **the yongeste** THE YOUNG (MEN).

As in PDE, so in Chaucerian English some *determiners* agree in number with the nouns they modify. As in PDE, some determiners inflect, for example **thise men** THESE MEN, cf. **this man** THIS MAN. However, most determiners, such as **the**, did not inflect in Chaucerian English, though some inflexions are still found in EME (see p. 108 below). The indefinite article **a(n)**, derived from the OE numeral **ān** ONE, was becoming more widespread along PDE lines: **an** was used when the following word began with a vowel, **a** elsewhere.

None of the cardinal numerals inflects in Chaucerian English, as a few did in OE, and their usage is much as in PDE. One common practice, which still occurs in certain PDE dialects, is the use of an endingless noun after a numeral, for example **foure and twenty yere** TWENTY-

FOUR YEARS. Such usages are generally accounted for as survivals of the OE numeral + genitive plural construction, or of OE Nouns with an endingless plural; they are distinct from the PDE attributive use in, for example, A FIVE-MILE DRIVE. The sequence of numbers in **foure and twenty** may also be noted. This construction is comparatively rare in present-day varieties of English, although not unknown; cf. also present-day German **vierundzwanzig**.

6.2.2 The verb phrase

Verb phrases function as predicators within the clause. The following verb phrase grammatical categories may be distinguished: *simple* and *complex verb phrases, person, number, tense, aspect, mood* and *voice*. Verbforms can be distinguished in terms of *finiteness*; verb phrases are also affected by *agreement (concord)*. There were also ME innovations, notably a considerable expansion in the use of *impersonal verbs*, and *the phrasal verb*. Also covered in this section, since it is usually expressed by means of a particle which is closely associated with the verb phrase, is *negation*; constructions of *interrogation*, since they are differently expressed in ME than in PDE, are also covered here.

As with the noun phrase, *agreement* is important for the ME verb phrase (as it is, indeed, in both OE and PDE). Subject and predicator in ME 'agree', for example **he bindeth** HE BINDS, beside **they binden** THEY BIND. Verbs can be inflected according to the person and number of the subject with which they agree, for example **I binde, thou bindest, he bindeth, they binden** and so on. Forms of verbs which undergo inflexion to agree with the subject are known as *finite* verbs; forms of verbs which do not so agree are known as *non-finite* verbs; thus **bindeth** in **he bindeth** is a finite verb-form, while **bounden** in **he hath bounden** is a non-finite verb-form.

As will be apparent from the previous example, ME, like PDE, uses both *simple* and *complex verb phrases*. A simple verb phrase in PDE consists of a simple verb, for example LOVES in HE LOVES; a complex verb phrase in PDE is HAS LOVED in HE HAS LOVED, consisting of an auxiliary and a main (lexical) verb. Similar constructions are found in ME, for example **he loueth, he hath loued**. A feature of OE often retained into ME is the 'split' between auxiliary and lexical verbs in complex verb phrases, with the lexical verb appearing at the end of the clause, for example **he kan no difference fynde** HE CAN FIND NO DIFFERENCE; this 'brace' construction is rare in PDE, but survives in such usages as WE CAN NEVER SING, with an intervening adverb. In complex verb phrases, the auxiliary verb agrees with the subject.

As in PDE, simple verbs are also inflected for the *present* and *preterite* (past) *tenses*, for example **sche loueth** SHE LOVES, **sche loued** SHE LOVED; the finite verbs in complex verb phrases can also be inflected in this way, for example **sche hath loued** SHE HAS LOVED, **sche hadde loued** SHE HAD LOVED. The 'historic present', whereby a formal present tense is used with a past-tense meaning, is not found in OE. However, it is common in Chaucerian English, for example **This yongeste, which that wente to the toun, ful ofte in herte he rolleth up and doun** ... THIS YOUNGEST (MAN), WHO WENT TO THE TOWN, VERY OFTEN HE REVOLVES IN HIS HEART ...

Complex verb phrases can also be used to express tense distinctions. With regard to the future tense, in ME, **wol/schal** etc. (the reflexes of OE **willan, sculan** and so on) frequently retain the lexical significance they carried in OE, that is volition and obligation respectively, for example **Oure sweete Lord God of hevene** ... **wole that we comen alle to the knowleche of hym** OUR SWEET LORD GOD OF HEAVEN ... WISHES THAT WE ALL COME TO KNOWLEDGE OF HIM; ... **he shal first biwaylen the synnes that he hath doon** HE MUST FIRST BEWAIL THE SINS THAT HE HAS DONE. However, it could be argued that they are used simply as future auxiliaries in examples such as **Now wol I yow deffenden hasardye** NOW I ?SHALL/WANT TO FORBID YOU (FROM PURSUING) GAMBLING. Since volition generally implies futurity, the extension of the construction to take over expression of the simple future tense was always a potential development. Future time could also, as in OE, be expressed by the simple present tense. **Gan** (from OE **ginnan** BEGIN) is sometimes used as a past tense auxiliary, as in, for example, **This olde man gan looke in his visage** THIS OLD MAN LOOKED INTO HIS FACE.

Aspectual distinctions can be expressed in ME, as they are in PDE, with the use of auxiliaries followed by lexical verbs, although the range of forms is not as large; thus the common PDE AM + -ING construction (such as I AM GOING, I WAS GOING), used to express progressive aspect, is not common in ME, and simple verb phrases are used instead. Perfect aspect combined with past tense can be expressed, as in PDE, by means of complex verb phrases. When the lexical verb is transitive, that is, capable of governing a direct object, then reflexes of OE **habban** are used, as in **whan a man hath dronken draughtes thre** WHEN A MAN HAS DRUNK THREE DRAUGHTS. When the verb is intransitive (that is, not capable of governing a direct object) the reflexes of PDE BE are used, as in **At nyght was come into that hostelrye wel nyne and twenty in a compaignye** AT NIGHT ABOUT TWENTY-

NINE (FOLK) IN A COMPANY HAD COME INTO THAT HOSTELRY.

Reflexes of the OE 'auxiliary' **weorþan** BECOME are still found occasionally in Chaucerian English (ME **worthe(n)** and so on) within a complex verb phrase to express the *passive voice*. However, the usual methods for expressing the passive voice in ME are either by using the auxiliary verb derived from OE **ben/wesan**, as in PDE, for example **He is ... yholde the lasse in reputacioun** HE IS CONSIDERED ... THE LESS IN REPUTATION, or, as in OE, by using the indefinite pronoun **man**. The PDE construction linking passive and progressive elements, for example WAS BEING BOUND, is unknown in ME; instead the construction **be** + past participle is employed, for example **Biforn a cors, was caried to his graue** IN FRONT OF A CORPSE [WHICH] WAS BEING CARRIED TO ITS GRAVE.

Mood is a grammatical category to do with possibility. *Indicative* mood verb forms are used when the speaker regards the action referred to as a real action; *subjunctive* mood verb forms are used to suggest hypothesis, conjecture or volition; *imperative* mood verb forms are used for commands, and were much as in PDE, for example **Binde!** BIND! In OE, indicative and subjunctive moods were formally marked in the simple verb paradigms, for example **hīe bundon** THEY BOUND (indicative), **hīe bunden** THEY MIGHT HAVE BOUND (subjunctive), whereas in PDE the distinction is generally made by using auxiliaries in the subjunctive, for example I LOVE YOU (indicative), I MIGHT LOVE YOU (subjunctive). The change took place during the ME period, although vestiges of the older usage remain, as in PDE, in some Chaucerian usages, for example **if that yow be so leef to fynde Deeth** IF YOU ARE (cf. PDE formal BE) SO DESIROUS OF FINDING DEATH.

The reflexes of PDE MAY, MIGHT – in Chaucerian English **may** and **might(e)** – became extended in meaning during the course of the ME period. Their original sense was CAN, COULD, and they usually retain these meanings in Chaucerian English, for example **the feend ... putte in his thoughte that he sholde poyson beye, with which he myghte sleen his felawes tweye** THE DEVIL ... PUT INTO HIS THOUGHT THAT HE SHOULD BUY THE POISON, WITH WHICH HE COULD KILL HIS TWO COMPANIONS. However, there is an obvious semantic overlap between MAY/MIGHT 'hypothesis' and CAN/COULD 'possibility' even in PDE, and thus, as the old formal subjunctive disappeared, ME **may/might** and so on were extended to take over the functions of that construction. An example such as **Thanne may we bothe oure lustes al fulfille** ... THEN WE

?MAY/CAN BOTH FULFIL ENTIRELY OUR DESIRES ... demonstrates the overlap.

The main syntactic innovation in the verb phrase during the ME period was the rise of two kinds of construction: *the impersonal verb* and *the phrasal verb*. The former – although certainly found in OE – became greatly extended in use during the ME period. It may be exemplified by **us thynketh** IT SEEMS TO US, **hem thoughte** IT SEEMED TO THEM; however, the construction had become highly restricted in context by EModE times, and has now largely disappeared. The latter construction, still common in PDE, consists of a verb followed by another element which seems closely tied to it semantically, for example GET UP, WAKE UP, LOOK UP. Typically, as mentioned on p. 75 above, phrasal verbs in PDE are rather colloquial in register; typically also, they tend to have formal-register near-synonyms, cf. ARISE, AWAKE, CONSULT.

As in OE, *negation* is expressed in ME by the negative particle **ne**, frequently assimilated to following weak-stressed words with initial vowel or /w-/ (for example **nis** = **ne** + **is**); cf. **nas** WAS NOT. In ME it is often reinforced by a postverbal particle **nat, nought** and so on; towards the end of the ME period, and usually in Chaucerian English, it became common to drop **ne** and use **nat, nought** and so on, alone, as in, for example, **if he wol nat tarie** IF HE DOES NOT WISH TO WAIT. It will be noted that, as in OE, multiple negation was not stigmatised in ME, **he nevere yet no vileynye ne sayde** HE NEVER YET SPOKE ANY COARSE SPEECH.

In PDE, *interrogation* is expressed prototypically using the so-called 'dummy DO', for example DO YOU WANT ...? DON'T YOU SING ...? In ME (as in OE), questions were commonly expressed by the element-order Predicator-Subject (PS); see p. 100 below.

6.2.3 Sentence structure

This section deals with *word-order*, *clauses* and *some distinctive ME constructions*.

Since in ME the OE inflectional system broke down, *word-order patterns* are much like those of PDE with the same range of prototypical and deviant usages. The most common order of elements, in both main and subordinate clauses, is – like PDE – SP (Subject-Predicator), where the predicator (= the verb-phrase) immediately follows the subject, for example **If that a prynce useth hasardye** ... IF A PRINCE PRACTISES GAMBLING ... This usage can, as in PDE, sometimes be deviated from for stylistic reasons in order to place some other element in the thematic position in a clause or sentence, or in order to sustain a rhyme, for example **This tresor hath Fortune unto us yiven, in myrthe and joliftee oure lyf to lyven** FORTUNE HAS GIVEN TO US THIS TREASURE IN ORDER TO LIVE OUR LIFE IN MIRTH AND JOLLITY. Since ME is intermediate between PDE and OE, it is not surprising that some older constructions are still found; in Chaucerian English these practices are plainly useful when the poet wishes to sustain a rhyme. Thus, when a complex verb phrase is employed, the lexical element has a tendency to appear at the end of the clause, as in **hath ... yven** above, or as in **the feend ... putte in his thought that he sholde poyson beye** THE DEVIL PUT INTO HIS MIND THAT HE SHOULD BUY POISON.

An older usage, S ... P (Subject ... Predicator), is still sometimes found in Chaucerian usage, especially when the object of the clause is a pronoun, as in **This olde man ful mekely hem grette** THIS OLD MAN GREETED THEM VERY HUMBLY. Furthermore, as in OE, a delayed verb phrase can still appear occasionally in subordinate clauses, for example **Whan that Aprill with his shoures soote/ The droghte of March hath perced to the roote ...** WHEN APRIL WITH ITS SWEET SHOWERS HAS PIERCED TO THE ROOT THE DROUGHT OF MARCH ...

The OE usage PS is found when the clause begins with an adverbial, for example **unnethe ariseth he out of his synne** HE SCARCELY RISES OUT OF HIS SIN (with a simple verb phrase), **at many a noble armee hadde he be** HE HAD BEEN ON MANY A NOBLE MILITARY EXPEDITION (with a split in the complex verb phrase). The PS-construction meant that the verb would still be in 'second position', a prototypical feature of OE main clauses. PS is also found in questions, for example **Why lyvestow so longe in so greet age?** WHY DO YOU LIVE SO LONG IN(TO) SUCH GREAT AGE? The 'dummy DO', characteristic of PDE in such constructions, appears in EModE; it is not a feature of ME question-constructions.

As have OE and PDE, ME has a range of different *clause-types*, *main* and *subordinate*. Main clauses can stand on their own as a well-formed sentence; subordinate clauses cannot stand on their own, and are semantically dependent on main clauses. Thus, in a sentence such as THE MAN WAS RUNNING ALONG THE ROAD WHILE HE WAS BEING CHASED BY A TIGER, there are two clauses: 1. THE MAN WAS RUNNING ALONG THE ROAD and 2. WHILE HE WAS BEING CHASED BY A TIGER. Clause 1 is a main clause, because it could potentially stand on its own as a well-formed English sentence; clause 2 cannot stand on its own as a well-formed English sentence since it begins with the 'subordinating conjunction' WHILE; the information subordinate clause 2 contains supports and supplements that provided by the main clause 1.

Main clauses can be linked together through *coordination*, for example BILL WAS EATING A BANANA AND TOM WAS EATING AN APPLE. In this sentence, BILL WAS EATING A BANANA and TOM WAS EATING AN APPLE are both main clauses; AND is a coordinating conjunction. *Coordinating conjunctions* in ME include **and** and **but**, as in PDE, for example **And forth he gooth** ... **into the toun, unto a pothecarie, and preyde hym that he hym wolde selle som poyson** ... AND HE GOES FORTH ... INTO THE TOWN, TO AN APOTHECARY, AND BEGGED HIM THAT HE WOULD SELL SOME POISON ...

Subordinate clauses can be introduced, as in OE, by a range of *subordinating conjunctions*. The forms of these conjunctions are much as in PDE, except that the particle **that** often (although not always) appears along with **if, whan** and so on, for example **Whan that Aprill** ... WHEN APRIL ..., **If that a prynce** IF A PRINCE, **how that the seconde heeste** HOW THE SECOND COMMANDMENT ... **whil that thou strogelest** ... WHILE YOU STRUGGLE ... **er that he dide** ... BEFORE HE DID ..., **beside whan he came** ... WHEN HE CAME ..., **if he be baptized** IF HE IS BAPTISED ... The option of using **that** has obvious metrical advantages, and there is evidence that metre seems to have been a determining factor in Chaucer's selection or omission of **that** in such constructions.

As in OE and PDE, there is in ME a range of subordinate clauses: *relative*, *adverbial* and *comparative*. Relative clauses (that is 'WHO/ WHICH and so on clauses' in PDE) are commonly introduced by **that** in ME. A slightly confusing feature of ME is that these clauses can sometimes be separated from the noun phrases they modify, something not possible in PDE, for example **God save yow, that boghte agayn mankynde** MAY GOD, WHO REDEEMED MANKIND, SAVE YOU. For other relative pronouns, see p. 94 above. Sometimes a relative clause is used without a relative pronoun when that pronoun is to be expected in subject position; this usage occurs in OE and EModE, but is not known in PDE, for example **Biforn a cors, was caried to his graue** IN FRONT OF A CORPSE, (WHICH) WAS BEING CARRIED TO ITS GRAVE. Adverbial clauses without subordinating conjunctions are also found in ME, for example **Bledynge ay at his nose in dronkenesse** CONTINUALLY BLEEDING AT HIS NOSE IN DRUNKENNESS. Comparative usages are common in ME, for example **And two of vs shul strenger be than oon** AND TWO OF US MUST BE

STRONGER THAN ONE. Sometimes the conjunctions characteristic of comparative clauses are used correlatively, for example **right as they hadde cast his deeth bifoore, right so they han hym slayn** JUST AS THEY HAD PLANNED HIS DEATH EARLIER, JUST SO THEY HAVE SLAIN HIM.

Chaucerian English still retains some special features of OE sentence-structure which are not a prototypical feature of PDE usage: *recapitulation and anticipation* and *the splitting of heavy groups*. A third feature of OE syntax, *parataxis*, is not so salient a feature of Chaucer's practice, but is found in some varieties of ME and will therefore be discussed here.

Recapitulation and anticipation was a feature of OE whereby an anticipatory noun phrase was recapitulated later in the clause by a pronoun. Such constructions also occur in Chaucerian English, for example **This yongeste, which that wente to the toun, ful ofte in herte he rolleth up and doun** THIS YOUNGEST (MAN), WHO WENT TO THE TOWN, VERY OFTEN HE REVOLVES IN SPIRIT ..., **The worste of hem, he spak the first word** THE WORST OF THEM, HE SPOKE THE FIRST WORD, **alle the gretteste that were of that lond, pleyynge atte hasard he hem fond** ALL THE GREATEST WHO WERE FROM THAT LAND, HE FOUND THEM PLAYING AT GAMBLING.

The splitting of heavy groups was a characteristic of OE, whereby long phrases and modifiers, which were apparently regarded as clumsy, could be broken up, or 'split'. Thus a PDE usage such as BILL AND TOM WERE EATING CAKE would be expressed (in OE-fashion) as BILL WAS EATING CAKE, AND TOM. This construction still appears in PDE, but as a stylistically marked usage; in what appears to be an unmarked form it survives into ME, for example **Thy tonge is lost, and al thyn honeste cure** YOUR TONGUE AND YOUR CARE FOR HONOURABLE THINGS ARE LOST, **An oold man and a povre with hem mette** AN OLD AND POOR MAN MET WITH THEM.

Parataxis means the juxtaposition of two or more main clauses rather than the subordination of one clause to another (which is called *hypotaxis*). Parataxis can be of two kinds: *syndetic* (with coordinating conjunctions such as AND) and *asyndetic* (without such conjunctions). The three patterns might be illustrated as follows:

1. BECAUSE HE WAS BEING CHASED BY A TIGER, HE CLIMBED THE TREE (hypotaxis)
2. HE WAS BEING CHASED BY A TIGER AND HE CLIMBED THE TREE (syndetic parataxis)

3. HE WAS BEING CHASED BY A TIGER; HE CLIMBED THE TREE (asyndetic parataxis)

As these examples demonstrate, the use of parataxis requires readers to make causational links which are not made explicitly by writers, whereas writers who employ hypotaxis make such links explicit. In OE literature, parataxis was more commonly employed than it is in PDE. During the ME period, writers could choose between the older paratactic style characteristic of OE and the newer hypotactic style which seems to have been brought into English through contact with French. Chaucer's usage was basically hypotactic, often with quite complex subordination. However, some writers, such as Malory, seem consciously to have sustained the older paratactic usage as a sign of their ideological commitment to traditional values. The following passages may be taken to illustrate the two styles. The first passage is from William Caxton's Preface to his version of Malory's *Morte Darthur*; the second is a passage from Malory's own text as it survives in the Winchester Manuscript.

Passage 1
And I, accordyng to my copye, haue doon sette it in enprynte to the entente that noble men may see and lerne the noble actes of chyualrye, the jentyl and vertuous dedes that somme knyghtes vsed in thos dayes, by whyche they came to honour, and how they that were vycious were punysshed and ofte put to shame and rebuke, humbly bysechyng al noble lordes and ladyes wyth al other estates, of what estate or degree they been of, that shal see and rede in this sayd book and werke, thagh they take the good and honest actes in their remembraunce, and to folowe the same; wherein they shalle fynde many joyous and playsaunt hystoryes and noble and renomed actes of humanyte, gentylnesse, and chyualryes.

Passage 2
And ryght thus as they were at theyr seruyce, there came syr Ector de Maris that had seuen yere sought al Englond, Scotlond and Walys, sekyng his brother syr Launcelot; and whan syr Ector herde suche noyse and lyghte in the quyre of Joyous Garde, he alyght and put his hors from hym and came into the quyre; and there he sawe men synge and wepe, and al they knewe syr Ector, but he knewe not them.

6.3 Morphology

The inflexional morphology of a language may be defined as the set of *paradigms* which it contains. Paradigms are model patterns for the various word-classes; once a set of paradigms is established, it is possible to use these paradigms as grammatical templates. For example, knowing that the plural of STONE is STONES enables us to predict that the likely plural of BEAN is BEANS, even though there are of course irregular paradigms in PDE, such as the alternation CHILD - CHILDREN. In this section of Chapter 6 we will be establishing the paradigms of ME. Although the main reference-point is the Ellesmere MS of *The Canterbury Tales*, examples are also drawn from other texts so that a broad characterisation of ME patterns can be given.

This section is divided into subsections in the following sequence: *nouns, adjectives, (adjectival) adverbs, determiners, pronouns, numerals* and *verbs*. It should be noted that paradigmatic choice depends on syntactic function, cross-references are made throughout.

6.3.1 Nouns

By the time of Chaucer, there was a *Basic Noun Declension*, and a set of *Irregular Noun Declensions*. Nouns took on special forms depending on number and case (see pp. 93–4 above).

The *Basic Noun Declension* in Chaucerian English was as follows:

Number	Singular	Plural
Case		
Nominative	**stoon** STONE	**stoones**
Accusative	**stoon**	**stoones**
Genitive	**stoones**	**stoones**
Dative	**stoon(e)**	**stoones**

This system derived from the most common OE noun-paradigm, the so-called 'strong masculines'; the paradigm was extended to other nouns by analogy, and the process is earliest recorded in Northumbrian varieties of late OE.

It will be noted that the plural and genitive singular forms are indistinguishable and could only be disambiguated by syntactic context. Most ME nouns are declined on this pattern, for example **fish** FISH, **bo(o)k** BOOK, **lond** LAND. A sub-group where the nominative singular ends in -e follows a generally similar pattern, for example **herte(s)** HEART(S), **soule(s)** SOUL(S). Sometimes the inflexional -e- is replaced by -y-, as in **swevenys** DREAMS; sometimes it is dropped altogether, especially in nouns of more than one syllable, such as **naciouns** NATIONS. It will be observed that -e occasionally appears in the dative case; this use is largely restricted in the Ellesmere MS to what seem to have been a few formulaic expressions, for example **in londe** IN (THE) LAND. A few nouns have forms of the genitive which differ from that of the basic declension. Some are endingless, for example classical names whose nominative forms end in -s, such as **Epicurus owene son** EPICURUS' OWN SON, and some native forms, such as **my fader soule** MY FATHER'S SOUL. Uninflected forms also occur frequently after numerals, as in **ten fot** TEN FOOT, **hundred pound** HUNDRED POUNDS. The Chaucerian pattern of inflexion may be taken as characteristic of late ME, though endings in **-us** for Chaucerian **-es** are common in Western varieties, and **-is, -ys** appear for **-es** in Older Scots and Northern ME, and fifteenth-century varieties of Southern ME.

In Chaucerian English, there are only a few exceptions to this paradigm; and these may be termed the *Irregular Declensions*. In general these paradigms are marked by deviant plural forms (genitive singular forms follow the basic paradigm). Examples are: **oxen** OXEN, **eyen** EYES and the variant form **foon** FOES (beside **foos**); **feet** FEET beside **foot** FOOT, **gees** GEESE beside **goos** GOOSE; and nouns with endingless plurals such as **sheep** SHEEP, **deer** DEER, **thyng** THINGS, **hors** HORSES (beside **thynges, horses**). It will be observed that many of these exceptions are also found in PDE, although some only in nonstandard varieties. Other varieties of late ME have a few more exceptions, such as **berien** BERRIES, **eiren** EGGS (both beside forms with -s) and some of these survive into PDE dialects (cf. non-standard PDE **childer**, from OE **cildru** CHILDREN). These irregular declensions derive from alternative paradigmatic patterns in OE.

Conservative usages were retained until quite a late date in the south of England. Grammatical gender is flagged inflexionally, for instance, in Kentish texts from the late thirteenth and early fourteenth centuries. Further, there is good evidence in southern dialects of the EME period for the extension of **-en** endings as a paradigm rivalling the **-s** type (cf. Bennett and Smithers 1974: 392, note 23); although the **-s** genitive was dominant throughout the ME period, **-ene** appears for the genitive plural in many EME texts.

6.3.2 Adjectives

As indicated on p. 95 above, Chaucerian English sometimes distinguishes between strong and weak paradigms of adjectives, although the range of inflexional distinctions is considerably smaller than it was in OE times. Adjectives may be classified into the following groups:

1. Adjectives derived from OE which distinguish strong and weak paradigms. These are reflexes of OE adjectives such as **eald** OLD, **gōd** GOOD, **lang** LONG, **geong** YOUNG. In Chaucerian English the paradigm is as follows: **old** OLD (strong singular), **olde** (strong plural), **olde** (weak singular), **olde** (weak plural).

2. Adjectives derived from OE which do not distinguish strong and weak paradigms. These fall into two subgroups: (a) adjectives whose OE nominative masculine singular strong ended in -e, such as **wilde** WILD, **swēte** SWEET, **clǣne** CLEAN, **grēne** GREEN; cf. Chaucerian **wilde, sweete, clene, grene**, and (b) adjectives which were polysyllabic in OE, such as **hālig** HOLY, **lȳtel** LITTLE; cf. Chaucerian **hooly, litel**. These adjectives are indeclinable in Chaucerian English.

3. Adjectives derived from other languages, for example **large** AMPLE, GENEROUS. Such adjectives are indeclinable in Chaucerian English. The only forms in this group which occasionally inflect are those where French practices of inflexion have been transferred to English, for example **weyes espirituels** SPIRITUAL PATHS.[6, 7]

The distinction between strong and weak adjectives is a Germanic innovation, but the distinction began to break down in English during the transition from OE to ME. In EME, a version of the system can still be distinguished in texts such as *The Owl and the Nightingale* (Caligula MS), with forms such as **godne** (GOOD, strong masculine singular), **þat grete heued** (THAT LARGE HEAD, weak). However, in Northern dialects, which were inflexionally innovative, the distinction had disappeared by the beginning of the fourteenth century. A weak/strong distinction survived in southern English into the fifteenth century, but was vestigial by that date; it disappeared entirely in all varieties of English during the course of the fifteenth century. Chaucerian English is one of the last forms of the language to retain the old strong/weak and singular/plural distinctions in adjectival inflexion.

Comparison of adjectives in Chaucerian grammar follows a simple pattern, for example **depe, depere, depest** (cf. PDE DEEP, DEEPER, DEEPEST); these three forms of the adjective are known as the *positive*, *comparative* and *superlative* forms respectively. As in PDE, there are some irregular forms, such as **god(e), bettre, best(e)**. Comparative forms were always inflected according to the weak declension in OE, so no distinction between strong and weak forms was made with this category in ME; however, ME superlative forms could be marked for definiteness in those varieties where the strong/weak distinction was made, such as **yongest** beside **the yongeste**.

In PDE, an alternative method of comparison is periphrastic, using MORE and MOST. In OE, an equivalent construction occasionally appeared, using the adverbs **swiþor/swiþost** or **bet/betst**; these words were still used in periphrastic constructions in EME but were replaced in late ME by **ma/mo/mare/more** MORE and **mast/most** MOST. Such periphrastic constructions tended to be used with adjectives whose stems were polysyllabic, for example **most despitous** CRUELLEST. Words borrowed into ME followed both patterns: **fyner, fynest(e)** beside **mo(o)re precious, moost precious.**

Irregular comparative and superlative forms derive from OE patterns, such as **gōd** GOOD, **bet(e)ra/sēlra, betst/sēlest** (cf. PDE GOOD, BETTER (vs. *GOODER), BEST (vs. *GOODEST)). The most important of these exceptions were those where a different vowel appeared in the root-vowel of the comparative and superlative forms as a result of an OE sound-change called **i**-mutation or **i**-umlaut (Hogg 1992: 121–38), cf. OE (WS) **eald** OLD, **ieldra, ieldest.** In ME, the mutated comparatives and superlatives are also found, for example **elder, eldest** (beside positive **old**); but forms without mutation modelled on the positive also occur as analogous formations, for example **older, oldest.**

6.3.3 Determiners

Determiners in PDE form a special class of modifiers. The most important members of the class are the *definite* and *indefinite articles* (A(N), THE), and the *demonstratives* (THIS, THESE, THAT, THOSE). Chaucerian English differed from OE in possessing an indefinite article, **a(n)** whose distribution was the same as in PDE, that is **an** prevocalically and **a** elsewhere (see p. 95 above). The definite article in Chaucerian English was **the,** and was indeclinable. The demonstrative determiners were, however, inflected, agreeing as in PDE with their headword in number: **that** THAT, **tho** THOSE; **this** THIS, **thise/these** THESE. There is uncertainty as to the pronunciation of **-e** in **thise.** Metrical evidence suggests that the **-e** on **thise/these** was not pronounced, and was simply a written-mode marker of plurality.[8]

OE did not really have a category 'article' in the same way that PDE does; indeed, determiners are often omitted where they would be expected in PDE. Thus there was no indefinite article such as PDE A(N); **ān** was primarily a numeral ONE, and **sum** A CERTAIN had distinct semantics (see Mitchell 1985: 153 and references there cited). The form **se, seo** and so on, often translated as THE, is equally well-translated as THAT. It is probably best to argue that, where PDE has a three-way system of 'defining words' (THE; THAT/THOSE; THIS/THESE), OE had a two-way one (**se** etc.; **þes** etc.) (see Hogg forthcoming, Mitchell 1985: 132 and references there cited). There is still of course a semantic overlap between THAT/THOSE and THE in PDE (see Mitchell 1985: 132).

The PDE system of a distinct system of definite and indefinite articles, separate from the demonstratives, arose during the ME period. An indefinite article is present in EME texts from the South of England such as the Caligula MS of *The Owl and the Nightingale*. In this text what is clearly an indefinite article is found in a variety of inflected forms, for example **one** (dative singular, modifying an historically neuter noun), **ore** (dative singular, modifying an historically feminine noun). However, indeclinable **a** is also found, pointing forward to future developments. By Chaucer's time, the present-day configuration of demonstratives and articles was in place, though in Northern dialects – as in fifteenth-century Scots – **ane** had developed as the prototypical form in all phonetic environments.

Chaucerian **the** seems to descend, ultimately, from part of the **se**-type demonstrative paradigm which characterised OE; nominatives with initial þ-/ð- are already recorded in Northumbrian OE (Campbell 1959: 290-291, Mitchell 1985: 102), and, given the speed of their adoption, þ-/ð-types were probably already present in spoken OE over a fairly widespread area. These þ-type nominatives presumably derive from analogy with other parts of the paradigm.[9]

In the EME period two systems are in competition: the (ultimately successful) indeclinable **the**-type, and one where the definite article still has a variety of inflected forms. In the Caligula MS of the EME poem *The Owl and the Nightingale* a definite article **þe** appears beside forms **þane, þare, þas** and so on, and such systems are also recorded in Southern dialects well into the fourteenth century. However, the inflected forms of the definite article have disappeared from the written record by the time of Chaucer.[10]

For THIS/THESE in *The Owl and the Nightingale* (Caligula MS) we find **þis/þ(e)os**, with various inflected forms (such as **þisse**); this pattern may be taken as broadly prototypical for EME practice. For THAT/THOSE, **þat** – in origin the neuter singular of the **se**-paradigm – seems to have taken on its PDE demonstrative meaning during the EME period. *The Ormulum*, an East Midland text of *c.*1200, has examples of **þat**-type forms modifying all genders and without case-inflexion: **i þatt tun** IN THAT TOWN (cf. OE **tūn** masculine), **o þatt illke nahht** IN THAT SAME NIGHT (cf. OE **niht** feminine). *The Ormulum* has **þa** for THOSE; *The Owl and the Nightingale* (Caligula MS) has **þo(o)/þeo**. By the Late ME period, the PDE system was more or less in place. The demonstratives of Chaucerian English were inflected for number, agreeing with their headword as in PDE: **that** THAT, **tho** THOSE; **this** THIS, **thise/these** THESE. However, as in *The Ormulum*, there were no case-distinctive inflexions. Metrical evidence (see p. 107 above) suggests that the **-e** on **thise/these** was not pronounced, and was simply a written-mode marker of plurality; **these**-type forms became dominant from the early fifteenth century onwards. PDE THOSE arose, it seems, in the late Middle Ages through analogy: a prototypically plural inflexion, -s(e), was added to earlier tho (from OE þā), and the resulting form has been accepted into PDE standard usage. Other forms for THESE are also recorded in late ME; of special interest is the þir-type for THESE, which remains in northern varieties of PDE, and in present-day Scots (cf. the entry for 'this' in CSD).[11]

Other important determiners in ME were:

1. Reflexes of OE **se ilca** etc. THE SAME. OE **ilca** was inflected like a weak adjective, and only appeared in combination with a preceding **se**-form. ME reflexes were **þe ilke, þilke** and so on.

2. The form **ȝon** YON(DER). This demonstrative derives from an OE adjective ****geon** (only attested in its West Saxon feminine dative singular form **geonre**).

6.3.4 Pronouns

ME *pronouns*, as those of PDE, retain *number, person* and *case* distinctions, and are also used to signal the *gender* of their referents when in the third person. However, the gender reference is rarely in ME based on grammatical gender, as it was in OE, but instead is based on so-called *natural gender*, that is sex-distinctions. There are four sets of pronouns: (1) *personal* (cf. PDE I, YOU, SHE, IT, THEY and so on, and including *possessive* pronouns such as MINE and so on); (2) *reflexive* (cf. PDE MYSELF and so on); (3) *relative* (cf. PDE WHO in THE GIRL WHO HAD SHORT HAIR WAS ON THE BUS); (4) *interrogative* (cf. PDE WHO in WHO DID THAT?).

The Chaucerian pronoun-paradigms are as follows:

(1) First Person

Number / Case	Singular	Plural
Nominative	I (rarely **ich**)	**we**
Accusative	**me**	**us**
Genitive	**my(n)(e)**	**our(e)(s)**
Dative	**me**	**us**

(2) Second Person

Number / Case	Singular	Plural
Nominative	**thou/thow**	**ye**
Accusative	**the(e)**	**you/yow**
Genitive	**thy(n)(e)**	**your(e)(s)**
Dative	**the(e)**	**you/yow**

(3) Third Person

Number		Singular		Plural
Gender	Masculine	Feminine	Neuter	All genders
Case				
Nominative	he	s(c)he	it/hit	they etc.
Accusative	hym/him	hir(e) etc.	it/hit	hem
Genitive	his	hir(e)(s)	his	hir(e)(s)
Dative	hym/him	hir(e) etc.	it/hit	hem

It will be observed that the accusative and dative in all pronoun-paradigms are the same; this is because these two categories of pronoun may be considered to have merged in Chaucerian English.[12]

The inflexion of the *relative* pronoun **which(e)** was discussed on p. 94 above. The pronoun **who** had the following paradigm: **who, whom** (accusative), **whos** (genitive). All three forms could be used as *interrogative* pronouns; **whom** and **whos** were used as *relative* pronouns, but **who** seems not to have been so used. By far the most common relative pronoun was **that**, which was indeclinable. The forms **-self, -seluen** commonly appear for the reflexive pronoun in Chaucerian English. In some varieties of EME, this form was inflected in the same way as adjectives, that is as strong/weak (see p. 95 above).[13]

During the transition from OE to Late ME a series of major changes took place, at different speeds in different dialects. OE had a distinct paradigm for *duals* (WE TWO, YOU TWO and so on, see Note 12 below), and this paradigm disappeared. The dative and accusative forms were merged, generally on the dative. The feminine nominative singular pronoun **hēo** was generally replaced by various forms in **sch-, sh-**; the OE third person plurals in **h-** gave way to forms in **þ-/th-**. In the transition from ME to EModE, new genitive forms arose, notably the neuter possessive **its**.

The Chaucerian system clearly represents a position a good distance along the cline of change just described. The only exceptions to the list just given are in the third person plural pronoun, where only the nominative form of the third person plural pronoun is in **th-** (**here, hem** appear for the other cases), and in the neuter possessive, where **its** does not appear (Chaucer uses the older, ambiguous **his**, and periphrases such as **tharof**). Chaucerian pronouns, like those of PDE, retain number, person and case distinctions, and are also used to signal the natural gender of their referents when in the third person.

The following notes on pronominal changes indicate diatopic and diachronic developments:

1. The *dual number* was lost during the Early ME period. The system is evidently already in decay in *The Owl and the Nightingale*, where **we** (referring to two persons) can appear beside **wit** for WE TWO; it is possible that **unker** OF US TWO, the most common form of the dual in this poem, is retained for metrical reasons.

2. The dative and accusative forms were already merged in OE, in the first and second persons of the pronoun (see Note 12). The extension of the merger to the third person based on the dative use would seem a logical development, given that formal distinctions between subject and object would be functionally necessary.

3. The feminine nominative singular pronoun **hēo** was generally replaced in late ME by various forms in **sch-, sh-**. In the North the reflex was generally **scho**; in the Midlands and South **s(c)he** is prototypical. The earliest spelling which seems to reflect this development is **scæ** in the Final Continuation to the *Peterborough Chronicle*; the annal for 1150, where this form appears, which seems to have been written not long after the events it describes. However, **h**-type forms lasted for quite a long time in Southern and Western dialects, and apparently intermediate forms (such as **ȝho**) are also recorded in a number of texts, especially from the Early ME period. The origins and evolution of PDE SHE is a classic problem of English historical linguistics; it is discussed in detail in Chapter 7 below.

4. The OE third person plurals in **h-** gave way, ultimately, to forms in **þ-/th-**, which appear to derive from Old Norse. Again, innovation happened earliest in the North, and the **h-** types continued in the South for quite some time.

5. The rise of **its** is really an issue relating to EModE. The form seems to have developed as an analogical creation, simply adding the genitive suffix **-s** to **it**. It was evidently regarded as colloquial in EModE, because it is often avoided in favour of the periphrastic **therof**.

6. The following minor developments might also be noted:

OE **ic** (later spelt **ich**) was gradually replaced by **I** during the course of the ME period. The form **i** began to be used in the North and Midlands from the thirteenth century onwards, at first, it seems, as an unstressed variant; forms in **ich** lasted longer in the South, and indeed the form was still recorded in the late nineteenth century (Wright and Wright 1928:

159), particularly in contracted forms such as **cham** I AM. Chaucer generally has **I**, but **ich** occurs as a minor variant. PDE I is a restressed variant of the originally unstressed ME **i**.

Thou, ye and so on had special uses in ME. The distinction was roughly comparable with the **tu/vous** distinction in present-day French; in ME **thou** was not only singular but also intimate and **ye** was regarded as more formal as well as plural.

OE **hit** survives in ME, particularly in the South and West; but in the North and East it is replaced by the advancing form **it**. In border areas between the two forms, a semantic distinction has been noted, whereby **hit** is more stylistically marked and **it** is less marked.

When the pronouns were used reflexively in OE the word **self** was often added for emphatic purposes – although it could be omitted, a usage which remained into EModE (cf. Bunyan's **I dreamed me a dream**). Various forms were current in OE varieties (**sylf, silf, seolf**); it is not surprising, therefore, that various reflexes appear in ME.

In OE the indeclinable particle **þe** had a relative function, particularly when used in conjunction with the determiners of the **se**-group. It was distinguished from the OE interrogative pronouns used in questions, that is **hwā** WHO, **hwelc** WHICH. In some EME texts **þe** was retained as the relative particle, but in most others it was replaced by **þat/that**. In some other texts, variant forms of **which(e)** were used. The pronoun **who** had the following paradigm: **who, whom** (accusative), **whos** (genitive). All three forms could also be used as interrogative pronouns; as noted on p. 94 above, **whom** and **whos** were used as relative pronouns, but **who** seems not to have been so used. Forms such as **quhilk** WHO, WHICH are recorded in Northern varieties.

6.3.5 Adverbs

In general, Chaucerian *adverbs* end in **-e**, **-ly** and (rarely) **-liche**, for example **brighte** BRIGHTLY, **unkyndely** UNNATURALLY, **roial-liche** ROYALLY. Adverbs, like adjectives, have *comparative* and *super-lative* forms. In OE, forms such as **heardor, heardost** appear, and these are reflected in ME as **harder, hardest** and so on.

Adverbs fall into two groups: *adjectival* and *non-adjectival*. Adjectival adverbs seem to have originated in Indo-European languages as deriva-tives of adjectives (see further Lass 1994: 207–8), and in OE this re-lationship between adjectives and adverbs is fairly transparent. Adverbs were prototypically formed in OE by adding **-e** to the adjectival stem, for example **hearde** SEVERELY, BRAVELY beside the adjective **heard** SEVERE, BRAVE. When **-e** was added to the very common adjectival ending **-lic**, the resulting ending **-lice** was reinterpreted as an adverb-marker: thus doublets such as **hearde, heardlice** appear (although, interestingly, they develop distinct semantics; cf. the PDE distinction between HARD in HE WORKS HARD and HARDLY in HE HARDLY WORKS). Such pairs also appear in ME; cf. Chaucerian **softe/softely** SOFTLY. In this case, the **-ly** ending is probably a reduced reflex of the OE form, although it may derive from Old Norse **-ligr**; the Northern usage in **lik** derives from Old Norse (cf. **-líkr**).

6.3.6 Prepositions

The growth in use of prepositions during the ME period has already been noted (see p. 94 above). The category 'preposition' shades into that of 'adverb', as is demonstrated by the way in which they can still be used as such in PDE; we might compare, for instance, TO in I WENT TO THE HOUSE and in HE WALKED TO AND FRO. The evidence is that in early forms of Indo-European, prepositions were originally an 'extra', adjunct element which started to be used commonly as gram-matical markers when inflexional systems began to decay. In form, the ME prepositions resemble those of PDE, although there are some which are no longer found, or which have or had a dialectal restriction in ME or PDE, for example **fort** UNTIL, which is common in Southern varieties of ME, for example in *The Owl and the Nightingale* (Caligula MS), but has died out since.

6.3.7 Numerals

As in PDE, ME *numerals* are divided into *cardinal* (ONE, TWO and so on) and *ordinal* (FIRST, SECOND and so on) categories. Here are the ME cardinal numbers ONE to TEN, 100 and 1000, and equivalent ordinals for FIRST to TENTH in the variety of language represented by the Ellesmere MS:

	Cardinal	*Ordinal*
1	oon	first(e)
2	two(o)	seconde, secunde
3	thre(e)	thridde, thirde
4	four	ferthe, fourthe
5	five	fifthe
6	sixe	sixte
7	sevene	seventhe

8	eighte	eighthe
9	nine	ninthe
10	ten	tenthe
100	houndred	
1000	thousand	

In OE, **ān** ONE was declined like the adjectives, both strong and weak, and declined forms are still recorded in Early ME. Similarly, **twā** TWO declined in OE thus: Nominative/Accusative **twēgen** (Masculine), **twā** (Feminine), **twā/tū** (Neuter); Genitive **twēgra/ twēg(e)a** (all genders); Dative **twǣm** (all genders). **þrēo** THREE declines thus: Nominative/Accusative **þrīe** (Masculine), **þrēo** (Feminine/Neuter); Genitive **þrēora** (all genders); Dative **þrim** (all genders). Elements of these inflected forms are sporadically recorded in EME, but the PDE configuration is in position by Chaucer's time. All other cardinal numbers are generally indeclinable. These forms are commonly used in most varieties of ME, although **hundreth** (from the Old Norse cognate for HUNDRED) is common in northern varieties.

In the ordinals, the most interesting change is the replacement of OE **ōþer** by ME **seconde** and so on. **Oþer** could be used for OR, OTHER in OE; the use of the French-derived form, which itself derives from the Latin verb **sequor** FOLLOW, resolved the potential ambiguity.[14]

6.3.8 Verbs

As in OE and PDE, ME verbs fall into three categories: *weak*, *strong* and *irregular*, and the assignment of verbs to these categories is broadly in line with the assignment of such verbs in earlier and later states of the language. As is the case in OE and PDE, ME verb paradigms take account of person, number, tense and mood.

The various categories of verb just described derive from patterns established in the OE period. The distinguishing feature of the *strong verb*, variation in the stressed vowel, derives from alternations which existed in Proto-Indo-European, known as *Ablaut* or *gradation*. The original pattern distinguished between front vowels and back vowels; there seems to have been a related semantic correspondence between front vowels and the present tense/progressive aspect, and back vowels with past tense/perfect aspect (see further Prokosch 1938: 122, Samuels 1972: 170). Although subsequent sound-changes obscured this pattern, elements of the system remain, for example WRITE/WROTE, TREAD/TROD and so on. *Contracted verbs* are strong verbs whose inflexional systems have been disturbed by certain kinds of sound-change.[15]

The **weak verbs** were a Germanic innovation; their origins have not been clearly determined by scholars, but it is commonly suggested that they derive from the combination of a lexical element and a verb related to PDE DO. Weak verbs are the main productive verb paradigm in PDE, and new verbs are generally conjugated weak, for example JIVE, JIVED. Some verbs which were strong in OE and ME have subsequently been transferred to the weak conjugation, for example HELP, HELPED, cf. ME **help(en)**, **holp(en)** and so on.

Irregular verbs fall into various categories, and raise numerous problems of classification. As with the strong verbs, it seems likely that semantic considerations underlie their formal appearance; the fact that they are non-prototypical in verb-form, and that in many cases they overlapped semantically with verbal categories such as subjunctivity and modality made them ripe for grammaticalisation, that is for use as grammatical rather than lexical items (see Warner 1993).

Here are three model conjugations in the forms found in the Ellesmere MS: **binde(n)** TO BIND, a typical strong verb; **love(n)** TO LOVE, a typical weak verb; and the most important irregular verb, **be(e)(n)** TO BE. It may be noted that the present-tense forms of the strong and weak conjugations are the same.[16]

1. **binde(n)** TO BIND

	Indicative	*Subjunctive*
Present		
1st person singular	**binde**	**binde**
2nd person singular	**bindest**	**binde**
3rd person singular	**bindeth**	**binde**
All persons plural	**binde(n)**	**binde(n)**
Preterite		
All persons singular	**bounde, bounde**	
All persons plural	**bounde(n) bounde(n)**	

Imperative: **bind** (singular), **bindeth** (plural)

Participles
Present **bindyng(e)**   Past **(y)bounde(n)**

2. **loue(n)** TO LOVE

	Indicative	*Subjunctive*
Present		
1st person singular	**loue**	**loue**
2nd person singular	**louest**	**loue**
3rd person singular	**loueth**	**loue**
All persons plural	**loue(n)**	**loue(n)**

Preterite

1st/3rd persons singular	**louede**	**louede**
2nd person singular	**louedest**	**louede**
All persons plural	**louede(n)**	**louede(n)**

Imperative: **loue** (singular), **loueth** (plural)

Participles
Present **louyng(e)**   Past **(y)loued(e)**

3. **be(e)(n)** TO BE

	Indicative	*Subjunctive*
Present		
1st person singular	**am**	**be**
2nd person singular	**art**	**be**
3rd person singular	**is**	**be**
All persons plural	**be(e)(n)/ be(e)(n)/ar(e)(n)**	**ar(e)(n)**
Preterite		
1st/3rd persons singular	**was**	**were**
2nd person singular	**were**	**were**
All persons plural	**were(n)**	**were(n)**

Imperative: **be** (singular), **be(th)** (plural)

Participles
Present **beyng(e)**   Past **be(e)(n)**

Binden can act as the general model for all strong verbs; however, as in OE and PDE, there are several classes of strong verb in ME marked by varying patterns of alternation in stem vowels. It is possible to generate a complete paradigm from the ***principal parts*** of a strong verb, that is the infinitive, the third person present singular, the third person preterite singular, the preterite plural and the past participle. **Louen** may act as a general model for all weak verbs.[17]

Here are the principal parts of some common ***irregular verbs***, plus the third person present singular ('no pp.' = no recorded past participle).

KNOW **wite(n)**; **wo(o)t**; **wiste**; **wiste(n)**; **(y)wist**
OWE (cf. OE OWN) no infin.; **oweth**; **oughte**; **oughte(n)**; **owed**
KNOW **conne(n)**; **can**; **coude**; **coude(n)**; **coud**
BE ABLE TO **mowe(n)**; **may**; **myghte**; **myghte(n)**; no pp.
BE OBLIGED TO no infin.; **shal**; **sholde**; **sholde(n)**; no pp.
BE ALLOWED no infin.; **moot**; **moste**; **moste(n)**; no pp.
WANT TO no infin.; **wil(e)/wol(e)**; **wolde**; **wolde(n)**; no pp.
NOT WANT TO no infin.; **nil(e)**; **nolde**; **nolde(n)**; no pp.

DO **doon**; **doth**; **dide**; **dide(n)**; **(y)don**
GO **goon**; **goth**; **yede/wente**; **yede(n)/wente(n)**; **(y)gon**

As has already been indicated (p. 115 above), the paradigms just given are those of the Ellesmere MS; other paradigms are found in other varieties of ME. Very broadly speaking, a distinction may be made between *Northern*, *Midland* and *Southern* paradigms, as follows:

Northern

bind (infinitive), **bindand** (present participle), **bindis** (third person present singular), **binde/bindis** (present plural), **bounden** (past participle). Most scholars derive the endings **-and** and **-is** from Old Norse. A peculiarity of Northern ME – and Older Scots – is the 'Northern Personal Pronoun Rule'. Relics of this system remain in certain rural varieties of present-day American English. The system works as follows: *if the subject of the clause is a personal pronoun, and comes immediately before or after the verb*, the paradigm is as follows:

Singular	1	**I keip**
	2	**thou keipis**
	3	**he/scho/it keipis**
Plural		**we/ȝe/thai keip**

Otherwise *the* **-is** *form is used throughout the paradigm*; cf. Barbour, *Bruce* I: 487–8, **Thai** *sla* **our folk but enchesoune,/ And** *haldis* **this land agayne resoune** THEY *SLAY* OUR PEOPLE WITHOUT CAUSE, / AND *HOLD* THIS LAND CONTRARY TO REASON.

In the irregular verbs, the most distinctive feature of Northern ME is the use of **sal/suld** for SHALL/SHOULD, cf. Ellesmere **s(c)hal/ s(c)holde**. The evidence from later dialect usage is that **sal** and so on was pronounced as [sal]. This Northern usage seems divergent if seen within the range of ME dialects, but is much less so from a broader Germanic perspective; cf. Dutch **zal**, German **sol**. (For the distinctive Norfolk form **xal** and so on, see p. 62 above.)

Midland

binde(n) (infinitive), **bindende/bindinge** (present participle), **bindeþ/bindes** (third person present singular), **binden** (present plural), **bounden** (past participle). The inflexion **-ende** for the present participle appears in EME. However, it was replaced in later ME by **-inge**, which derives from the OE *gerund* or verbal noun (cf. PDE *THE SINGING* WAS VERY LOUD), which, in constructions such as OE **on bindunge**, was synonymous with the present participle; the construction remains in archaistic use in PDE (for example A-SINGING). The reason for the disappearance of -ende seems to be to do with its potentiality for confusion with the -en form of the present plural, which was commonly used in Midland varieties of ME and which seems to have derived from a variant form comparatively rarely recorded in OE (cf. WS bindaþ). -es-type forms of the third person present singular are found in varieties of ME from the North Midlands.

Southern

binde(n) (infinitive), bindende/bindinde (present participle), bint (third person present singular), bindeth (present plural), ybounde (past participle). The Southern verb-paradigm was the most conservative within the ME dialects. The retention of the older form of the present participle seems to be connected with the retention of a distinct form of the present plural, while the common use of contracted verbs such as bint (cf. Midland bindeth) disambiguated singular and plural forms of the present tense. It is noticeable that Southern varieties were the last to adopt distinct forms of the third person pronoun, and it is usually argued that there is a connection here with the conservative verb-paradigm – though of course Southern dialects had least contact with the advancing þ-forms, which seem to derive from Old Norse (see further Samuels 1972: 85–6).

Exercises

Questions for review

1. It is sometimes said that the history of English grammar has direction but no pre-determined goal. Write on EITHER the shift from synthesis to analysis in Old and Middle English OR the history of the Old and Middle English determiners in the light of this saying.

2. 'Old English speakers could tolerate a confusing system of third-person pronouns, but Middle English speakers could not.' Discuss.

Other question

In the passage below, from Chaucer's *Pardoner's Tale*, find the following constructions:

a noun phrase containing a weak adjective
a verb phrase containing a strong verb
an adjective phrase containing a strong adjective
a subordinate clause acting as an adverbial

Whan they han goon nat fully half a mile,
Right as they wolde han troden ouer a stile,
An oold man and a poure with hem mette.
This olde man ful mekely hem grette,
And seyde thus, 'Now, lordes, God yow see!'

Recommendations for reading

All the major surveys have extensive discussion of ME grammar; the best discussions in the general histories are probably those contained in the *Cambridge History*, but there are also sections in Strang (1970), Barber (1993) and Smith (1999). For the origins of the ME system, see Lass (1994), Hogg (2002), and also much discussion in Samuels (1972).

ME morphology has always received a fair amount of attention in the standard handbooks (such as Brunner 1963, Fisiak 1964, Wright & Wright 1928), although, disappointingly, there is no large-scale recent comprehensive survey drawing upon diatopic as well as diachronic perspectives; the handbook planned by Jordan (see the Recommendations for reading at the end of Chapter 5) was never completed. Some of the articles collected by Laing (1989) are on morphological subjects, from a diatopic point of view. The listing of forms given in this chapter is of course hardly comprehensive, and could not be otherwise in such a small space. Although not primarily a grammatical survey, LALME is the richest available source of morphological detail.

The best modern survey of English historical syntax (apart from those already mentioned), which includes much discussion of ME, is Denison (1993), which includes a full bibliography and offers a wide range of research questions. Denison's work takes an eclectic approach to theoretical issues. Generative approaches are offered by Lightfoot (1979) and Traugott (1972). Special issues in ME syntax, within the same overall theoretical framework as Lightfoot, are pursued by Warner (1982, 1993); the latter publication, interestingly, takes on notions derived from 'protoype theory'. The standard work on ME syntax ('parts of speech') is Mustanoja (1959), but the second volume has not yet appeared.

Notes

1. The grammatical terminology used in this chapter is widely adopted by linguists; more detail will be given as it is needed, but students are recommended to consult a standard grammar, such as Leech *et al.* 1982 (which supplies the model used here), or Greenbaum and Quirk 1990.

2. As in earlier chapters, 'Chaucerian usage' is shorthand for 'the usage of the Ellesmere MS'. However, it seems likely that the grammar of the Ellesmere MS is pretty close to Chaucer's own; where the two varieties deviate, Chaucerian use can be reconstructed by referring to the poet's handling of metre; see further Chapter 7.

3. At various places, comparisons are made with earlier and later forms of the English language; for further information, students should refer to the companion volumes in this series. Citations from OE are generally, because of its familiarity for students, given in WS although, of course, this variety was not the ancestor of the best-known varieties of ME.

4. There was also a special *dual* form of the pronoun; this usage survived into a few early varieties of ME, but had died out before the time of Chaucer. The dual number in English is a fossil category, deriving ultimately from Proto-Indo-European. The loss of the dual must have been encouraged functionally by semantic overlap, and formally by the fact that, in many of the Indo-European languages, the old distinctive verbal inflexions were lost and the dual pronouns started to be used with the forms of verbs governed by the singular and plural first- and second-person pronouns.

5. Gender is perhaps the most problematic of categories in the history of English. It is traditional to state that OE had grammatical gender. In other words, OE nouns, and the pronouns referring to them, were assigned to certain paradigmatic patterns on the basis of a system of semantic classification inherited from Proto-Indo-European.

The established terminology for the three genders is to refer to masculine, feminine and neuter, but in many ways these terms are unfortunate because they confuse grammatical and sexual distinctions. However the three categories emerged, they overlapped with, but did not coincide with, the natural sexual distinctions between male, female and neuter. In OE, **wer** MAN is masculine but so is **stān** STONE; both **hlǣfdige** LADY and **giefu** GIFT are feminine; **wīf** WOMAN and **þing** THING are both neuter.

One view of the emergence of grammatical gender is that the original semantic distinction was between animate and inanimate categories, and that the animate set of forms subsequently split into what became masculine and feminine genders. Another view (not necessarily opposed to the twofold view) holds that a three-way distinction developed between individual, general and objective-collective. For a discussion of the origins and/or functions of grammatical gender, see Hogg forthcoming, Jones 1988, Lass 1994: 126 and references there cited. See also the classic account by Prokosch 1938: 228–9, esp. p. 228. Szemerényi 1996: 156–7 gives a very full bibliography on the subject, as does Mitchell 1985: 29.

In principle, OE pronouns referring to the categories masculine, feminine, neuter were regularly **hē** HE, **hēo** SHE and **hit** IT respectively; thus (for example) **hit** could refer back to a sexually female referent if that referent were expressed using a grammatically neuter noun (for instance **wīf** WOMAN).

However, there are many indications that the system was breaking down towards the end of the OE period, with (for example) **hēo** being used for sexually female referents however those referents might be classified according to grammatical gender (see further Mitchell 1985: 36–7).

6. Relics of the old genitive plural are occasionally found, for example **Oure Hoost ... was oure aller cok** OUR HOST ... WAS (AWAKENING) COCKEREL FOR ALL OF US, where **aller** is the reflex of OE **ealra**. The expression seems to be a formulaic one, and no longer productive in ME.

7. For a discussion of the evolution of the adjective, see the brief account in Lass 1994: 146–50 and the more comprehensive account in Prokosch 1938: 259–66; see also Hogg 2002.

8. For the relationship between determiners and pronouns, see Note 12 below. In some handbooks, the distinction is collapsed; see, for example, Wright and Wright 1928: Chapter IX.

9. For further discussion of the OE paradigm, see Hogg forthcoming. It may be convenient for readers to have the OE paradigms for the demonstratives in a footnote:

(a) Equivalent to PDE THAT, THOSE:

Number	Singular			Plural
Gender	Masculine	Feminine	Neuter	All genders
Case				
Nominative	se	sēo	þæt	þā
Accusative	þone	þā	þæt	þā
Genitive	þæs	þ ǣre	þæs	þāra
Dative	þ ǣm	þ ǣre	þ ǣm	þ ǣm

A distinct *instrumental* form is occasionally found in the singular: **þ ȳ** (masculine), **þ ȳ/þon** (neuter), **þ ǣre** (feminine).

(b) Equivalent to PDE THIS, THESE:

Number	Singular			Plural
Gender	Masculine	Feminine	Neuter	All genders
Case				
Nominative	þes	þēos	þis	þās
Accusative	þisne	þās	þis	þās
Genitive	þisses	þisse	þisses	þissa
Dative	þissum	þiss	þissum	þissum

10. A few fossil forms remain in Chaucerian usage, but these are simply formulaic survivals. One such is **for the nones** FOR THE TIME BEING, a line-filler which Chaucer and other late medieval poets frequently employ for metrical reasons. The usage descends from an earlier **for þen ones** FOR THE ONE, with an inflected determiner **þen**. The transfer of -n from the end of one word to the beginning of another is a fairly commonplace phenomenon, known as *metanalysis*, an example in reverse is the form AN ADDER (cf. OE **nǣdre** SNAKE, present-day German **Natter**).

11. There remain many interesting questions about the form of the plural demonstratives in comparison with both OE and PDE. It will be recalled that the nominative plural forms for THOSE, THESE in OE were **þā, þās** respectively. Now, most OE words with ā have <oCe, oa, o> and so on (where C = consonant) in PDE, for example **stān** STONE, **bāt** BOAT, **swā** SO; if OE **þā, þās** had followed this pattern then we would expect *THO, *THOSE in PDE. THOSE as the plural of THAT seems to have emerged analogically; -S(E), as the prototypical marker of plurality, was simply extended as an ending for the original **tho**-type form. (Something similar can be seen in the PDE non-standard **youse** for the plural of YOU.) For a suggestion as to the origins of this form, see Smith 1996: 46, which derives from Samuels 1972: 171.

It is an interesting fact that THOSE, although adopted in the standard language, has been resisted in non-standard usage. The *Survey of English Dialects: Dictionary and Grammar* (1994: 485, 489) records a range of forms, for example **yon turnips** (Yorkshire), **they turnips** (Somerset), **them turnips** (Durham), **them there turnips** (Wiltshire). A **yon**-type form is recorded as a demonstrative **ʒond** in *The Ormulum* and *The Owl and the Nightingale*, but the usage seems to be 'more distal' in comparison with THAT/THOSE. For a helpful outline of this problem with special reference to Older Scots, see King 1997: 168.

12. The category 'pronoun', historically, overlapped with that of determiners; as Lass (1994: 139) puts it,

> Proto-Germanic did not inherit a fully coherent pronoun or determiner system; nothing quite like this reconstructs even for proto-I[ndo-]E[uropean]. Rather the collections labelled 'pronouns' or 'articles' or 'demonstratives' in the handbooks represent dialect-specific selections out of a mass of inherited forms and systems.

And indeed these systems vary across the Germanic languages, with cognate forms taking on distinct roles in different Germanic dialects. Thus, for instance, it is conventional for linguists to note that the Old Icelandic neuter singular pronoun is þat, cognate with the OE neuter singular determiner þæt. Clearly the division between categories is a fuzzy one, and it was therefore possible in OE for the determiners se and so on to be employed occasionally where pronouns would be used in PDE; such usages occur in the earliest varieties of EME. There is evidence for the converse use of (for example) Old Icelandic þat. It is probably more accurate a characterisation of the difference to argue that Old Icelandic þat was prototypically a pronoun, and OE þæt prototypically a determiner. During the transition from OE to ME non-prototypical usages became steadily less common, but the cross-over between categories has relevance for understanding the processes of change.

It may be helpful to give an outline of the OE system in a footnote; because of its comparative familiarity, the WS paradigm is given here. OE pronouns, like nouns, had number and case, and, in the third person, gender; like nouns, they declined. The OE pronoun-paradigms were as follows:

First Person

Number	*Singular*	*Plural*
Case		
Nominative	ic	wē
Accusative	mē	ūs
Genitive	mīn	ūre
Dative	mē	ūs

Second Person

Number	*Singular*	*Plural*
Case		
Nominative	þū	gē
Accusative	þē	ēow
Genitive	þīn	ēower
Dative	þē	ēow

Third Person

Third Person Pronouns were distinguished not only by number and case, but also by gender:

Number		*Singular*		*Plural*
Gender	*Masculine*	*Feminine*	*Neuter*	*All genders*
Case				
Nominative	hē	hēo	hit	hīe
Accusative	hine	hīe	hit	hīe
Genitive	his	hiere	his	hiera
Dative	him	hiere	him	him

In OE there were also dual forms of the first and second person pronouns:

Person	*First*	*Second*
Case		
Nominative	**wit** WE TWO	**git** YOU TWO
Accusative	unc	inc
Genitive	uncer	incer
Dative	unc	inc

13. When the subject-form of the second person singular pronoun is preceded by its verb, it frequently merges with that verb, thus: **lyuestow?** DO YOU LIVE?

14. In some varieties of EME, notably that found in the WM dialect of *Ancrene Wisse*, an interesting graphic distinction was maintained whereby **oþer** was used for OTHER but **oðer** for OR.

15. The origin of contracted verbs lies in pre-OE. A good example is OE **slēan** SLAY, ME **slee(n)**; this verb derives from a pre-OE form *slahan, which underwent a change known as 'first fronting' to produce *slæhan (Hogg 1992: 80–1). The sound-change known as 'breaking', which seems to have occurred soon after the Anglo-Saxons arrived in Britain, meant that *ea appeared in the environment of a following -h-, thus: *sleahan (Hogg 1992: 87). At a somewhat later date, -h- was lost and the vowel lengthened to compensate, producing the historical form **slēan** (Hogg 1992: 173–6).

16. Optional elements in a number of places in these paradigms may be noted, for example the **y-** prefix on past participles (descended from OE **ge-**). In Chaucerian English, these optional elements were frequently employed for metrical reasons. Some optional elements were only found in certain dialects; thus, for instance, **y-** does not appear in Northern varieties of ME.

17. In OE, strong verbs were classified into seven groups; for the origins of this system, see Hogg forthcoming. For comparative purposes, the Chaucerian forms are given here, according to their *principal parts* (that is (1) the infinitive, (2) the third person preterite, (3) the plural preterite and (4) the past participle). Some of the distinctions between classes of strong verbs which occur in OE have disappeared as a result of sound-changes.

I: WRITE **write(n), wroot, write(n), (y)write(n)**
II: CREEP **crepe(n), crepte, crepe(n), (y)cropen, cre(e)pe**
III: BIND **binde(n), bounde, bounde(n), (y)bounde(n)**
IV: BEAR **bere(n), ba(a)r, bare, (y)bore(n)**
V: TREAD **trede(n), trad, trode(n), (y)troden**
VI: SHAKE **shake(n), shook, shoke(n), (y)shake(n)**
VII: HOLD **holde(n), held, helde(n), (y)holde(n)**
KNOW **knowe(n), knew, knewe(n), (y)knowe(n)**

Some verbs which were contracted in OE appear as follows in Chaucerian English. Not all variants are given.

V: SEE **se(n), saugh, sawe(n), (y)seyn**
VI: SLAY **slee(n), slough, slowe(n), (y)slayn**

The OE class-distinctions in weak verbs had largely died out by Chaucer's time. The only common form to display a distinctive paradigm is **have(n)** HAVE, which belonged to the OE weak class III:

III: HAVE **have(n), hadde, hadde(n), (y)had**

The distinction between weak classes I and II had disappeared by Chaucer's time, although there are occasional relicts of a distinctive class II paradigm in earlier fourteenth-century texts such as the Auchinleck MS of *Sir Orfeo*, which represents London usage of the generation before Chaucer, for example **aski** ASK (infinitive); such forms were even more common in EME, for example **louien** LOVE (infinitive) in the thirteenth-century West Midland dialect of the Corpus Christi College, Cambridge MS of *Ancrene Wisse*.

7 Looking forward

So far, our discussion has concentrated on the description of the English language during the ME period. In this final chapter, an attempt is made to look forward, to show how knowledge of ME can be harnessed to engage with broader issues of linguistic evolution, and how an understanding of the ME language can contribute to other areas (literary, cultural, textual) in ME studies. The chapter therefore falls into two parts: *language change* and *language and text*. Obviously in such a small space it is not possible to cover all aspects of such matters, or for that matter any aspects in much depth, but it is hoped that this chapter may be regarded as a 'bridge' to more advanced books, for which see the Recommendations for reading at the end of the chapter.

7.1 Language change

ME is an ideal focus for a central endeavour of historical linguistics: the study of the processes involved in language change. Almost all students of linguistic change are agreed that a key mechanism is the pool of variants to be found in natural languages. Since ME is, for reasons discussed in Chapter 3, the period when diatopic variation is so richly recorded, it supplies scholars with an important resource which can (among other things) be compared with the set of variants to be found in PDE.

To demonstrate these processes, two extended examples will be discussed: a change in the *EME determiner-system* which eventually died out, and a change in the system of *pronouns* which resulted in the usage found in PD 'standard' English. In conclusion, these two examples will be placed within the general context of a third change in the history of English: *the synthetic-analytic shift*.

7.1.1 Determiners in EME

In OE, case, as has been stated on p. 93 above, provided a useful syntagmatic tracking device, marking the functions of noun-phrases, and relating determiners and adjectives to nouns at a time when element-order was more fluid than in PDE. However, although the system has survived in modern German, it largely died out in English during the EME period and, with the exception of the optional genitive in 'S – alongside the singular/plural number-distinction – it is no longer a feature of PDE.

The breakdown of the Old English system is well illustrated in the language of the *Peterborough Chronicle Continuations* (MS Oxford, Bodleian Library, Laud Misc. 636), which date from the twelfth century; the First Continuation contains records for the years 1121–32, while the Final Continuation consists of annals for the period 1133–54. One especially controversial area of the language of the First Continuation relates to the reflexes of the OE determiners **sē, sēo, þæt** and so on, and also with the system of adjectival agreement. In this portion of the *Peterborough Chronicle*, the OE distinctions of grammatical gender have almost completely disappeared. However, there is evidence in the First Continuation that an attempt has been made to retain and reorganise the inter-phrasal tracking device, that is the case-system. The pattern is illustrated in Figure 7.1, with the Late WS equivalents provided for the sake of comparison; the masculine accusative singular ending -**ne** appears in originally feminine and neuter contexts, the masculine/ neuter genitive singular -**s** appears modifying historically feminine nouns, while the feminine dative singular -**re** is used to modify masculines and neuters.

Such patterns appear in the First Continuation (Annals 1121–31) of the *Peterborough Chronicle*, for example **on þone mynstre** IN THE MINSTER, **tō þ̄re mynstre** TO THE MINSTER, where **mynster** is an historically neuter noun, but where **þone** is historically masculine and **þ̄re** is historically feminine. The new system has obvious advantages, not least because the selection of forms can be accounted for as being based on phonetic distinctiveness; a comparison of the incipient EME system with that of Late WS suggests that selection of forms was based upon the singular/plural distinction. Thus **þ̄re** has been dropped as the feminine singular genitive because of potential overlap in form with the similar genitive plural **þāra**, whereas **þ̄m** has disappeared in the masculine and neuter dative singular because of overlap with the dative plural form. Feminine **þā** was dropped in the accusative because of overlap with the plural form; the selection of **þone** rather than **þæt** seems most probably to be because **þæt** was beginning to perform a number of other useful functions, notably as a relative marker.

However, this system was beginning to break down even in the First

Figure 7.1

Late West Saxon system

Number	Singular			Plural
Gender	Masculine	Feminine	Neuter	
Case				
Accusative	þone	þā	þæt	þā
Genitive	þæs	þǣre	þæs	þāra
Dative	þǣm	þǣre	þǣm	þǣm

Incipient Early Middle English system

Number	Singular			Plural
Gender	Masculine	Feminine	Neuter	
Case				
Accusative	þone —————————————>			þā
Genitive	þæs —————>< ————þæs			þāra
Dative	<————— þǣre —————>			þǣm

Continuation of the *Peterborough Chronicle*, where 'false' (that is unhistorical) case-forms appear, such as **þurh se Scotte kyng** 'by the action of the king of Scots' Annal 1126 (with nominative **se** for the expected accusative singular), **þone abbotrice** THE ABBACY Annal 1127 (in subject position, and thus for nominative singular). By the time of the Final Continuation (Annals 1132–54), the determiner was invariably **þe** – the ancestor of PDE THE – whatever the historical case required. In short, the restructured system was not, in the long term, a 'successful' development.

7.1.2 Third-person pronouns in ME

In contrast with the incipient restructuring of the determiner system, EME developments in third-person pronouns resulted – eventually – in the PDE usage; these developments were therefore, in historical terms, 'successful'. In brief, much of the OE system was replaced by forms which derive (it is generally, though not universally, acknowledged) from Old Norse.

The OE system was as in Figure 7.2 (in early WS). This system evidently worked well for the Anglo-Saxons, but during the course of the transition from OE to ME it was replaced by the system which obtains in PDE, as in Figure 7.3.

The main difference between the OE and PDE systems is that PDE third-person pronouns are more phonetically distinctive, especially in

Figure 7.2

Number		Singular		Plural
Gender	Masculine	Feminine	Neuter	All genders
Case				
Nominative	hē	hēo	hit	hīe
Accusative	hine	hīe	hit	hīe
Genitive	his	hiere	his	hiera
Dative	him	hiere	him	him

Figure 7.3

Number		Singular		Plural
Gender	Masculine	Feminine	Neuter	All genders
Case				
Nominative	he	she	it	they
Accusative/Dative	him	her	it	them
Genitive	his	her	its	their

the important nominative cases which play a key role in the discourse-structure of connected speech. Whereas OE pronouns all begin with [h-], PDE nominative pronouns begin with acoustically distinctive sounds which have a wide articulatory distribution: [h-, θ-, ʃ-].[1]

As was discussed in Chapter 5, before the Conquest, standardisation kept most of the Norse wordstock out of the Old English written record. However, from the late eleventh and twelfth centuries, Norse forms became much more widespread in writing, and this change must reflect (however belatedly) a development in the spoken mode. Norse-derived words seem, unlike French vocabulary, to have been treated sociolinguistically as equivalent to items of English lexis, and thus available for use within the core vocabulary of the language.

It was from Norse that the new, phonetically distinctive third-person pronouns seem to have been derived. As might be expected, these pronouns appear first in the written record in texts localised or localisable in the areas with densest Scandinavian settlement, the Danelaw (the extent of which is indicated, for instance, by the evidence of place-names). However, the process was not one of simple transfer; the selection of variables followed complex and not always straightforward paths. Two sets of forms are relevant in this connection: 1. the third person plural pronouns and 2. the third person feminine singular.

In the plural paradigm, the new Norse-derived forms with initial þ- appeared first in texts from the Danelaw, and slowly spread south.

Thus *The Ormulum*, a Lincolnshire text of *c*.1200, has **þeȝȝ** THEY, **þeȝȝre** THEIR; the usual form for THEM was **hemm**, but **þeȝȝm** appeared after a vowel to prevent elision. However, it may be noted that the replacement of pronouns in ME did not happen simultaneously; thus (for instance) the Chaucerian plural pronouns were **they** (nominative), **hem** (accusative/dative) and **here** (genitive).

The speed of adoption of Norse-derived forms, it would seem, varied both diatopically and in terms of function. Thus, for instance, in Northern ME and Scots the Norse forms were adopted – it seems – in a group, whereas in Midland and Southern dialects the nominative forms were adopted first and the other cases at a later date; in PDE native-derived **em** still appears as a spoken-language informal variant of THEM. It is as if the crucial problem was to do with the nominative form, and that **their, them** were adopted, perhaps, by analogy. It is possible that this priority makes sense in discourse terms, since the theme of a text – the central piece of information which a text tries to put across – is usually focused upon the subject of the sentence or clause. However, there were pressures for the disambiguation of the oblique (that is 'non-nominative') forms of the third person plural pronoun; it is noticeable that the native **em**-type, which has survived longest, was disambiguated even in the Ellesmere text by the choice of different vocalisms in **hem** THEM and **him** HIM and so on.[2]

More controversial is the problem of SHE (ME **sche** and so on). Most modern scholars hold that PDE SHE derives from OE **hēo, hīe**, although some still hold that a derivation is possible from the determiner **sēo** (which could be used pronominally in OE). Few still hold that it is the result of some sandhi (word-boundary) articulation, a view on the origin of the form offered in, for example, the OED. Arguments about the origins of the form are based essentially upon three observations of correspondences:

1. The form is found first in ME texts from the North and Midlands and then spreads South. The geographical patterning would seem to resemble that for the **þ**- forms for the plural third-person pronoun and a Norse connection would therefore seem to be likely on *a priori* grounds;

2. In Northern ME and in older Scots, the form is **scho**. In the South, the usual adopted form is **sche, she**, giving the current Present-Day standard English form;

3. In ME, border forms such as **ȝho, ȝeo** appear in the South-East Midlands and South-West Midlands respectively; **ȝho** is recorded in *The Ormulum*.

The evidence of the correspondences suggests strongly that the form derives from Norse and, if so, the process must have operated something as follows:

1. It seems that Norse-speakers had a series of 'rising' diphthongs (that is with stress on the second element), as opposed to the 'falling' diphthongs of Old English, which appear to have had stress on the first element; we might compare Old Norse **kjōsa** CHOOSE with its OE cognate **cēosan**. In such circumstances, and given the close relationships between English and Scandinavian in the North of England, a 'resyllabification' of OE **hēo** to *****hjō** would seem a fairly straightforward contact blend, whereby a Norse pronunciation was transferred to an English context – rather as English spoken in parts of Wales is spoken with a Welsh accent.

2. The phonetic sequence [hj-] is comparatively rare in PDE, and was also rare in OE. That it has a persistent tendency to change to the much more common [ʃ] is exemplified by, for example, present-day Scots **Shug** [ʃʌg] HUGH, a personal name which is common in Scotland; since SHE is a common item (whereas other '[-hj]-words' are less so) we can suppose a parallel development. The place-names **Shap** (< **hēap**), **Shetland** (< **Hjaltland**) and so on also exemplify this tendency. There is no need to posit any other influence to account for the development; it represents an accommodation of a marginal form to one much more commonly attested in the language, namely [ʃ]. The resulting form, **scho**, is of course that attested in the North and North Midlands.

3. The movement to [ʃ] probably took place via the palatal fricative [c]. The evidence of Orm's spelling-system may be relevant here; his **ȝho** seems to be an attempt to reproduce [coː]. His graph-cluster **ȝh**, only used in this word, contrasts with **ȝʰ**, which he uses for [ɣ].

7.1.3 From synthesis to analysis

At first sight, the reasons why the innovation in the determiner-system 'failed' whereas that in the pronoun-system 'succeeded' might seem obscure. However, in the light of other linguistic developments the differing outcomes become more explicable, since it seems that 'success' and 'failure' in linguistic change is to do with the way in which an innovation correlates with the larger contextual drift of the language. The larger context within which both developments should be studied is the overall movement from *synthesis* to *analysis* in grammatical relations, that is from a language which marked relationships between words by special endings to one which used a comparatively fixed word-order and separable morphemes such as prepositions.

Three related – and interacting – grammatical changes are relevant here:

(a) *the obscuration and loss of inflexional endings*
(b) *developments in the use of prepositions*
(c) *changes in element order.*

(a) The *obscuration of inflexions* is a characteristic of a number of Germanic languages, and seems to derive from the shift to fixed stress which took place during the proto-Germanic period, that is soon after the birth of Christ. This stress-shift seems to have become diffused gradually across the various dialects of Germanic; scholars have argued that it derived from contact with non-Indo-European peoples.

However it arose, this shift of stress away from inflexional endings made them vulnerable to 'phonetic attrition', that is loss of distinctiveness, or loss altogether. OE was already some way down this path; ME simply continued the trend. At later stages in the history of English, the loss of inflexions was probably encouraged through interaction with Norse, particularly in the Northern and North Midland varieties of English, where contact with Norse was closest (and where inflexional innovation seems to have been always most advanced).

(b) The rise in the use of *prepositions* during the ME period was flagged on p. 113 above, where there was also some discussion of their origins. In OE times, prepositions became more important as the period went on; they are certainly more salient a part of the grammar of (for instance) late OE verse such as *The Battle of Maldon*, which can be dated to after 991 AD, than of a poem like *Beowulf* which is generally accepted by most scholars to be much older than the date (*c.*1000) of the sole manuscript in which it survives. Prepositions were available to express grammatical relations hitherto catered for by inflexional endings, and their use naturally increased iteratively as the inflexional system decayed.

(c) OE *word-order* is certainly more flexible than that of PDE, but there were certain usages which had become prototypical in different clause-types: SP in main clauses, and PS in questions or when the clause was preceded by adverbials (such as OE þā THEN), and S … P in subordinate clauses. Deviation from these patterns was certainly easier than in PDE, but it had a stylistic function. With the loss of inflexions, the SP element-order, which expressed a clear relationship between two key elements in a sentence (subject, predicator) became more fixed and was extended to take over other functions – to such an extent that, even in questions, PDE uses a 'dummy' auxiliary verb in order to retain the SP relationship between subject and lexical verb, as in DO YOU COME HERE OFTEN?

In the light of the synthetic-analytic shift, it is fairly easy to understand why the innovation in the determiners 'failed' but the innovation in pronouns 'succeeded'. The loss of inflexions to act as 'tracking devices' meant that pronoun-differences became more important in discourse terms, and thus the pronominal system was modified – through the adoption of more distinctive variant forms – as a compensatory, therapeutic reaction. However, the case distinction between determiners was no longer necessary given the establishment of a more fixed element-order in ME, and thus that innovation failed.

It is worth pondering explicitly on the mechanisms of language change which have just been discussed. Linguistic change seems to relate to three mechanisms: (a) *variation*, (b) *contact* (between languages and between varieties of the same language) and (c) *systemic regulation*. These three mechanisms interact in complex and (except in the most general terms) practically unpredictable (though not inexplicable) ways to produce linguistic change. New variants are produced, and are imitated through contact, but they are constrained (generally unconsciously) by the changing systems of which they are a part.

7.2 Language and text

Another area where some linguistic knowledge of ME is invaluable is in literary study, for the analysis of *style*. Style was discussed in Chapter 5 above in particular (see pp. 81–4). It is a notion which attracts a good deal of sloppy use, but most scholars agree that it is essentially about choice amongst available options – in literature, between forms available in each level of language (sound-patterns, lexis, grammatical constructions). Another term, which a medieval scholar would have understood, is *rhetoric*; literary authors in ME were highly conscious of the rhetorical structures which they adopted, and they drew upon an extensive tradition of rhetorical handbooks which, though originally devised for Latin, were easily extended to the vernaculars.

An appreciation of style is important for ME studies for at least two reasons. First, literary scholars, in order to arrive at a proper appreciation of authors' achievements, need to know the baseline from which those authors departed; for no author works in a vacuum and all literary art (and perhaps arguably all art) draws upon traditions even when it subverts them. Secondly – and this will be the concern of the remainder of this chapter – there is a problem which characterises ME studies and which is not so obvious in present-day conditions. Modern authors, through (for example) proof-reading, have at least some control over the production of their books; though commonplace, the intervention of publishers is in general discreetly done. ME texts were, however, copied by scribes, who very frequently had no compunction about changing the texts before them to reflect their own concerns and circumstances, as well as making simple errors. The question therefore arises: given the activity of scribes, how far do surviving texts reflect authorial intentions?[3]

In the nineteenth century, it was believed that the application of certain rules of what came to be called *textual criticism* would solve the editorial problem objectively. The achievements of this editorial approach were formidable, not least in the textual criticism of the Bible. However, it is now generally accepted that the critical edition, once the primary goal of any editor who wanted to reconstruct authorial practice, raises many theoretical problems; when editors choose a particular reading, or make an emendation of the text before them, how do they judge that it is plausible? As J. N. Jacobs has noted, 'in the case of the most commonly studied medieval English texts it is generally not intelligibility but literary quality that is in question, and here judg[e]ment becomes subjective' (1998: 4). The question is one of style; and since style is a linguistic phenomenon, editors need an acute sense of the structure of the language concerned in order to make good judgements.

In what follows, three small editorial problems in a range of ME texts are addressed. In themselves bordering on the trivial, they have, it is held here, a wider significance for editorial methodology, and all, it may be argued, are insoluble without linguistic knowledge. The problems relate to sounds and spellings, lexis and grammar respectively.

7.2.1 Sounds and spellings

The first problem comes from the ME *Pearl*, a religious dream-vision poem composed in the North-West Midlands some time during the second half of the fourteenth century. The anonymous poet, who (most scholars agree) also composed three other poems in MS Cotton Nero A.x (*Patience, Cleanness* and *Sir Gawain and the Green Knight*) was a highly sophisticated artist, drawing upon a wide range of Biblical and patristic sources and engaging with a range of current theological issues.

Towards the end of the poem, the Dreamer is given a vision of the New Jerusalem, using language echoing the Book of Revelation. He tells us that the city of God was built from and adorned with precious stones;

and all things derived their light not from the sun and moon but from the presence of God. The following lines then appear:

Of sunne ne mone had þay no nede;
þe self God watȝ her lombe-lyȝt,
þe Lombe her lantyrne, wythouten drede;
þurȝ hym blysned þe borȝ al bryȝt.

(lines 1045–8)

['They had no need of sun or moon; God himself was their lamp-light, the Lamb their lantern, undeniably; through him the city shone brightly everywhere.']

These lines are taken from what is now one of the standard editions of the poem, by Gordon (1953). But one manuscript-reading, retained by Gordon, caused earlier editors problems: **lombe-lyȝt** LAMP-LIGHT (1046). Editors before Gordon had universally modified the form to **lompe lyȝt**, since **lombe** was felt to be an obvious scribal error, an example of a phenomenon known as 'eyeskip', where copyists pick up similar (but distinct) forms from elsewhere in their copy-texts ('exemplars') and use them instead of the forms of their exemplars.

However, Gordon kept the reading of the manuscript; and the reason for his decision derived from linguistic knowledge. There is good evidence that the voiced plosives [b, d, g] were unvoiced in final position in certain WM dialects, to [p, t, k], even when traditional spelling (**b, d, g**) was retained; this is indicated by rhymes such as **along** ALONG; **wlonc** NOBLE, by variant spellings for THING (**þyng, þynk**) and for LAMB (**lombe, lompe**). Thus there is no good reason for departing from the MS-reading; and, moreover, to do so makes less obvious the theological wordplay – characteristic of the poet's skill – on the identity of LAMB and LAMP.

7.2.2 Lexis

For our next example, we will move a little further back in time, to the EME period and *The Owl and the Nightingale*. This poem survives in two MSS, the Cotton MS (London, British Library, Cotton Caligula A.ix), which was copied by a scribe who attempted – albeit somewhat clumsily – to reproduce the forms of his exemplar, and the Jesus MS (Oxford, Jesus College 29), which was copied by an interventionist scribe who had no compunction in modifying his exemplar where he was puzzled by it, or where his own conception of how the poem should read differed.

The Owl and the Nightingale is a debate poem, in which the Owl and the Nightingale debate each other's qualities, notably the relative usefulness of each bird to humanity. The following lines (181–4) occur fairly early in the poem; after the initial argument, the Nightingale suggests that it would be better if they were to debate matters formally, and receive judgement from someone qualified to decide the matter.

Cotton MS:

þe3 we ne bo at one acorde,
we m[a]3e [MS: mu3e] bet mid fayre worde,
witute cheste, & bute fi3te,
plaidi mid fo3e [MS so3e] & mid ri3te ...

['Though we may not be at one accord, we can better with fair speech, without argument and without fighting, plead with fitness and with correctness ...']

Jesus MS:

þeyh we ne beon at one acorde,
We mawe bet myd fayre worde,
Wiþvte cheste, and bute vyhte,
Playde mid soþe & mid ryhte ...

['Though we may not be at one accord, we can better with fair speech, without argument and without fighting, plead with truth and with correctness ...']

The problem here is the form so3e in the Cotton MS (line 184). The form is apparently meaningless and unattested elsewhere in ME, and would seem to be an error requiring emendation. That the form was puzzling even to an EME reader is indicated by the reading offered by the Jesus scribe, where þ has been substituted for 3 – a practice which is attested elsewhere in ME, and occurs in one other place in the poem (3at for þat THAT, in line 506). This reading is plausible, if somewhat commonplace. Another emendation is suggested by Stanley (1972), who argues that so3e should be emended to fo3e; this emendation is simpler, since the ME letter f is often confused with an allograph of s, the so-called 'long-s' <<ʃ>>. The emendation is on balance a less radical one in terms of handwriting, and it is supported by linguistic knowledge of the history of the English lexicon; the form fo3e has a clear OE ancestry (cf. the OE phrase **mid gefo3e** FITTINGLY), and a cognate in modern German, cf. **mit Fug und Recht**, which is exactly parallel to **mid fo3e & mid ri3te**. A supporting argument in favour of **fo3e** rather than **soþe** would seem to be a Latin maxim of classical textual criticism: **difficilior lectio potior** I TAKE THE MORE DIFFICULT READING; scribes, it is generally held, attempted to simplify rare or old-fashioned forms which they encountered in favour of the more commonplace, and thus the 'difficult reading' was more likely to be the original one.[5] The choice of **foʒe** rather than **soþe** is therefore a matter of balancing one argument against another; but it is clear that without knowledge of the history of the lexicon the editor would be hard-put to make a proper decision.

7.2.3 Grammar

For our last editorial problem, we might turn to another late-fourteenth-century poet: Geoffrey Chaucer. Chaucer was, it is fairly clear, an innovative metrist. In his adoption of the iambic metrical unit (x /) he was, of course, simply following in the footsteps of, among others, the author of *Sir Orfeo*. Iambic rhythms became dominant in ME (and in subsequent verse) once inflexional attrition and the regular use of determiners and auxiliaries meant that the 'prototypical' noun and verb phrases consisted of an unstressed 'grammatical' word followed by a stressed word carrying lexical meaning.[4] However, in his later verse, such as *The Canterbury Tales* and *Troilus and Criseyde*, Chaucer innovated by introducing the iambic pentameter, based upon French and Italian models.

The advantage of the pentameter was that it aided *enjambement*; as Attridge (1982: 81–2) has pointed out, the prototypical clause-length in Indo-European languages contains four 'prominences' in terms of emphasis/stress. This means that ends of clauses in four-stress measures tend to coincide with ends of lines, producing a disjointed effect. The five-stress (pentameter) line allows for enjambements (run-ons) from line to line, and helps the poet avoid the choppy qualities of the tetrameter; it offers the poet an easy way of overcoming end-stopping by accommodating the four-stress sense-unit within a five-stress measure. The difference between the two metrical forms may be illustrated in two passages from Chaucer's poetry: 1. the earlier, four-stress measure with end-stopping and 2. the later, five-stress form where end-stopping is avoided. It will be observed that in 1, phrase- and clause-boundaries do not generally correspond with the ends of lines, whereas in 2 the correlation is much more common.

1. But at my gynnynge, trusteth wel,
   I wol make invocacion,
   With special devocion,
   Unto the god of slep anoon,
   That duelleth in a cave of stoon ...

   (*The House of Fame*, 66–70)

2. Glorye and honour, Virgil Mantoan,
   Be to thy name! and I shal, as I can,
   Folwe thy lanterne, as thow gost byforn,
   How Eneas to Dido was forsworn.

In thyn Eneyde and Naso wol I take
The tenor, and the grete effectes make.

(*Legend of Good Women*, 924–9)

However, although Chaucer's iambic pentameter line prototypically contained ten syllables, with alternating unstressed and stressed syllables, it is important to realise that not every line had to follow this stress-pattern; if it had done, the result would be monotonous (cf. what might be termed the 'minimalist' patterns of Longfellow's *Hiawatha*). The function of metre in verse has traditionally been taken as relating to the interplay of metrical norm and rhythmical deviation, intended to make the modulation between norm and deviation salient in terms of meaning – something which poets often emphasise by accompanying their metrical choices with other stylistic effects.

This metrical discussion has relevance for a grammatical problem faced by editors of Chaucer: the use of final -e in adjectives. The scribe of the Ellesmere MS of *The Canterbury Tales* had difficulties with -e in adjectives, apparently because it was not a living part of his own language (as it was with Chaucer's). However, Chaucer's adjectival usage can be reconstructed by reference to the metre, which shows fairly conclusively that he used -e with reference to the weak/strong adjective-system (see p. 95 above). Interestingly, the Hengwrt MS, which was almost certainly copied by the same scribe as Ellesmere, reproduces the presumed Chaucerian of adjectival -e pretty accurately, thus indicating that the reproduction of -e was probably related to its reproduction in the scribe's exemplars (and, incidentally, supporting the usefulness of the Hengwrt MS as a witness for the text of *The Canterbury Tales*).

The standard critical edition of Chaucer's works remains *The Riverside Chaucer* (1987). The Riverside editors based their text of *The Canterbury Tales* on the Ellesmere MS, cross-referring to the Hengwrt MS but carrying out certain emendations on the grounds of metre. One such emendation appears in *The Reeve's Tale*, line 4175, in the context of the passage below; the reading in the Hengwrt MS is also supplied.

Ye, they sal have the flour of il endyng.
This lange [Hengwrt: lang] nyght ther tydes me na reste;
But yet, na fors, al sal be for the beste.

(lines 4174–6)

['Yes, they must have the best of a bad end. No rest is permitted me for (all) this long night. But still, no matter, everything must be for the best.']

The effect of the Riverside emendation of line 4175 is to produce a line with a regular iambic stress-pattern, and the insertion of a weak -e ending on **lange** regularises the adjectives in the *Tale* in line with

Chaucer's usage elsewhere. In doing so, the Riverside edition is simply following the decisions taken by earlier editors, notably W. W. Skeat (1912). But the evidence of the MSS tells against this editorial decision, and this is supported if we consider further some facts about the grammars of ME. In the Hengwrt MS, -e is omitted in weak adjectives only in *The Reeve's Tale* – and only there in the speech of the young Northern students whom Chaucer is mocking. Such a usage is a genuine feature of Northern ME in Chaucer's time, for adjectival -e disappeared in Northern dialects long before it disappeared in the South. The Skeat/ Riverside emendation, **lange**, mixes a Northern spelling of the stem (**lang-**) with a Southern inflexion (-e); the result is an unhistorical form. One of the most salient features of Northern pronunciation for Southerners must have been its prosodic structure; it seems likely, therefore, that phrases such as **This lang nyght**, deviating from the iambic pattern which Chaucer prototypically adopted, are stylistically marked. Thus knowledge of the differences between Northern and Southern dialects makes it possible for us to appreciate another aspect of Chaucer's 'good ear' (see further Everett 1955a, 1955b).

Exercises

Questions for review

1. (On language change) 'There is no more reason for languages to change than there is for automobiles to add fins one year and remove them the next, for jackets to have three buttons one year and two the next' (P. M. Postal, *Aspects of Phonological Theory* 1968: 283). Discuss, drawing your examples from the ME evidence.

2. (On language and text) 'The traditional task of the editor, that of reconstructing as far as possible the original version of the text … remains a legitimate objective' (J. N. Jacobs, in McCarren and Moffat 1998: 12). Discuss, with special reference to the textual history of *one* ME poem.

Recommendations for reading

The bibliography for this chapter is necessarily somewhat eclectic, and clearly very partial, since the purpose of the chapter is to begin discussion and suggest ways forward rather than present conclusive results; in other words, it is designed to indicate the sorts of problem that historical linguists and philologists investigate rather than present 'party lines'.

The subject of linguistic change is notoriously controversial. Beginners might find Aitchison (1991) useful, since it assumes no very great level of theoretical sophistication. Other important and/or useful books, at varying levels of sophistication, are Keller (1994), Lass (1980) and Samuels (1972). Smith (1996) takes a text-focused 'philological' approach which correlates quite closely with that taken in the present book; an important alternative line of argument, with a more 'linguistic' skew, is taken in McMahon (1994). Questions of style and text are similarly problematic. On the style of ME texts, the best starting-point remains Burnley (1983), which is the most thoroughgoing and convincing survey of Chaucer's language, from a literary-stylistic viewpoint, yet produced. Burnley gives full references to both medieval and present-day thinking on rhetorical and stylistic matters. On metrical theory, Burnley's study might be supplemented by Attridge (1982), which is a sensitive linking of linguistic and literary concerns. On textual criticism, the best introduction is Reynolds and Wilson (1974), chapter 6; although this book draws its examples from Greek and Latin literature, it has a much wider significance for the study of scribal culture. On the editing of ME texts, the best introduction is McCarren and Moffat (1998), which contains a series of important essays on all aspects of the editing process; for the general theory of textual criticism, particularly useful (and a sound corrective to much current thinking) are the papers by J. N. Jacobs and J. Fellows. All scholars interested in textual issues should also read two classic essays: A. E. Housman's introduction to his edition of Juvenal's *Satires* (1905), and E. T. Donaldson's essay 'The Psychology of Editors of Middle English Texts' (in Donaldson 1970: 102–18).

Arguably the most complex issues in the critical editing of ME texts in recent years have been raised with the appearance of the great Athlone edition of William Langland's versions of *Piers Plowman*, under the general editorship of G. Kane with assistance from E. T. Donaldson and G. H. Russell. A useful starting-point for discussion of this edition and the theoretical questions it raises is L. Patterson's essay 'The Logic of Textual Criticism and the Way of Genius: The Kane-Donaldson *Piers Plowman* in Historical Perspective' (Patterson 1987: 77–113).

Notes

1. Obviously there are other differences between the OE and PDE systems, for example the use of **its**, which seems to have arisen analogically in EModE to replace the older (and potentially confusing) **his**.

2. It is interesting in this context that **heom** THEM is a comparatively late

form, in West Saxon at any rate, only found in texts dating from after *c.* 1000, and similarly disambiguating **heom** THEM from **him** HIM.

3. It is usual to state that there are two kinds of scholarly editions of ME texts: the critical edition, where the editor attempts to reconstruct the authorial original, and the diplomatic edition, where the editor presents a transcription of one MS accompanied by an appropriate commentary elucidating difficulties raised by the text in question. A good example of a critical edition is G. Kane's and E. T. Donaldson's edition of the B-text of *Piers Plowman* (1975); a good example of a diplomatic edition is E. J. Dobson's edition of the Cleopatra MS of *Ancrene Riwle* (1972). See further the Recommendations for reading for this chapter.

4. The dominant trochaic metre of OE verse (/ x) derives from the distinct nature of OE grammar, where stressed stem is followed by unstressed inflexional ending. See Millward 1989: 134 for a very precise and concise statement of this issue.

5. For a clear discussion of the doctrine of **difficilio lectio potior**, see Reynolds and Wilson (1974: 199).

Appendix:
Middle English texts

Text 1. The *Peterborough Chronicle*

Introduction

The *Peterborough Chronicle* is a descendant of the Anglo-Saxon Chronicle which was instituted during the reign of King Alfred. This chronicle was copied at a number of different monasteries during the Anglo-Saxon period although few survived the Norman Conquest of 1066. Following the conquest the few surviving chronicles began to be copied in Latin, and the *Peterborough Chronicle* is the only survivor to continue to be copied in English. The *Peterborough Chronicle* continued into the twelfth century, longer than any other chronicle. The final entry is dated 1154, a date which marks the end of the reign of King Stephen (1135–54) and the accession of King Henry II (1154–89). The manuscript of the chronicle was destroyed by a fire in the monastery at Peterborough in 1116, but this was replaced by the copying of a Southern version. The annals for 1122 to 1154 are divided into two 'continuations'. The First Continuation covers the entries from 1121 to 1132 and was compiled by a single monk working on six separate occasions. The Final Continuation, from which the following extract is taken, was written in a single hand in a continuous retrospective account in 1155.

The standard edition of the *Peterborough Chronicle* is Clark (1970).

Text

MCXXXVII Ðis gære *for* þe king Stephne ofer sæ to Normandi, and ther wes *underfangen* forþi ðat hi *uuenden* ðat he sculde ben *alsuic* also the *eom* wes, and for he hadde *get* his tresor; ac he *todeld* it and scatered sotlice. *Micel* hadde Henri king gadered gold and syluer, and na god ne dide me for his saule tharof. (5)

þa þe king Stephne to Englalande com, þa *macod* he his gadering æt

Oxeneford; and þar he nam þe biscop Roger of Serebyri, and Alexander biscop of Lincol, and te canceler Roger-hise neues-and dide ælle in prisun til hi iafen up here castles. þa the *suikes undergæton* ðat he milde man was, and softe and god, and na iustise ne dide, (10) þa diden hi alle *wunder*. Hi hadden him *manred* maked and athes suoren, ac hi nan treuthe ne heolden. Alle he wæron forsworen and here treothes forloren. For æuric *rice* man his castles makede and agænes him heolden, and fylden þe land ful of castles. Hi *suencten suyðe* þe uurecce men of þe land mid castel-weorces. (15) þa þe castles uuaren maked, þa fylden hi mid deoules and yuele men. þa namen hi þa men þe hi wenden ðat ani god hefden-bathe be nihtes and be dæies, carlmen and wimmen-and diden heom in prisun, and *pined* heom efter gold and syluer untellendlice *pining*: for ne uuæren næure nan martyrs swa *pined* alse hi wæron. (20) Me henged up bi the fet and smoked heom mid *ful* smoke. Me henged bi the þumbes other bi the hefed, and hengen *bryniges* on her fet.

Notes

line 1. þe
The use of the indeclinable form of the determiner is consistent throughout this text.

line 1. þe king Stephne
This construction seems to be modelled on French syntax, cf. **le roi Charles**. Compare this structure with **Henri king** (line 4) which preserves the OE construction, for example **Alfred cyning**.

line 1. ofer
This word preserves the OE practice of using <f> to represent the voiced labio-dental fricative, although there are examples of <u> in these positions, for example **syluer**.

line 2. sculde
This text also preserves the OE use of <sc> to represent /ʃ/; see also **biscop** (line 7).

line 3. tresor
This text has a large number of French loanwords, many of which belong to the domains of law and government, for example **canceler** (line 8), **prisun** (line 9), **castles** (line 9), **iustise** PUNISHMENT (line 10). Many of these are first recorded in the *Peterborough Chronicle*.

line 8. **te**
This is a regular form of the determiner apparently showing the assimilation of an initial dental fricative to a preceding dental plosive.

line 8. **dide ælle in prisun**
This phrase appears to be modelled upon the French construction **faire en prison**. We might compare also **na iustise ne dide** (line 9) which follows the French phrase **faire justice**.

line 9. **hi, here, heom**
Despite its composition in an area of Norse settlement the text employs a native OE third person plural pronominal system, rather than using the forms adopted from ON found in later texts.

line 9. **iafen up**
Verbs with prepositions, known as 'phrasal verbs', seem to be the result of interaction with ON.

line 9. **he milde man was, and softe and god**
This construction derives from a characteristic feature of OE syntax known as the *splitting of heavy groups*.

line 11. **wunder**
Most nouns in this text carry the <-es> inflexion as a plural marker, for example **neues, castles, suikes**. However this noun is derived from the OE neuter declension and is therefore endless in the plural.

line 17. **carlmen**
This form is derived from ON **karl** and is cognate with OE **ceorl**. There are a number of Norse words in this text, although these belong to a different register to the French words identified above, for example **bathe, syluer, bryniges**.

Glossary

alsuic Adj JUST SUCH (OE **al swilc**)
bryniges N COAT OF MAIL (ON **brynja**)
eom N UNCLE (OE **ēam**)
for V 3 sg pret TO TRAVEL (OE **faran**)
ful Adj FOUL (OE **fūl**)
get Adv STILL (OE **gīet**)
macod V 3 sg pret TO MAKE, HOLD (OE **macian**)

manred N HOMAGE (OE manrǣden)
Micel Adj MUCH (OE micel)
pined V 3 pl pret TO TORTURE (OE pīnian)
pinung N TORTURE (OE pīnung)
rice Adj POWERFUL (OE rīce)
suencten V 3 pl pret TO OPPRESS (OE swencan)
suikes N TRAITORS (OE swica)
suyðe Adv GREATLY (OE swīþe)
todeld V 3 sg pret TO DISPERSE, DIVIDE (OE tōdǣlan)
underfangen V past participle TO RECEIVE (OE underfōn)
undergæton V 3 pl pret TO REALISE (OE undergietan)
uuenden V 3 pl pres TO THINK (OE wēnan)
wunder N ATROCITIES (OE wundor)

Text 2. The Owl and the Nightingale

Introduction

The Owl and the Nightingale is a debate poem surviving in two contemporary late thirteenth-century manuscripts. Its genre derives from Latin rhetorical traditions and its metrical form, octosyllabic couplets, belongs among the French narrative poems. The reference to a dead King Henry is usually taken to refer to Henry II and this has led scholars to date the poem's composition to the period 1189–1216. However this traditional dating has recently been questioned and a date after the death of Henry III in 1272 has been proposed. The unanimous praise for a Master Nicholas of Guildford is interpreted by some as a reference to the poem's author, although others have seen this as a joke at Nicholas' expense by a close friend.

Two editions of *The Owl and the Nightingale* might be recommended: Stanley's critical edition of 1972, and Atkins' parallel-text edition of 1922.

Text

Ich was in one sumere *dale*
in one suþe *diзele hale*
iherde ich holde grete *tale*
an *hule* and one niзtingale
þat *plait* was stif & starc & strong   5
sum wile softe & lud among
an aiþer aзen oþer *sval*

    & let þat *vuele mod* ut al
    & eiþer seide of oþeres *custe*
    þat alre worste þat hi *wuste*   10
    & *hure & hure* of oþeres songe
    hi holde plaiding *suþe* stronge
    þe niʒtingale bigon þe speche
    in one *hurne* of one *breche*
    & sat up one vaire *boʒe*   15
    þar were abute blosme inoʒe
    in ore uaste þicke hegge
    imeind mid *spire* & grene *segge*
    Ho was þe gladur uor þe *rise*
    & song a *uele* cunne wise   20
    Bet þuʒte þe *dreim* þat he were
    of harpe & pipe þan he nere
    bet þuʒte þat he were *ishote*
    of harpe & pipe þan of þrote
    þo stod on old stoc þarbiside   25
    þar þo vle song hire *tide*
    & was mid iui al bigrowe
    hit was þare hule *earding-stowe.*

Notes

line 1. **one**
This is an inflected form of the indefinite article (derived from OE **ān**
ONE) used after prepositions.

line 8. **vuele**
This spelling shows the retention of the rounded vowel as a reflex of OE
y which is a characteristic of Western dialects. However the rhyming
evidence shows OE **y** reflected in <e>: a typically South-Eastern
feature. It is therefore likely that the author's dialect was that of the
South-East, while the Western spellings belong to the scribe.

line 10. **þat alre worste**
Alre is a genitive plural form (cf. OE **ealra**) and the construction therefore means THE WORST OF ALL.

line 10. **hi**
This form is used both for the feminine third singular pronoun and the
third plural pronoun (all genders); see line 12.

line 17. **ore**
This is the dative singular feminine form of the indefinite article, which agrees with the feminine noun **hegge**.

line 17. **uaste**
The presumed voiced reflex of the initial fricative, spelled <u, v>, is a feature of the scribe's Southern dialect which is commonly attested in this text; see also **vaire** (line 15), **uele** (line 20).

line 19. **Ho**
This is the feminine third person singular pronoun SHE (OE **hēo**) used as both birds are feminine. The reflection of OE /eo/ in <o> is common in this text and found in words such as **flo** (OE **flēogan**, PDE FLEE) and **bo** (OE **bēon**, PDE BE).

line 26. **þo**
In this text the determiner (> definite article) is frequently inflected according to case and number as in OE. The form **þo** is a reflection of OE **sēo**, the feminine singular nominative form of the definite article, agreeing with **vle** OWL.

line 28. **þare**
This is the genitive singular form of the definite article, identical in form to that of the dative singular. See the discussion of the determiners in Chapter 7 above.

Glossary

bet Adv RATHER (OE **bet**)
boȝe N BOUGH, BRANCH (OE **bog**)
breche N CLEARING (OE **bræc**)
custe N CHARACTER (OE **cyste**)
dale N VALLEY (OE **dæl**)
diȝele Adj HIDDEN, SECLUDED (OE **diegol**)
dreim N SOUND (OE **drēam**)
earding-stowe N DWELLING-PLACE (OE **eardung-stōw**)
hale N NOOK, CORNER (OE **halh**)
hule N OWL (OE **ūle**)
hure & hure Adv ESPECIALLY (OE **hūru**)
hurne N CORNER (OE **hyrne**)
ishote V past participle TO SEND OUT (OE **scēotan**)
mod N FEELING, SPIRIT (OE **mōd**)

plait N DEBATE (OE **plaid**)
rise N BRANCH, TWIG (OE **hris**)
segge N SEDGE (OE **secg**)
spire N REEDS (OE **spir**)
suþe Adv GREATLY, VERY (OE **swiþe**)
sval V 3 sg pret TO SWELL UP (OE **swellan**)
tale N DEBATE (OE **talu**)
tide N CANONICAL HOURS (OE **tid**)
uele Adj MANY (OE **fela**)
vuele Adj EVIL, MALICIOUS (OE **yfel**)
wuste V 3 sg pret TO KNOW (OE **witan**)

Text 3. Ancrene Wisse

Introduction

Ancrene Wisse is a work of spiritual guidance written for three noble sisters who had become anchoresses. The text survives in Corpus Christi College, Cambridge 402: a manuscript copied in the West Midlands dialect in the early thirteenth century, close to the place and date of the composition of the text. Revised versions of the text were also produced for larger communities of recluses, known to modern scholars as *Ancrene Riwle*, and these were also translated into Latin and French. *Ancrene Wisse* shares a number of lexical, stylistic and thematic features with other early ME didactic prose works written for women, such as *Hali Meiðhad*, *Sawles Warde* and the lives of female saints.

All texts of *Ancrene Wisse/Ancrene Riwle* have been edited diplomatically for EETS. The best edition of part of the text is by G. T. Shepherd (1991).

Text

Aȝein alle temptatiuns, ant nomeliche aȝein fleschliche, *saluen* beoð ant *bote* under Godes grace-halie meditatiuns, inwarde ant *meadlese* ant angoisuse *bonen*, hardi bileaue, redunge, veasten, *wecchen*, ant *licomliche swinkes*, oþres *froure* forte speoke toward i þe ilke *stunde* þet hire stont stronge. (5) *Eadmodnesse*, freolec of heorte, ant alle gode þeawes beoð armes i þis feht; ant *anrednesse* of luue ouer alle þe oþre. Þe his wepnen warpeð awei, him luste beon iwundet.

Hali meditatiuns beoð *bicluppet* in a uers þet wes ȝare itaht ow, mine leoue sustren:

(10) Mors tua, mors Cristi, nota culpe, gaudia celi, Iudicii terror, figantur mente fideli-

þet is:

þench ofte wið sar of þine sunnen;
þench of helle wa, of heoueriches *wunnen*;
þench of þin ahne deað, of Godes deað o rode; (15)
þe grimme dom of Domesdei munneð ofte ofte i mode;
þench hu fals is þe worlt, hwucche beoð hire meden;
þench hwet tu ahest Godd for his goddeden.

Euchan of þeose word walde a long hwile forte beo wel iopenet; ah ʒef Ich *hihi* forðward, *demeori* ʒe þe lengre. A word Ich segge. (20) Efter ower sunnen, hwen se ʒe þencheð of helle wa ant of heoueriches wunnen, understondeð þet Godd walde o sum wise schawin ham to men i þis world bi worltliche pinen ant worltliche wunnen, ant schaweð ham forð as schadewe; for na lickre ne beoð ha to þe wunne of heouene ne to þe wa of helle þen is schadewe to þet þing þet hit is of schadewe. (25) ʒe beoð ouer þis worldes sea upo þe brugge of heouene: lokið þet ʒe ne beon nawt þe hors *eschif* iliche, þe *schuncheð* for a schadewe ant falleð adun i þe weater of þe hehe brugge. To childene ha beoð þe fleoð a peinture þe þuncheð ham grislich ant *grureful* to bihalden: wa ant wunne i þis world - al nis bute peintunge, al nis but schadewe. (30)

Notes

line 1. **nomeliche**
This form shows a rounded vowel before a nasal consonant which is a characteristic feature of the West Midlands dialect, cf. **mon, lond** and so on.

line 3. **veasten**
This form shows the voicing of initial fricatives which was another Western characteristic, although it is also found in the South. However it is not a consistent feature of *Ancrene Wisse* (AW) which has a number of voiceless initial fricatives, such as **forte, forðward** and so on.

line 4. **swinkes**
This form shows that the strong plural **-es** has been extended to the OE neuter declension, although this process is not as widespread as in many other ME texts of this date. See **wepnen** in line 7 for an example of a neuter noun with a weak **-en** plural.

line 5. **heorte**
The OE <eo> digraph is consistently written in AW although the diphthong was no longer reflected in the spoken language. The use of the
<eo> digraph to represent [ø] in OF loanwords, for example **demeori**
(line 20), suggests that <eo> represents long and short [ø] in native
words.

line 7. **wepnen**
This noun has the weak plural ending -en although it was a strong neuter
noun in OE (**wæpen**). This ending has also been extended to nouns
belonging to the strong feminine declension in OE, such as **sunnen** (line
13). Major exceptions are strong feminine nouns ending in -ung which
take the strong plural in -es, for example **fondunges**.

line 8. **Hali**
This spelling shows that the rounding of OE ā found in Southern
dialects of ME had probably not occurred in this language. However
there is evidence from other texts that this change had occurred in the
West Midlands and this is therefore evidence of the archaic nature of
AW language. Other examples of the unrounded vowel are as follows:
sar (line 13), **wa** (line 14).

line 8. **wes**
This form shows the characteristic West Mercian sound change known
as 'second fronting', found also in a Mercian OE text, the *Vespasian Psalter
Gloss* [VP].

lines 10–11. **Mors tua, mors Cristi, nota culpe, gaudia celi, Iudicii
terror, figantur mente fideli-**
'Your death, the death of Christ, the stain of sin, the joys of heaven, the
terror of judgement, are fixed in the minds of the faithful.'

line 13. **sunnen**
This spelling shows the characteristic West Midlands reflex of OE **y**,
written <u> – presumably reflecting a rounded sound. Other examples
are **wunnen** (line 14), **grureful** (line 29).

line 18. **hwet**
Another conservative feature of the language of AW is the preservation
of OE <hw-> which is commonly reflected as <wh->, <w-> in other
ME dialects.

line 23. ham
The third person plural pronouns have the initial <h-> form derived from OE: **ha, ham, hare**. However the consistent appearance of the <a> in these forms is more difficult to explain. The similarity of the form **hare** with **heara** in the OE *Vespasian Psalter Gloss* [VP] suggests a possible explanation. The VP form **heara** is derived analogically from the demonstrative form **ðeara** and it is possible that analogy with the determiner paradigm explains the AW forms. Therefore **ha** may derive by analogy with **þa, har** from **þara** and **ham** from **þam**. This explanation is supported by the use of **ha** for both SHE and THEY in AW: a similar function was also performed by **þa**.

line 26. lokið
This form shows the preservation of the <i> in the endings of OE weak class 2 verbs.

line 29. bihalden
This form shows lack of diphthonisation ('breaking') of æ before <-ld> characteristic of Anglian dialects of OE. The spelling <a> implies that this vowel was retracted rather than broken.

Glossary

anrednesse N STEADFASTNESS, CONSTANCY (OE ānrǣdnes)
bicluppet V past participle TO EMBRACE, CONTAIN (OE beclyppan)
bonen N PRAYER, REQUEST (ON bón)
bote N RELIEF, CURE (OE bōt)
demeori V Imperative TO STAY, DELAY (OF demurer)
eadmodnesse N HUMILITY (OE ēadmōdnes)
eschif Adj EASILY FRIGHTENED, SHY (OF eschif)
froure N COMFORT, HELP (OE frōfor)
ӡare Adv LONG AGO (OE gēara)
grureful Adj TERRIBLE (OE gryre)
hihi V 1 sg pres TO HASTEN, HURRY (OE hīgian)
licomliche Adv BODILY, PHYSICAL (OE līchamlic)
meadlese Adj UNLIMITED, CONTINUAL (OE mǣþlēas)
saluen N REMEDY, OINTMENT (OE sealf)
schuncheð V 3 sg pres TO SHY, START ASIDE (?OE *scyncan)
swinkes N LABOUR, TOIL (OE swinc)
stunde N TIME, WHILE (OE stund)
þeawes N VIRTUE (OE þēaw)

wecchen V TO KEEP VIGIL (OE **wæccan**)
wunnen N JOY, PLEASURE (OE **wynn**)

Text 4. *Piers Plowman*: two parallel texts

Introduction

Piers Plowman is an alliterative poem composed during the latter half of the fourteenth century by William Langland. Although he seems to have spent some time in London, Langland's origins were in the West Midlands. There are references in the poem to the Malvern Hills and a note on the earliest surviving manuscript of the poem links the poet with an Oxfordshire family. Scholars distinguish three major versions of the poem, known as A, B and C (the identification of a fourth – the so-called Z-text – remains controversial). The A-text, the shortest of the three versions, was completed around 1370, while the B-text presents a revision and continuation of A completed at the end of the 1370s. The C-text is a further revision of the B-text which was left incomplete at Langland's death in about 1385.

There are over fifty surviving manuscripts of the three versions of the poem, copied in a variety of ME dialects. The following extracts are taken from two manuscripts of the B-text of the poem, copied in different parts of the country. The first of these, taken from Trinity College, Cambridge B 15.17 [Trinity], was copied in a variety of London English similar to that of the Hengwrt and Ellesmere manuscripts of Chaucer's *The Canterbury Tales*. The scribe of the Trinity manuscript also shares a number of palaeographical features with the scribe of the Hengwrt and Ellesmere manuscripts. The second extract is drawn from Cambridge University Ll. 4.14 [Ll], a manuscript copied using the dialect of Ely.

The most useful student edition of *Piers Plowman* is that by A. V. C. Schmidt (1978). The accompanying text has been presented in a way which reflects ME punctuation, that is with the mid-line point to indicate a caesura.

A note on alliterative metre

There is no formal handbook of alliterative poetry surviving from the ME period. One key principle, however, seems to be accepted by modern scholars: it seems almost certain that, as in other kinds of poetry, a framework of modulation between norm and deviation, linked to literary salience, lies at the heart of alliterative verse-practice. This view has been argued very effectively by (among others) G. Kane, who points out (1981: 46) that a poet's success derives from the way in which

> his versification exists as part of the meaning of his poetic statements, not merely because the verse is effective in making that meaning more emphatic, clearer, more evidently interrelated, but also because it will engage the reader's auditory interest and confer the combination of physical and intellectual pleasure experienced when pattern and meaning are simultaneously apprehended.

Kane and Donaldson (1974) establish that the normative alliterative pattern of Langland's verse is of what is generally termed the '*aa/ax*' variety, but that there are numerous deviant patterns (such as *aa/aa*, *aaa/ax*, *aa/bb* and so on), including lines with so-called 'supplementary' alliteration. Thus a line such as

In habite as a hermite vnholy of workes

(Langland, *Piers Plowman* B Prol. 3), which follows the normative pattern *aa/ax*, may be compared with deviant lines such as the opening of the poem:

In a somer seson whan soft was the sonne

(Langland, *Piers Plowman* B Prol. 1) (*aa/aa*). In the latter line, the extra alliteration may be interpreted as a prominent metrical signal, appropriate at the beginning of a poem and underlined by the quasi-formulaic conventionality of the lexis adopted.

Texts

Trinity College, Cambridge B 15.17 (London)

Passus Tercius de Visione vt supra

Now is Mede þe mayde . and namo of hem alle
Wiþ *bedeles* and with *baillies* . brouȝt bifore þe kyng
The kyng called a clerk . *kan* i noȝt his name
To take mede þe maide . and maken hire at ese
I shal assayen hire my-self . and sooþliche appose   5
What man of þis *moolde* . þat hire were leuest
And if she werche bi *wit* . and my wil folwe
I wol forgyuen hire þis gilt . so me god helpe
Curteisly þe clerk þanne . as þe kyng hiȝte
Took mede bi þe *myddel* . and broȝte hire into chambre   10
And þer was murþe & mynstralcie . mede to plese

They þat wonyeþ in Westmynstre . worshipeþ hire alle
Gentilliche wiþ ioye . þe iustices somme
Busked hem to þe bour . þer þe *burde* dwellede
To conforten hire kyndely . by clergies leue   15
And seiden . mourne noȝt mede . ne make þow no sorwe
For we wol *wisse* þe kyng . and þi wey shape
To be wedded at þi wille . and wher þee leef likeþ
For al consciences *cast* . or craft as I *trowe*
Mildely mede þanne . *merciede* hem alle   20
Of hire grete goodnesse . and gaf hem echone
Coupes of *clene* gold . and coppes of siluer
Rynges wiþ rubies . and richesses manye
The leeste man of hire *meynee* . a moton of golde
Thanne *lauȝte* þei leue . þise lordes at mede   25
Wiþ þat comen clerkes . to conforten hire þe same
And beden hire be bliþe . for we beþ þyne owene
For to werche þi wille . þe while þow myȝt laste
Hendiliche heo þanne . *bihiȝte* hem þe same
To louen hem *lelly* . and lordes to make   30
And in þe consistorie at þe court . do callen hire names
Shal no lewednesse *lette* . þe *leode* þat I louye
That he ne worþ first auaunced . for I am *biknowen*
Ther konnynge clerkes . shul *clokke* bihynde

CUL Ll 4.14 (Ely)

Passus Tercius de Visione

Now is Mede the maide . and na ma of hem alle
With bedelles and with baillifs . brought bifore the kyng
The kyng called a clerc . kan I naught his name
To take mede the maide . and make hir at ese
I schal assaie hir myself . and sotheliche appose   5
What man of molde . that hir were leuest
And if sho worche by my wit . and my wille folwe
I wole for-gyue hir this gilte . so me god help
Curteisliche the Clerc . as the kyng hight
Toke Mede by the midel . and brought hir into chambre   10
And thare was mirthe and mynstralcye . mede to plese
Thay that wonyeth in Westmynstre worschiped hir alle
Gentiliche with ioie . the iustices somme
Busked hem to the boure . ther the birde dwelled
To conforte hir kyndly . by clergies leue   15

And saiden morne nouhte mede . ne make thow no sorwe
For we wisse the kyng and thy way schape
To be wedded at thy wille . and wher the leue liketh
For al conscience caste or craft as I trowe
Mildeliche mede thanne . mercied hem alle   20
Of thayr grete goodnesse. and gaf hem echone
Coupes of clene gold . and coppis of siluer
Rynges with rubies . and riches manye
The leste man of hir meynge . a moton of golde
Thanne laughte they leue . thise lordes at mede   25
With yat comen clerkes to conforte hir the same
And biden hir be blithe . for we beth thyn owene
For to wirche thy wille . the while thow myght laste
Hendeliche sho thanne . bihyghte hem the same
To loue hem lealy . and lordes to make.   30
And in the consistorie atte courte . do calle youre names
Schal no lewednesse . lette the leode that I louye
That he ne worth first auanced . for I am biknowen
Ther konnyng clerkes . schul clokke bihynde

Notes

line 1. namo
Trinity shows the rounded reflex of OE ā, spelled <o>, while the Ll
scribe has the unrounded vowel, spelled <a>, common to Northern
dialects during this period.

line 2. brouȝt
The Trinity scribe uses the letter <ȝ> to represent /x/: a letter which is
not found in the Hengwrt and Ellesmere manuscripts. The Ll scribe uses
both <gh> and <h> (see nouhte, line 16) for this sound.

line 5. asseyen
The Trinity manuscript has a form of the infinitive with an -(e)n
inflexion, while the final -n is not found in the Ll manuscript. This
inflexion is a feature of more conservative Midlands dialects and is also
a necessary part of the metre of this poem, preventing elision between a
vowel and a following vowel or aspirate.

line 5. sooþliche
The Trinity scribe frequently adopts the practice of doubling vowels as
a marker of length, while the Ll manuscript marks length by adding a

final -e as a diacritic thus: VCe, for example **sotheliche**. Compare also **Took** with **Toke** in line 10.

line 7. she

The Trinity scribe has the regular London form for the feminine pronoun while the Ll scribe has the Northern form of the pronoun **sho**. However at line 29 the form **heo** is found in Trinity, a conservative form which is found only in the West Midlands during this period. Given that William Langland seems to have been a native of the West Midlands it is likely that this is the authorial form, and this is confirmed by the fact that a form of the pronoun with initial h- is required by the alliteration. It is interesting to notice that the Ll scribe uses the **sho** form in this line, thereby spoiling the alliterative patterning.

line 11. murþe

The Trinity form with <u> shows the preservation of a rounded reflex of OE **y**, a feature common to West Midlands dialects and therefore probably an archetypal form. The Ll scribe has a form with medial <i>, probably flagging a pronunciation with an unrounded vowel which was, it seems, common in the East Midlands. Compare also **burde** and **birde** in line 14.

line 21. hire

The Trinity manuscript has the native form of the pronoun with initial <h->, while the Ll manuscript has a form derived from ON: **thayr**.

line 26. þat

The Trinity scribe uses a form of the letter thorn that is graphically distinct from the letter <y>. However the Ll scribe uses the letter <y> to represent /ð, θ/ and /j/: a characteristic of Northern dialects of ME.

Glossary

baillies N BAILIFFS (OF **baili**)
bedeles N BEADLES (OE **bydel**)
bihiȝte V 3 sg pret TO PROMISE (OE **behātan**)
biknowen V infin TO ACKNOWLEDGE (OE **becnāwan**)
burde N LADY (OE **byrdu**)
busked V 3 pl pret TO HASTEN TO, REPAIR TO (ON **búask**)
cast N INTENTION, PURPOSE (ON **kast**)
clene Adj PURE (OE **clǣne**)
clokke V infin TO LIMP (OF **clochier**)

coupes N BOWLS (OE **cuppe**)
hendiliche Adv GRACIOUSLY (OE **hende**)
hiȝte V 3 sg pret TO COMMAND (OE **hātan**)
kan V 1 sg pres TO KNOW (OE **cunnan**)
lauȝte V 3 pl pret TO TAKE (OE **læccan**)
lelly Adv LOYALLY (OF **leal**)
leode N MAN, PERSON (OE **lēod**)
lette V infin TO HINDER, IMPEDE (OE **lettan**)
moolde N WORLD, EARTH (OE **molde**)
merciede V 3 sg pret TO THANK (OF **mercier**)
meynee N FOLLOWERS, RETINUE (OF **meine**)
myddel N WAIST (OE **middel**)
trowe V 1 sg pres TO BELIEVE (OE **trēowan**)
wisse V infin TO GUIDE (OE **wīsian**)
wit N WISDOM, INTELLIGENCE (OE **witt**)

Text 5. *Cursor Mundi*: two parallel texts

Introduction

The *Cursor Mundi* covers the spiritual history of mankind from the
Creation to the Day of Judgement in over 30,000 lines, and survives in
nine manuscripts. The following texts are taken from two manuscripts
copied by scribes using different ME dialects. The first extract is from
British Library Cotton Vespasian A.iii, copied in the dialect of the West
Riding of Yorkshire in the early fourteenth century. The second is from
Trinity College, Cambridge R.3.8, copied in the Staffordshire dialect in
the late fourteenth century.

All the versions of *Cursor Mundi* were edited for EETS by R. Morris
in a parallel-text edition (1874–93).

Texts

British Library Cotton Vespasian A.iii

The Cursor o the world

Man *yhernes* rimes for to here,
And romans red on maneres *sere*,
Of Alisaunder þe conquerour;
Of Iuly Cesar þe emparour;
O grece and troy the strang strijf,   5
þere many thosand lesis þer lijf;

O brut þat *bern* bald of hand,
þe first conquerour of Ingland;
O kyng arthour þat was so *rike*,
Quam non in hys tim was like,   10
O *ferlys* þat hys knythes fell,
þat aunters *sere* I here of tell,
Als wawan, cai and oþer stabel,
For to were þe ronde tabell;
How charles kyng and rauland faght,   15
Wit sarazins wald þai na *saght*;
[Of] tristrem and hys leif ysote,
How he for here becom a sote,
Of Ionek and of ysambrase,
O ydoine and of amadase   20
Storis als o *ferekin* thinges
O princes, prelates and o kynges;
Sanges *sere* of *selcuth* rime,
Inglis, frankys, and latine,
to rede and here Ilkon is *prest*,   25
þe thynges þat þam likes best.

Trinity College, Cambridge R.3.8

Here bigynneþ þe boke of storyes þat men callen cursor mundi

Men ȝernen iestes for to here
And romaunce rede in dyuerse manere
Of Alisaunder þe conqueroure
Of Iulius cesar þe emperoure
Of greke & troye þe longe strif   5
þere mony mon lost his lif
Of bruyt þat baron bolde of honde
Furste conqueroure of engelonde
Of kyng Arthour þat was so *riche*
Was noon in his tyme him liche   10
Of wondris þat his knyȝtes felle
And auntres duden men herde telle
As wawayn kay & oþere ful abul
For to kepe þe rounde tabul
How kyng charles & rouland fauȝt   15
Wiþ Sarazines nole þei [neuer be] sauȝt
Of tristram & of Isoude þe swete
How þei wiþ loue firste gan mete

Of kyng Ion and of Isombras
of Idoyne and of amadas 20
Storyes of dyuerse þinges
Of princes prelatis & of kynges
Mony songes of dyuerse ryme
As englisshe frensshe & latyne
To rede & here mony are prest 25
Of þinges þat hem likeþ best

Notes

line 5. **strang**
This form shows the Northern unrounded reflex of OE ā̄. Another example of this is **bald** in line 7. However, this usage is not entirely consistent as the form **non** (line 10) has the rounded vowel characteristic of Southern dialects of ME. The more southerly language of the Trinity manuscript shows rounded reflexes of OE ā̄ in <o>, <oo>, for example **bolde, noon.**

The form **strang** also shows the loss of the distinction between weak and strong adjectives. Here the adjective appears after a determiner and we would therefore expect to find the inflexion **-e**. However, this weak adjectival ending was lost earlier in the North of England. The stress pattern of the verse suggests that the original text probably did have the final **-e** inflexion, as preserved in the Trinity manuscript: **þe longe strif.**

line 6. **lesis**
This form shows the Northern present plural indicative inflexion **-is**. The Trinity manuscript shows the Midland inflexion in **-en, callen, ȝernen, duden.**

line 6. **þer**
This text also shows the adoption of Norse-derived third person plural pronouns **þer** and **þam** (line 26). Compare this with the Trinity manuscript which retains the OE-derived form **hem.**

line 21. **ferekin**
This is a scribal error for the word **serekin** caused by confusion over initial <f> and 'long-s' <<ſ>>. The scribe was perhaps unfamiliar with this rare Northern word. The Trinity scribe replaced this form with an equivalent with a diatopically more widespread currency, **dyuerse.**

line 23. **sere** (see also lines 2 and 12)
The use of this word of ON origin is another feature of a Northern
provenance; the Trinity scribe substitutes the word **mony.**

Glossary

bern N WARRIOR, MAN (OE **beorn**)
ferekin see **sere**
ferlys N MARVELS, WONDERS (ON **ferligr**)
prest Adj READY (OF **prest**)
rike, riche Adj POWERFUL (OE **rice**)
saght N PEACE, RECONCILIATION (ON **satt**)
selcuth Adj STRANGE, WONDERFUL (OE **seldcuð**)
sere Adj MANY, VARIOUS (ON **ser**)
yhernes V 3 sg pres TO LIKE (OE **gyrnan**)

Text 6. The Proclamation of Henry III

Introduction

The Proclamation of Henry III was issued in 1258, one of the few official
documents to be written in English during the thirteenth century. The
text was produced in both French and English and copies were sent to
every English county. The version printed below is thought to have been
the exemplar from which all other copies were made, and its language
represents the earliest evidence for the London dialect of ME.

An accessible text of the *Proclamation*, with a translation, appears in
Burnley (1992: 113–16).

Text

Henri, þur3 Godes *fultume* King on Engleneloande, Lhoauerd on
Yrloande, Duk on Normandi, on Aquitaine, and Eorl on Aniow,
send igretinge to alle hise holde, ilærde and ileawede, on
Huntendoneschire. þæt witen 3e wel alle þæt we willen and vnnen
þæt, þæt vre *rædesmen* alle, oþer þe moare *dæl* of heom, (5) þæt beoþ
ichosen þur3 us and þur3 þæt loandes folk on vre *kuneriche*, habbeþ
idon and shullen don in þe worþnesse of Gode and on vre treowþe,
for þe *freme* of þe loande þur3 þe besi3te of þan toforeniseide
redesmen, beo stedefæst and ilestinde in alle þinge a buten ænde.
And we *hoaten* alle vre treowe, in þe treowþe þæt heo vs o3en, (10)
þæt heo stedefæstliche healden and swerien to healden and to

werien þo isetnesses þæt beon imakede and beon to makien, þurȝ toforeniseide rædesmen, oþer þurȝ þe moare dæl of heom, alswo alse hit is biforen iseid; and þæt æhc oþer helpe þæt for to done bi þan ilche oþe aȝenes alle men riȝt for to done and to foangen. And noan ne *nime* of loande ne of *eȝte* wherþurȝ þis besiȝte muȝe beon ilet oþer iwersed on onie wise. (15) And ȝif oni oþer onie cumen her onȝenes, we willen and hoaten þæt alle vre treowe heom healden deadliche ifoan. And for þæt we willen þæt þis beo stedefæst and lestinde, we senden ȝew þis writ open, iseined wiþ vre seel, to halden amanges ȝew ine *hord*. Witnesse vsseluen æt Lundene þane eȝtetenþe day on þe monþe of Octobre, (20) in þe two and fowertiȝþe ȝeare of vre cruninge. And þis wes idon *ætforen* vre isworene redesmen, Boneface Archebischop on Kanterburi, Walter of Cantelow, Bischop on Wirechestre, Simon of Muntfort, Eorl of Leirchestre, Richard of Clare, Eorl on Glowchestre and on Hurtford, Roger Bigod, Eorl on Northfolke and Marescal on Engleneloande, (25) Perres of Sauueye, Willelm of Fort, Eorl on Aubermarle, Iohan of Plesseiz, Eorl on Warewik, Iohan Geffrees sune, Perres of Muntfort, Richard of Grey, Roger of Mortemer, Iames of Aldithele, and ætforen oþre inoȝe.

And al on þo ilche worden is isend into æurihce oþre shcire ouer al þære kuneriche on Engleneloande, and ek in tel Irelonde (30).

Notes

line 1. Lhoauerd
This word shows the reflection of OE ā in <oa>, a common development in this text, for example **loande, hoaten**. However there are examples showing OE ā reflected in <o> and <a>, such as **oþe, amanges**. This form also shows OE /hl/ reflected as <lh>, suggesting that the fricative is retained in pronunciation.

line 6. kuneriche
This form shows the preservation of a rounded reflex of OE **y**: a feature of the West Midlands dialect of ME (see *Ancrene Wisse*). However, other examples provide evidence of the reflection of OE **y** in <i> and <e>, such as **king, iwersed**; features common to the Midlands and South-Eastern dialects respectively. Spellings showing all three reflexes are common in London texts throughout the ME period.

line 9. ænde
This form shows the characteristic Essex i-mutated reflex of Germanic

a before nasals, which was not raised to <e> as in all other dialects of OE. This <æ> was subsequently retracted and is found written as <a> in later Essex and London texts.

line 10. healden

This form shows the retention of the <ea> diphthong and suggests that it is derived from a form which had undergone 'breaking', an OE sound-change whereby monophthongs became diphthongs before certain consonant groups. However the single occurrence of **halden** (line 19) shows a monophthong, suggesting that this form may be derived from an Old Anglian ancestor, as breaking did not occur before <-ld> in the Old Anglian dialect.

line 17. ifoan

This form shows the weak plural inflexion <-n>, which is also preserved in **worden** (line 29). These endings were a common feature of Southern and Western dialects of ME and are found commonly in the language of *Ancrene Wisse*.

line 20. þane

There are several examples of inflected forms of the determiner system. Here the masculine accusative singular form has been selected, while dative plural form **þan** is used in line 8 and the feminine dative singular form **þære** in line 29.

line 19. æt Lundene

Nouns appearing after prepositions show the dative singular inflexion <-e>.

line 29. shcire

The change in the representation of /ʃ/ from OE <sc> to ME <sch, sh> is clearly in a state of transition. There are examples of both <sh> and <sch> while the spelling <shcire> suggests that the adoption of the ME convention had not yet been completely established.

Glossary

ætforen Prep BEFORE, IN THE PRESENCE OF (OE **ætforan**)
dæl N PORTION, PART (OE **dǣl**)
eȝte N PROPERTY (OE **æht**)
freme N ADVANTAGE, BENEFIT (OE **fremu**)
fultume N HELP SUPPORT (OE **fultum**)

hoaten V 1 pl pres TO COMMAND, ORDER (OE hātan)
hord N ARCHIVE (OE hord)
kuneriche N RULE, SOVEREIGNTY (OE cynerīce)
nime V 3 sing pres TO SEIZE (OE niman)
rædesmen N COUNSELLORS (OE radesmann)

Text 7. The Ormulum

Introduction

The Ormulum was written in the last quarter of the twelfth century, *c*. 1180. In the preface the author dedicates the work to his brother Walter and tells us that his name is Orm: **þis boc iss nemmned Orrmulum forþi þat Orm itt wrohhte**. It is thought that Orm was an Augustinian canon from Bourne in Lincolnshire, an area of dense Norse settlement in the Danelaw; the name Orm is of Scandinavian origin. *The Ormulum* is a collection of metrical homilies containing numerous Biblical stories with many personal illustrations. The exisiting work is 20,000 lines long although this is only about an eighth of the planned work. The text survives in a single manuscript, Bodleian Library Junius I which is in the author's own hand. *The Ormulum* is one of very few autograph manuscripts of ME works and is therefore extremely important for historical linguists.

There is no complete modern edition of *The Ormulum*, but there are useful selections in Dickins and Wilson (1952: 81–5), in Bennett and Smithers (1974: 174–83), and in Burnley (1992: 79–87, including a plate illustrating Orm's handwriting).

Text

An Romanisshe kaserr-kinḡ
Wass Auḡusstuss ȝehatenn,
Annd he wass wurrþenn kasserr-kinḡ
Off all mannkinn onn erþe,
Annd he ḡann þennkenn off himmsellf 5
Annd of hiss miccle riche.
Annd he biḡann to þennkenn þa,
Swa summ þe ḡoddspell kiþeþþ,
Off þatt he wollde witenn wel
Hu mikell fehh himm come, 10
ȝiff himm off all hiss kinedom
Illc mann an peninnḡ ȝæfe.

Annd he badd settenn upp o writt,
All mannkinn forr to lokenn,
Hu mikell fehh he mihhte swa   15
Off all þe werelld sammnenn,
Þurrh þatt himm shollde off illc an mann
An peninḡ wurrþenn reccnedd.
Annd ta wass sett tatt iwhillc mann,
Whær summ he wære o lande,   20
Ham shollde wendenn to þatt tun
þatt he wass borenn inne,
Annd tatt he shollde þær forr himm
Hiss hæfedd peninḡ reccnenn,
Swa þatt he ȝæn þe kaserr-kinḡ   25
Ne felle nohht i wíte.
Annd i þatt illke time wass
Iosæp wiþþ Sannte Marȝe
I Ḡalilew, annd i þatt tun
þatt Nazaræþ wass nemmnedd.   30
Annd ta ðeȝȝ baþe forenn ham
Till þeȝȝre baþre kinde;
Inntill þe land off Ȝerrsalæm
þeȝȝ forenn samenn baþe,
Annd comenn inn till Beþþleæm,   35
Till þeȝȝre baþre birde
þær wass hemm baþe birde to,
Forr þatt teȝȝ baþe wærenn
Off Dauiþþ kinḡess kinnessmenn,
Swa summ þe ḡoddspell kiþeþþ.   40
Annd Dauiþþ kinḡess birde wass
I Beþþleæmess chesstre;
Annd hemm wass baþe birde þær
þurrh Dauiþþ kinḡess birde;
Forr þatt teȝȝ baþe wærenn off   45
Dauiþess kinn annd sibbe.
Annd Sannte Marȝess time wass
þatt ȝho þa shollde childenn,
Annd tær ȝho barr Allmahhtiȝ Godd
Ðatt all þiss werelld wrohhte,   50
Annd wand himm sone i winnde-clút,
Annd leȝȝde himm inn an cribbe;
Forr þi þatt ȝho ne wisste whær
Ȝho mihhte himm don i bure.

Notes

line 2. **Wass**
Double consonants are used to indicate that the preceding vowel is short. However, this practice only applies after short vowels in closed syllables, cf. **Annd** (line 3), **Off** (line 4), **onn** (line 4) and so on. A closed syllable is made up of a vowel and a consonant, whereas an open syllable ends with a vowel and begins with an optional consonant. For example, the first syllable of the word FATHER is open, CV-, while the second syllable is closed, -VC (where V represents any vowel and C any consonant). Therefore in Orm's system the word FATHER is written **faderr**.

Where a single consonant appears in a closed syllable this indicates that the preceding vowel is long. As as result of this Orm's system provides much information concerning the late OE lengthening of short vowels before certain consonant groups, known as 'homorganic lengthening' (see p. 58 above). For example, we might compare the forms **land** and **lanng**. Both of these vowels appear in closed syllables and we may therefore assume that the vowel in **land** is long, while that in **lanng** is short. It seems therefore that in Orm's idiolect lengthening had taken place before <-ld> but not before <-ng>.

In addition to the doubling of consonants, Orm also used diacritics to mark vowel length in order to distinguish homographs. This information is also useful in reconstructing vowel quantity in Orm's linguistic system. For instance a diacritic mark over the initial vowel of **tákenn** TAKE indicates that this vowel is short, thereby distinguishing it from **takenn** TOKEN, where the vowel is long. As the <a> in **tákenn** TAKE was later subjected to ME Open Syllable Lengthening we know that this sound change had not yet occurred in Orm's language.

line 5. **ḡann**
The superscript line over the <g> represents a distinct letter-form in Orm's own written practice. Orm uses a number of distinct graphemes and combinations of graphemes to represent different sounds, as follows:

> <ḡ> represents the velar stop [g]
> <ȝ> represents the palatal approximant [j]
> <gg> represents the palato-alveolar affricate [dȝ]
> <ȝh> represents the velar fricative [ȝ]

line 26. **wíte**
Orm uses a number of brevigraphs to indicate length and to distinguish homographs. Here the brevigraph over the <i> graph indicates a long vowel and thereby distinguishes this form (derived from OE **wite**

BLAME) from **wite** where the vowel is short (derived from OE **witan** TO KNOW).

line 34. þeȝȝ

The Ormulum is the earliest text to record 'th-'-type forms of the third person plural pronouns (cf. PDE THEY, THEIR, THEM), generally assumed by scholars to be borrowed from ON. See line 32 for the form **þeȝȝre**. However, the dominant form for the pronoun THEM is **hemm** (see line 37) although the form **þeȝȝm** is used following vowels, to prevent elision.

line 35. till

This is a word of probable ON origin, meaning TO (ON **til**). Given that *The Ormulum* was composed in Lincolnshire, situated in the Danelaw, it is not surprising that Orm uses a large number of ON loanwords.

line 48. ȝho

The use of the initial <ȝh> in the word **ȝho** SHE is distinct from all other occurrences of these graphs. In all other lexemes the <h> is written superscript while in the single item **ȝho** the <h> is written on the line. The consistency of this practice suggests that this represents a phonetic distinction. It seems likely that in **ȝho** the <ȝh> graphs represent the palatal fricative [ç]. This form appears to be a transitional stage in the development from OE **hēo**, **hīe** to Modern English SHE.

Glossary

baþre Adj gen. pl. BOTH (ON **báðir**)
birde N FAMILY (OE **byrd**)
bure N LODGING (OE **būr**)
chesstre N CITY, TOWN (OE **ceaster**)
childenn V GIVE BIRTH (cf. OE **cild**)
fehh N MONEY, WEALTH (OE **feoh**)
ȝæn Prep WITH RESPECT TO, TOWARDS (OE **ongēan**)
hæfedd-peninnḡ N POLL-TAX (OE **hēafod-pening**)
ham N HOME (OE **hām**)
iwhillc Adj EVERY (OE **gehwilc**)
kiþþeþ V 3 sg **kiðen** TO RELATE, MAKE KNOWN (OE **cȳðan**)
miccle Adj GREAT, MUCH (ON **mikil**)
mikell See **miccle**
nemmnedd V past participle TO NAME (OE **nemnan**)
reccnedd V past participle TO PAY (OE **recenian**)

riche N KINGDOM (OE rīce)
samenn Adv TOGETHER (OE samen)
sammnenn V infin TO GATHER, COLLECT (OE samnian)
sibb N FAMILY, STOCK (OE sibb)
till Prep TO (ON til)
winnde-clút N SWADDLING CLOTH (OE windan-clūt)
wíte N BLAME (OE wīte)
writt N LETTER, o writt IN WRITING (OE writ)

Text 8. The Equatorie of the Planetis

Introduction

The Equatorie of the Planetis survives in a single manuscript copied in the late fourteenth century, now Peterhouse College, Cambridge 75.I, which has been identified by some scholars as the author's own copy. The text describes the production and use of an instrument for calculating the motions of the planets. The calendar references in the text suggest that it was produced in 1393, while the reference to a 'radix Chaucer' has led to the suggestion that the text was composed and copied by Chaucer himself. However recently scholars have questioned this identification and argued that the manuscript is neither of a Chaucerian text nor an autograph. The language of the scribe belongs to the London dialect of the late fourteenth century and therefore shows a number of similarities with that of Chaucer. Characteristic of this dialect are a mixture of features showing the influence of the Midlands and South-Eastern dialects which appeared in London English as a result of large-scale immigration into the capital.

The standard edition of *The Equatorie* is by D. J. Price (1955); for the authorship controversy, see the study by K. A. Rand Schmidt (1993).

Text

In the name of god pitos & merciable. Seide Leyk: the largere þat thow makest this instrument, the largere ben thi chef deuisions; the largere that ben tho deuisions, in hem may ben mo smale fracciouns; and euere the mo of smale fracciouns, the ner the trowthe of thy conclusiouns (5).

Tak therfore a plate of metal or elles a bord that be smothe shaue by leuel and euene polised. Of which, whan it is rownd by compas, the hole diametre shal contene 72 large enches or elles 6 fote of mesure. The whiche rownde bord, for it shal nat werpe or krooke, the egge of the circumference shal be bownde with a plate of yren (10) in maner of a karte whel. This bord, yif the likith, may be vernissed or elles glewed with *perchemyn* for honestyte.

Tak thanne a cercle of metal that be 2 enche of brede, and that the hole dyametre with in this cercle shal contene the forseyde 68 enches or 5 fote and 8 enches, (15) and *subtili* lat this cercle be nayled vpon the circumference of this bord, or ellis mak this cercle of glewed perchemyn. This cercle wole I clepe the 'lymbe' of myn equatorie that was compowned the yer of Crist 1392 complet, the laste meridie of Decembre.

This lymbe shaltow deuyde in 4 quarters by 2 diametral lynes in maner of the lymbe of a comune *astrelabye* – (20) and lok thy croys be trewe proued by geometrical conclusioun. Tak thanne a large compas that be trewe, and set the fyx point ouer the middel of the bord, on which middel shal be nayled a plate of metal rownd. The hole diametre of this plate shal contiene 16 enches large, for in this plate shollen ben perced alle the centris of this equatorie (25). And ek in proces of tyme may this plate be turned abowte after that auges of planetes ben moeued in the 9 spere: thus may thin instrument laste perpetuel.

Notes

line 1. **In the name of god pitos & merciable**
This invocation appears to be modelled on the Arabic **bismillah** meaning 'in the name of Allah'. Its use here suggests that the work is a translation of an Arabic text.

line 2. **thow**
The use of the second person pronoun as a form of address is a feature of medieval scientific texts.

line 3. **hem**
We might note the use of the <h-> form of the third person plural pronoun. London English in this period tended to show 'th-type' forms for the nominative pronoun THEY, and OE derived forms, namely **hem**, **her**, in oblique cases. See for instance the Chaucerian extracts in Chapters 2 and 3.

line 8. **enches**
The spelling with initial <e>, representing the reflex of OE **y**, is an

originally South-Eastern feature which is common in London texts of this period.

line 9. The whiche
The use of **the whiche** and **the forseyde** (see line 14) is a common cohesive device in ME technical and legal writing. It is probably modelled on the French usage **lequel, laquelle** and so on.

line 20. Astrelabye
An astrolabe is an instrument used to determine the positions and movements of celestial bodies and to calculate latitude and longitude and so on.

line 24. contiene
The spelling of this word with <ie> is another South-Eastern feature which is less commonly found in London English.

line 25. shollen
The use of the Midlands <-en> inflexion in plural forms of the present tense is a feature of the London dialect, and reflects the input from Midland dialects into London English during the fourteenth century.

Glossary

astrelabye N ASTROLABE (Lat **astrolabium**)
honestyte N GOOD APPEARANCE, FAIRNESS (OF **honeste**)
perchemyn N PARCHMENT (OF **parchemin**)
subtili Adv CAREFULLY (OF **sotil**)

Discussion of the exercises

Most of the chapters end with exercises. Most of these exercises consist of 'Questions for review', and the answers are to be found in the preceding chapter. These questions can be used as essay titles, or as questions to be pursued in seminar-discussion. These questions vary in aim; some are designed to encourage students to formulate descriptions, while others ask students to present an argument.

Other exercises ask the reader to carry out a specific task – perhaps a translation or a commentary of some kind, or perhaps a discussion of a particular linguistic development. Again, the answers should be clear from the preceding chapter, but in some cases we give below some hints on how to tackle the question.

Chapter 2

'The passage below contains the same Chaucerian text as on pp. 15–17 above, but using modern conventions of punctuation. Attempt a translation of this passage into PDE prose, using present-day grammar, vocabulary and conventions of punctuation.' Offering a translation here would rather defeat the purpose of this exercise! However, it is worth comparing your translation with those of others; recommended are Coghill (poetry, 1952) and Wright (prose, 1981).

Chapter 4: Other questions

1. 'Provide a phonemic transcription, in Chaucerian ME, of the following passage from Chaucer's *Pardoner's Tale*. Mark all long vowels. There are interpretative notes at the side to help you ...'

A suggested phonemic transcription appears below. There are of course debatable interpretations (for example, whether the final consonant was voiced in words such as **of**, **his**), and these can be used to trigger seminar discussion. Since the transcription is phonemic, some phenomena which were probably phonetic (such as [ŋ] in words such as **longe, rong**) have not been used; thus **longe** /lɔŋgə/ was probably realised phonetically as [lɔŋgə]. However, all long vowels are marked whether they are phonemic or not.

/bʊt siːrəz nu: wɔl i: tɛlə fɔrθ mɪ taːlə
ðɪz riːətuːrəz θreː ɔv ʍɪtʃ i: tɛlə
lɔng ɛrst ɛr priːmə rʊng ɔv anɪ bɛlə
weːr sɛt hɛm ɪn ə tavɛrnə toː drɪnkə
and az ðaɪ sat ðaɪ hɛrd ə bɛlə klɪnkə
bɪfɔrn ə kɔrs waz karɪd toː hɪz graːve
ðat ɔːn ɔv hɛm gan kalən toː hɪz knaːve
gɔː bɛt kwɔd heː and aksə rɛdɪlɪ
ʍat kɔrs ɪs ðɪs ðat pasəθ heːr fɔrbɪ
and loːkə ðat ðuː rəpɔrt hɪz naːmə weːl
siːrə kwɔd ðɪs bɔɪ ɪt neːdəθ nɛvər ə dɛːl
ɪt waz meː tɔːld ɛr jeː kam heːr twɔː huːrəz
heː waz pardeː an ɔld fɛlaʊ ɔv juːrəz
and sɔdaɪnlɪ heː waz ɪslaɪn toːnɪxt
fɔrdrʊnk az heː sat ɔn hɪz bɛntʃ ʊprɪxt/

2. 'Write notes on the history of the pronunciation of the following words from the late OE period to PDE. OE forms appear in the West Saxon variety.'

cild CHILD. In OE, **cild** was pronounced [tʃild]. Towards the end of the OE period, the vowel underwent Homorganic Lengthening, and [tʃiːld] resulted. The long vowel was diphthongised and underwent the Great Vowel Shift, to produce the PDE form [tʃaɪld].

nama NAME. In OE, **nama** was pronounced [nama]. By the year 1200, the pronunciation of final vowels was becoming obscured, and the word was pronounced [namə]. Through Middle English Open Syllable Lengthening after 1200, EME **name** was pronounced [naːmə]; when the 'final -e' was lost, earliest in the North but in the South by at least the beginning of the fifteenth century, full lengthening was carried out and the word was pronounced [naːm]. Subsequently the stressed vowel in this word was subjected to the Great Vowel Shift, yielding ultimately PDE forms such as [nɛːm], [neɪm] and so on.

Chapter 5: Other questions

1. 'Look up the following words in the OED and/or MED, and trace their meanings through time with special reference to the ME period ...'

2. 'Choose any passage from the writings of Geoffrey Chaucer (say ten lines from one of *The Canterbury Tales*). Make a list of the **lexical** (that is open-class words) in the passage, and use the OED and/or MED online to find other citations elsewhere in ME texts ...'

Both these exercises are fairly self-explanatory, and are designed to get students working with dictionaries (both in print-form and online), and to make them aware of the kinds of change in meaning which can take place.

Chapter 6: Other questions

'In the passage below, from Chaucer's *Pardoner's Tale*, find the following constructions ...'

a noun phrase containing a weak adjective: **This olde man**
a verb phrase containing a strong verb: **wolde han troden**
an adjective phrase containing a strong adjective: **An oold man/a poure**
a subordinate clause acting as an adverbial: **Whan they han goon nat fully half a mile** OR **Right as they wolde han troden ouer a stile.**

References

Aitchison, J. (1991), *Language Change: progress or decay?*, Cambridge: Cambridge University Press.

Attridge, D. (1982), *The rhythms of English poetry*, London: Longman.

Barber, C. L. (1993), *The English Language: a Historical Introduction*, Cambridge: Cambridge University Press.

Baugh, A. C. and T. Cable (1993), *A History of the English Language*, London: Routledge.

Bennett, J. A. W. and G. V. Smithers, with a glossary by N. Davis (1974), *Early Middle English Verse and Prose* (revised edn), Oxford: Clarendon Press.

Benskin, M. (1982), 'The letters <þ> and <y> in later Middle English, and some related matters', *Journal of the Society of Archivists* 7: 13–30.

Benskin, M. (1992), 'Some new perspectives on the origins of standard written English', in J. A. van Leuvensteijn and J. B. Berns (eds), *Dialect and Standard Languages in the English, Dutch, German and Norwegian Language Areas*, Amsterdam: Royal Netherlands Academy of Arts and Sciences, pp. 71–105.

Benson, L. (gen. ed.) (1988), *The Riverside Chaucer*, London: Oxford University Press.

Blake, N. (1996), *A History of the English Language*, Basingstoke: Macmillan.

Bloomfield, L. (1935), *Language*, London: Allen & Unwin.

Brunner, K. (trans. G. Johnston) (1963), *An Outline of Middle English Grammar*, Oxford: Blackwell.

Burnley, J. D. (1983), *A Guide to Chaucer's Language*, Basingstoke: Macmillan.

Burnley, J. D. (1992), *The History of the English Language: a source-book*, London: Longman.

Burrow, J. and T. Turville-Petre (1997), *A Book of Middle English* (revised edn), Oxford: Blackwell.

Campbell, A. (1959), *Old English Grammar*, Oxford: Clarendon Press.

Cannon, C. (1998), *The Making of Chaucer's English. A Study of Words*, Cambridge: Cambridge University Press.

Cawley, A. C. (ed.) (1958), *The Wakefield Pageants in the Townleye Cycle*, Manchester: Manchester University Press.

Chambers = *The Chambers Dictionary*, 1998.

CHEL = Hogg, R. (gen. ed.) (1992–), *The Cambridge History of the English Language*, Cambridge: Cambridge University Press.

Clanchy, M. (1993), *From Memory to Written Record* (2nd edn), Oxford: Blackwell.

Clark, C. (ed.) (1970), *The Peterborough Chronicle* (2nd edn), Oxford: Clarendon Press.

Coghill, N. (trans.) (1952), *The Canterbury Tales*, Harmondsworth: Penguin.

CSD = *Concise Scots Dictionary*.

Davis, N. (ed.) (1971–6), *Paston Letters and Papers from the Fifteenth Century*, Oxford: Clarendon Press.

Davis, N. (1974), 'Chaucer and Fourteenth-Century English', in D. S. Brewer (ed.), *Geoffrey Chaucer*, London: Bell, pp. 71–8.

Davis, N., D. Gray, P. Ingham and A. Wallace-Hadrill (1979), *A Chaucer Glossary*, Oxford: Clarendon Press.

Denison, D. (1993), *English Historical Syntax*, London: Longman.

Dickins, B. and R. M. Wilson (1952), *Early Middle English Texts*, London: Bowes and Bowes.

Dobson, E. J. (1962), 'Middle English lengthening in open syllables', *Transactions of the Philological Society*, pp. 124–48.

Dobson, E. J. (1968), *English Pronunciation 1500–1700* (2nd edn), Oxford: Clarendon Press.

Dobson, E. J. (ed.) (1972), *The English text of the Ancrene Riwle; edited from B.M. Cotton MS. Cleopatra C.vi*, London: Oxford University Press for EETS.

Donaldson, E. T. (1970), *Speaking of Chaucer*, London: Athlone Press.

Elliott, R. W. V. (1974), *Chaucer's English*, London: Deutsch.

Everett, D. (1955a), 'Chaucer's Good Ear', in *Essays on Middle English Literature* (ed. P. Kean), Clarendon Press: Oxford, pp. 138–48.

Everett, D. (1955b), 'Some reflections on Chaucer's "Art Poetical"', in *Essays on Middle English Literature* (ed. P. Kean), Oxford: Clarendon Press, pp. 149–74.

Fellows, J. (1998), 'Author, Author, Author … An Apology for Parallel Texts', in McCarren and Moffat (eds), pp. 15–24.

Fisher, J., M. Richardson and J. Fisher (1984), *An Anthology of Chancery English*, Knoxville: University of Tennessee Press.

Fisher, J. (1996), *The emergence of standard English*, Lexington: University Press of Kentucky.

Fisiak, J. (1964), *A short grammar of Middle English I: graphemics, phonemics and morphemics*, Warsaw: Polish Scientific Publishers/London: Oxford University Press.

Gimson, A. C. (rev. A. Cruttenden) (1994), *An Introduction to the Pronunciation of English*, London: Arnold.

Gordon, E. V. (ed.) (1953), *Pearl*, Oxford: Clarendon Press.

Graddol, D., D. Leith and J. Swann (1997), *English: History, Diversity and Change*, London: Routledge.

Greenbaum, S. and R. Quirk (1990), *A student's grammar of the English language*, Harlow: Longman.

Hall, J. (1921), *Early Middle English*, Oxford: Clarendon Press.

Hoad, T. (1994), 'Word Geography: previous approaches and achievements', in Laing and Williamson, pp. 197–203.

Hogg, R. (1992), *A grammar of Old English, volume I*, Oxford: Blackwell.

Hogg, R. (2002), *An Introduction to Old English*, Edinburgh: Edinburgh University Press.

Horobin, S. (forthcoming), *The Language of the Chaucer Tradition*, Cambridge: Brewer.

Housman, A. E. (ed.) (1905), *D. Junii Juvenalis Saturae*, London: Grant Richards.

Jacobs, J. N. (1998), 'Kindly Light or Foxfire? The Authorial Text Reconsidered', in McCarren and Moffat (eds), pp. 3–14.

Jones, C. (1972), *An introduction to Middle English*, New York: Holt, Rinehart and Winston.

Jones, C. (1988), *Grammatical Gender in English 950–1250*, London: Croom Helm.

Jones, C. (1989), *A History of English Phonology*, London: Longman.

Jordan, R. (trans. E. Crook) (1974), *Handbook of Middle English Grammar: Phonology*, The Hague: Mouton.

Kane, G., E. T. Donaldson and G. H. Russell (eds) (1960–75–97), *Piers Plowman: the three versions*, London: Athlone Press.

Kane, G. (1981), 'Music Neither Unpleasant nor Monotonous', in P. L. Heyworth (ed.), *Medieval Studies for J. A. W. Bennett*, Oxford: Clarendon Press, pp. 43–63.

Keller, R. (1994), *On Language Change*, London: Routledge.

King, A. (1997), 'The Inflectional Morphology of Older Scots', in C. Jones (ed.), *The Edinburgh History of the Scots Language*, Edinburgh: Edinburgh University Press, pp. 156–81.

Laing, M. (1989), *Middle English Dialectology*, Aberdeen: Aberdeen University Press.

Laing, M. and K. Williamson (eds) (1994), *Speaking in our Tongues*, Cambridge: Brewer.

LALME = McIntosh, A., M. L. Samuels and M. Benskin, with M. Laing and K. Williamson (1986), *A Linguistic Atlas of Late Mediaeval English*, Aberdeen: Aberdeen University Press.

Lass, R. (1980), *On Explaining Language Change*, Cambridge: Cambridge University Press.

Lass, R. (1987), *The Shape of English*, London: Arnold.

Lass, R. (1994), *Old English*, Cambridge: Cambridge University Press.

Leech, G., M. Deuchar and R. Hoogenraad (1982), *English Grammar for Today*, Macmillan: Basingstoke.

Lewis, R. E. (1994), 'Sources and techniques for the study of Middle English word geography', in Laing and Williamson, pp. 205–14.

Lightfoot, D. (1979), *Principles of Diachronic Syntax*, Cambridge: Cambridge University Press.

Luick, K. (1964), *Historische Grammatik der englischen Sprache*, Oxford: Blackwell.

McCarren, V. P. and D. Moffat (eds) (1998), *A Guide to Editing Middle English*, Ann Arbor: University of Michigan Press.

McIntosh, A. (1973), 'Word geography in the lexicography of medieval English', *Annals of the New York Academy of Sciences* 211, 55–66 (reprinted with corrections in Laing 1989, pp. 86–97).

McMahon, A. (1994), *Understanding Language Change*, Cambridge: Cambridge University Press.

MED = *Middle English Dictionary*.

Millward, C. (1989), *A Biography of the English Language*, Fort Worth: Holt, Rinehart and Winston.

Minkova, D. (1991), *The History of Final Vowels in English*, Berlin: Mouton de Gruyter.

Mitchell, B. (1985), *Old English Syntax*, Oxford: Clarendon Press.

Mitchell, B. and F. Robinson (1997), *A Guide to Old English* (6th edn), Oxford: Blackwell.

Morris, R. (ed.) (1874–93), *Cursor Mundi*, London: Paul, Trench and Trübner, for EETS.

Mossé, F. (trans. J. Walker) (1959), *A Handbook of Middle English*, Baltimore: Johns Hopkins University Press.

Mustanoja, T. (1959), *A Middle English Syntax, Vol. I* (all published), Helsinki: Société Néophilologique.

Norton-Smith, J. (ed.) (1966), *John Lydgate: Poems*, Oxford: Clarendon Press.

OED = *Oxford English Dictionary*.

Patterson, L. (1987), *Negotiating the past: the historical understanding of medieval literature*, Madison, WI: University of Wisconsin Press.

Pope, M. K. (1934), *From Latin to modern French with especial consideration of Anglo-Norman: phonology and morphology*, Manchester: Manchester University Press.

Price, D. J. (ed.) (1955), *The equatorie of the planetis; edited from Peterhouse MS.75.I*, Cambridge: Cambridge University Press.

Prins, A. A. (1952), *French Influence on English Phrasing*, Leiden: Leiden University Press.

Prins, A. A. (1972), *A History of English Phonemes*, Leiden: Leiden University Press.

Prokosch, E. (1938), *A Comparative Germanic Grammar*, Baltimore: Linguistic Society of America.

Rand Schmidt, K. A. (1993), *The authorship of the Equatorie of the planetis*, Cambridge: D. S. Brewer.

Reynolds, L. and N. G. Wilson (1974), *Scribes and scholars: a guide to the transmission of Greek and Latin literature* (2nd edn), Oxford: Clarendon Press.

Sampson, G. (1985). *Writing Systems*, Stanford: Stanford University Press.

Samuels, M. L. (1963), 'Some applications of Middle English dialectology', *English Studies* 44, 81–94 (reprinted with corrections and revisions in Laing 1989, pp. 64–80).

Samuels, M. L. (1972), *Linguistic Evolution*, Cambridge: Cambridge University Press.

Samuels, M. L. (1981), 'Spelling and dialect in the late and post-Middle English periods', in M. Benskin and M. L. Samuels (eds), *So meny people longages and tonges: philological essays in Scots and mediaeval English presented to Angus McIntosh*, Edinburgh: MEDP, pp. 43–54 (reprinted with corrections in Samuels and Smith 1988, pp. 86–95).

Samuels, M. L. (1983), 'Chaucer's Spelling', in D. Gray and E. G. Stanley (eds), *Middle English Studies Presented to Norman Davis*, Oxford: Clarendon Press, pp. 17–37 (reprinted in Samuels and Smith 1988, pp. 23–37).

Samuels, M. L. and J. J. Smith (1988), *The English of Chaucer*, Aberdeen: Aberdeen University Press.

Sandved, A. (1985), *Introduction to Chaucerian English*, Cambridge: Brewer.

Schmidt, A. V. C. (ed.) (1978), *William Langland: The vision of Piers Plowman: a critical edition of the B-text based on Trinity College Cambridge MS. B.15.17*, London: Dent.

Serjeantson, M. (1935), *A History of Foreign Words in English*, London: Kegan Paul.

Shepherd, G. T. (ed.) (1991), *Ancrene Wisse: parts six and seven* (revised edn), Exeter: University of Exeter.

Sisam, K. (1921), *Fourteenth-Century Verse and Prose*, London: Oxford University Press.

Smith, J. J. (1992), 'The Use of English: language contact, dialect variation and written standardisation during the Middle English period', in T. W. Machan and C. T. Scott (eds), *English in its Social Contexts*, New York: Oxford University Press, pp. 47–68.

Smith, J. J. (1996), *An Historical Study of English*, London: Routledge.

Smith, J. J. (1999), *Essentials of Early English*, London: Routledge.

Stanley, E. G. (ed.) (1972), *The Owl and the Nightingale* (2nd edn), Manchester: Manchester University Press.

Stockwell, R. and D. Minkova (1988), 'The English Vowel Shift: problems of coherence and explanation', in D. Kastovsky, G. Bauer and J. Fisiak (eds), *Luick Revisited*, Tübingen: Narr, pp. 355–94.

Strang, B. M. H. (1970), *A History of English*, London: Routledge.

Szemerényi, O. (1996), *Introduction to Indo-European Linguistics*, Oxford: Clarendon Press.

Traugott, E. C. (1972), *A History of English Syntax*, New York: Holt, Rinehart and Winston.

Upton, C., D. Parry and J. D. A. Widdowson (1994), *Survey of English Dialects: the Dictionary and Grammar*, London: Routledge.

Waldron, R. A. (1979), *Sense and Sense Development*, London: Deutsch.

Warner, A. (1982), *Complementation in Middle English and the Methodology of Historical Syntax*, London: Croom Helm.

Warner, A. (1993), *English Auxiliaries*, Cambridge: Cambridge University Press.

Wright, D. (1981), *Geoffrey Chaucer: The Canterbury Tales; translated into modern English prose*, London: Guild Publishing.

Wright, J. and E. M. Wright (1928), *An Elementary Middle English Grammar* (2nd edn), London: Oxford University Press.

Wyld, H. C. (1921), *A Short History of English*, London: Murray.

Wyld, H. C. (1936), *A History of Modern Colloquial English*, Oxford: Blackwell.

Index

For reasons of space and intelligibility, this index is selective. It gives references as follows:
• places, events, authors and texts (excluding bibliographical references)
• definitions of technical terms
• discussion of important categories and notions
• figures.
Since Chaucerian/Ellesmere MS usage is referred to very frequently, references to it are selective only. The Index generally gives no references to the Exercises, to the Recommendations for reading, or to the Appendix.